Pond Management in Rural Bangladesh: System Changes, Problems and Prospects, and Implications for Sustainable Development

Dissertation
in Partial Fulfilment of the Requirements for the Degree of Doctor of Philosophy
in the Graduate School (Philosophisch-Historische Fakultät) of
Basel University

presented by
Irène Kränzlin
from Luzern and Neuheim/Zug

Basel, 2000

Die Deutsche Bibliothek - CIP Einheitsaufnahme

Kränzlin, Irène:
Pond Management in Rural Bangladesh: System Changes, Problems and
Prospects, and Implications for Sustainable Development
Basel: Wepf, 2000
(Basler Beiträge zur Geographie; H.46)
Zugl.: Basel, Univ., Diss., 2000
ISBN 3-85977-234-1

Front Picture: Traditional Zamindar Pond in Saturia, Manikganj (by I. Kränzlin)

printed by Gissler Druck AG, Allschwil

with financial contribution from part of:
Prof. Dr. med. K. Gyr, Basel Cantonal Hospital
Geographisch-Ethnologische Gesellschaft, Basel
Mr. F. Kränzlin-Rast, Luzern

No hands, No feet,
Yet it goes smoothly,
At last resorts in a place.

(The Pond)

Introduction and Acknowledgements

When I decided to conduct research on ponds, specifically on pond management, for my PhD study I was surprised to see how enthusiastically Bangladeshi colleagues reacted. Many still remembered their daily bath in the pond during their childhood, some started to tell mysterious stories about ponds, others stressed the importance of ponds for fish production. Obviously, ponds were deeply embeded in the culture of this country.

Strangely enough, there were numerous verbal comments on the topic but hardly any written documents in English or studies about ponds in a wider cultural context. Pond studies had been limited to assessment reports on the role and the productive potential of ponds for fish production or as an alternative to tubewells for irrigation. However, the non-productive value of ponds and pond water for domestic purposes had been ignored. This was the first incentive to fill this gap of considerable importance. External circumstances have further raised the significance of the topic. The decline of the water table and more recently the arsenic contamination of the groundwater urge the country to find alternatives to meet the growing demand for water. Ponds present one alternative to relieve the pressure on groundwater.

My position posed a challenge to the work as I had to account to different parties: to the discipline of geography (as a geographer), to donors and to my partners in Bangladesh:

- As a geographer, my approach to the topic was driven by two motives: interdisciplinary and an integrative view. To understand and explain the complex issue of the pond, I had to consider its various aspects. Conscious about the fact that such an approach would remain incomplete I preferred to stimulate a research process which should motivate others to continue.
- A practical contribution to the research from part of the donors and the partners in Bangladesh was expected. This required an examination of development approaches on the one side and of problems and chances of ponds on the other side.

Regarding the many previous experiences where development interventions often brought more harm than help to developing countries, it may be questioned what foreign researchers – and also foreign development experts – could contribute to a developing country. With respect to this study I am quite sure that only the fact of being an outsider guided me towards the topic because insiders are too close to it. Therefore, this study can be considered as an example of cooperation between outsiders and insiders who can learn from each other – be it in the field of research or development practise. I learnt a great deal during my two years in Bangladesh and I hope that my study will also provide some useful information for the people of Bangladesh, for researchers, development practitioners and through them for the rural dwellers. Without the help and support of all of them this study would not have been possible.

Special thanks go to Prof. Dr. Klaus Gyr who encouraged me to conduct this study and who supported me with firm confidence throughout the three years of its duration. Through his efforts and the goodwill of the Swiss Development Cooperation I was able to undertake this study with the help of a scholarship. In this context I would also like to thank Peter Tschumi and Dr. Walter Meyer of the Swiss Development Cooperation in Bern and Dhaka for their support.

I want to express thanks to Prof. Dr. Rita Schneider-Sliwa for her guidance which was particularly helpful and valuable regarding the theoretical part of the study. Moreover, I very much appreciated her logistic support at the Department of Geography in Basel. Also, I would like to thank Leena Baumann for her meticulous cartographic work.

Warmest thanks also go to Dr. Bilqis Amin Hoque for her unbroken willingness to help and for providing all possible logistic and personal support in Dhaka and Singair which facilitated my work tremendously. I am also very grateful to the whole team of the Environmental Health Programme of ICDDR,B who always gave me the feeling of being a member of their family.

Further, I would like to particularly thank Ms. Shehla Parvin who assisted me during the entire period of fieldwork in different regions of Bangladesh. Her cheerful attitude, her curiosity and integrity not only facilitated the contact with people and obtaining information but also transformed fieldwork into a very valuable learning experience. I also want to express thanks to Alain Daumerie for his help in measuring the study village and drawing the map.

Although it cannot be perceived by most of them I do not want to miss thanking all the villagers of the study areas who always welcomed us and readily answered our questions. This study has not provided any material good to any of them, as many had expected, but I hope that many have realised their own strength and capacities.

Finally, so many friends in Bangladesh and Switzerland have continuously supported me during these years. I am very grateful to Dr. Bruce Currey for the intellectual and greatly stimulating dialogues, to Jane Crossley and Elizabeth Page for the accurate editing of this study and to Peter and Elisabet Eppler for the open door and their open minds. I would like to thank Shafiul Ahmed, Hasina Ahmed and Jennifer Duyne for their helpful advice, and Käthi Blumer for reviewing the paper. Last but not least the professional opinions of Claude André Ribaux, Prof. Dr. Verena Meier and Dr. Pierre Walther were important to me and deserve many thanks.

Irène Kränzlin, June 1999

Summary

The dissertation was part of an Interlinkage Programme between the University of Basel/Cantonal Hospital in Switzerland and the International Centre for Diarrhoeal Disease Research, Bangladesh (ICDDR,B) and was supported financially by the Swiss Development Cooperation (SDC). The study was carried out between January 1996 and December 1998. Regarding this administrative background the dissertation had to take into account the different interests of the parties involved.

The investigation of the problem required both a basic research component as well as an applied research component. The main objective of the study was to explore the importance of the traditional water resource pond in Bangladesh and its relevance for a future water sector policy in the country. The core of the research problem was a critique of the technocratic water policy, focusing on the introduction of the tubewell technology. Today, 96% of the population of Bangladesh drink groundwater from tubewells. However, the target of the Government, the reduction of the incidence of diarrhoeal diseases, could not be achieved. Furthermore, due to an increasing extraction of groundwater by deep tubewells for irrigation the water table is constantly declining. It can be assumed that there may be a connection between the excessive extraction of groundwater and the disastrous arsenic contamination of the groundwater in the country.

Therefore, the research on ponds was relevant for both theory and policy:

1. Significance of theory: Basic research on ponds was necessary because ponds represent a major water source for domestic purposes but have not yet been considered in water management research and policy in Bangladesh. Moreover, the research on ponds was used to develop and apply the integrative system approach, a methodological approach of recent social geography. Hence, the methodological relevance of social geography in the field of development should be demonstrated.
2. Significance of policy: Firstly, the problems of conventional development policy were addressed theoretically in order to propose alternatives that are more sustainable. Then, the theoretical discussion was applied to the context of water policy and pond management in Bangladesh, which has to find solutions for the acute groundwater problems.

A review of development theories over the past 50 years gives the theoretical framework of the study. The effects of capital- and technology-intensive development projects were outlined, taking the example of the tubewell introduction to Bangladesh and its effects on traditional pond management. In order to analyse the changes in pond management the integrative system approach, a working instrument in recent social geography, was used. The structural and functional changes of pond management over time were described and explained considering space as a product of human action.

The empirical study was based on two main hypotheses:

1. Pond management, defined as: the use, maintenance and control mechanism of ponds, has changed due to the introduction of hand tubewells in two ways. Firstly, pond maintenance has deteriorated which may augment the health risks of the users. Secondly, pond use is being commercialised. This may increase the social imbalance and conflicts between the different users.
2. Ponds may present a viable alternative for future water management if the inherent problems are dealt with. Ponds still are an important water source for domestic purposes in Bangladesh today. Local knowledge and local institutions should be considered as far as possible in future water management planning.

The explorative character of the study required a flexible research design. Due to an actor- and process orientation of the research an idiographic approach using mainly qualitative methods was needed. Besides several types of interviews, some quantitative methods were also used, such as water quality tests and mapping. Literature review and statistical analysis provided primary and supplementary information. According to the research design a case-study of one village was undertaken and later complemented with a short comparative study in two additional villages.

The main results of the study are as follows:

1. The first hypothesis was largely affirmed. The physical structure of the ponds in the study areas has deteriorated. Four firm high embankments were rarely detected, most ponds were too shallow and at risk of drying up. Many ponds were surrounded by dense vegetation which presents a preferred defecation place for villagers, especially the children. Former rules concerning the careful use of a pond were not respected anymore by the villagers. All the ponds analysed for faecal coliform bacteria counts were found to be highly contaminated. This can partially be explained by the fact that embankments are often flat and outlets into these ponds are common and so the risk of contaminated inflow is increased. Moreover, the understanding of the connection between water, health and human productivity is not sufficiently rooted in people's minds. Therefore, ponds remain a risky water source with regards to diarrhoeal diseases. Finally, it was confirmed that the introduction of hand tubewells directly caused the deterioration of pond maintenance as people no longer rely on ponds for drinking water. Thus, pond use has also changed remarkably. The secularisation of the ponds, the decline of the fish supply and a higher purchasing power have led to an increasing commercialisation and privatisation of the ponds for fish production. Although conflicts regarding the access or use of the ponds could not yet be observed, the competition for water may create problems in the future.
2. The second hypothesis could only partly be affirmed. Ponds still are an important domestic water source in Bangladesh. Pond water is particularly used for cooking, washing utensils and clothes, and for bathing. Multiple ownership, population pressure and the lack of financial resources are some of

the major problems that prevent an effective pond management. The disparity between the people's image of the *zamindar* pond and the real condition of the ponds poses another problem. If ponds are to be recommended for domestic use the water quality must be significantly improved. Traditional water improvement methods, such as potash alum or pond sand filters, might be considered, but their effectiveness and practical applicability need to be explored first. Regarding the further privatisation of ponds it may be useful for a community to manage one pond commonly for the use of domestic purposes (eventually even as a drinking water supply) since community management strategies have a long standing tradition in Bangladesh.

The results of the investigation imply the following conclusions for both theory and policy:

- Development problems are complex problems and therefore require a holistic, interdisciplinary approach to solve them. This is also the case with the water sector policy which is confronted with numerous problems in various countries, including Bangladesh. The integrative system approach, which was applied empirically in this study, proved to be a valid methodological tool to analyse and explain these complex problems. Furthermore, it is compatible with recent development approaches such as the community management approach.
- Regarding the critical groundwater situation in Bangladesh the country's water sector policy needs to be revised towards more sustainability. Respect for water as a scarce resource needs to be raised, and existing water resources must be used more efficiently. This implies equal consideration of the pond in the national water policy. Moreover, the importance of the domestic aspects of water management projects have to be emphasised and women should be involved in these projects since they are the main managers in this non-productive domain.
- The initiative to improve (or construct) a pond has to emerge from the community itself. External agencies should only act as facilitators in training and coordinating the different institutions. It would also be important to initiate a decentralised water quality monitoring system for ponds, based on appropriate technology. Finally, hygiene education will remain essential and should be linked with health messages and ecological messages. The understanding of the connections between environment, health and human productivity will improve the effectiveness and sustainability of development projects in general and pond projects in particular.

CONTENTS

List of Abbreviations

BMDA	Barind Multipurpose Development Authority
BRAC	Bangladesh Rural Advancement Committee (largest NGO in the country)
cfu	coliform unit
DANIDA	Danish International Development Agency
DTW	Deep tubewell
DPHE	Department of Public Health Engineering
EAWAG	Eigenössische Anstalt für Wasserversorgung, Abwasserreinigung und Gewässerschutz. Swiss Federal Institute for Environmental Science and Technology
EHP	Environmental Health Programme
FAP	Flood Action Plan
GNP	Gross National Product
HDI	Human Development Index
HYV	High Yielding Variety
ICDDR,B	International Centre for Diarrhoeal Disease Research, Bangladesh
IFADEP	Integrated Food Assisted Development Project
ILO	International Labour Organisation
IRRI	International Rice Research Institute, Manila
MLG, RD&C	Ministry of Local Government, Rural Development and Co-operatives
NADEL	Nachdiplomstudium für Entwicklungsländer
NGO	Non-Governmental Organisation
ORS	Oral Rehydration Solution
PRISM	Projects in Agriculture, Rural Industry, Science and Medicine
PSF	Pond sand filter
RWS	Rural Water Supply
SDC	Swiss Development Cooperation
SOC-MOB	Social Mobilisation
SODIS	Solar Water Disinfection
SPARSSO	Space Research and Remote Sensing Organisation
STW	Shallow tubewell
UNDP	United Nations Development Programme
UNICEF	United Nations Children's Fund
WATSAN	Water Supply and Sanitation
WHO	World Health Organisation
WPP	WATSAN Partnership Project

List of Maps, Tables, Figures, Photographs and Annex

List of Maps

List of Tables

List of Figures

List of Photographs

Annex

PART I PONDS AND SUSTAINABLE DEVELOPMENT – A CONCEPTUAL FRAMEWORK

1 Ponds and system changes

1.1
Introduction and conceptual background

Bangladesh is well-known throughout the world for its natural disasters and the extreme poverty of its people and, as a result of these adversities, Bangladesh is one of the target countries for international development aid. After the cyclone of 1970, the civil war in 1971 and a severe famine, international aid increased and Bangladesh has since received millions of dollars from donor countries for the victims of floods and cyclones. However, the country still has immense ecological and social problems that affect its people. Groundwater contamination, air pollution, rural-urban migration, political and economic instability, and violence against women are some of the many problems that face Bangladesh today.

It is argued that the present situation in Bangladesh partly reflects the failure of development aid. Although development aid should provide assistance to the country as a whole and to the poor in particular, its achievements are often double-sided, enhancing both economic growth and ecological and social imbalance. An example of this imbalance is the Flood Action Plan, a large-scale water management project. The project was aimed at protecting the land from floods and to modernise agricultural methods but the measures undertaken have adversely affected the hydrological system and the livelihood of the people who reside in the project area.

This dissertation is part of an interlinkage programme of the University of Basel/Cantonal Hospital in Switzerland and the International Centre for Diarrhoeal Disease Research, Bangladesh (ICDDR,B) with financial contribution from the Swiss Development Cooperation (SDC). During the research period in Bangladesh, the study was linked to the Environmental Health Programme (EHP) of ICDDR,B, which is actively researching on water supply and sanitation. Considering this administrative background, the dissertation embraces three different fields:

- the field of geography, which was the discipline of the principal investigator
- the field of public health through ICDDR,B and the Basel Cantonal Hospital
- in the field of development work through the relationship with SDC

The study had to take these considerations into account throughout the research period.

Figure 1.1 represents the position of the pond management study within EHP, ICDDR,B and external providers and specifies the locality and the scale in which the study took place. Accountability to ICCDR,B and to external providers and development agencies in general was a focal point of the study.

1.2
Objectives

The main objective of the study was to illustrate the shortcomings of development aid at the grassroots level and to ensure an integrative and actor-oriented perspective for pond management in rural Bangladesh.
    Two fields of objectives can be distinguished:

1. *Empirical objective – basic research on pond management:* Ponds are an important water source for domestic purposes. This is a fact that has only recently been recognised. Studies on ponds in general and changes in their management within the context of Bangladesh could not be ascertained. However, for the success of any pond intervention project, a knowledge of the use, maintenance and control of ponds and about the people's attitude to pond management is essential. Therefore, this study provides basic data on the past and the present structure of pond management and the processes of change through its empirical research. The study highlights the problems and opportunities of present pond management in order to lead to practical implementation by proposing recommendations for future pond management projects.
2. *Practical/project level – providing suggestions for development work:* As the Bangladesh Government is seeking alternative water sources to meet the groundwater problem of the country, ponds for domestic purposes must be given increased importance. Development agencies should support projects on pond improvement for domestic purposes. The empirical results of this study offers suggestions as to the future role ponds could play in sustainable water management in Bangladesh.

1.3
Relevance of the study

The topic of pond management is closely related to the tubewell policy in Bangladesh. The introduction of tubewells was an external intervention project with unforeseen consequences. UNICEF and the Government of Bangladesh started to systematically install hand tubewells in the 1970s with the aim of providing safe drinking water for the people. Mechanised tubewells were also introduced to increase crop production through large scale irrigation. Although the introduction of tubewells was considered to be successful, as today 96 percent of the population drink tubewell water and crop output has increased, there were adverse effects. The introduction of tubewells has resulted in a social and ecological imbalance. The impact of tubewells has been a social polarisation at

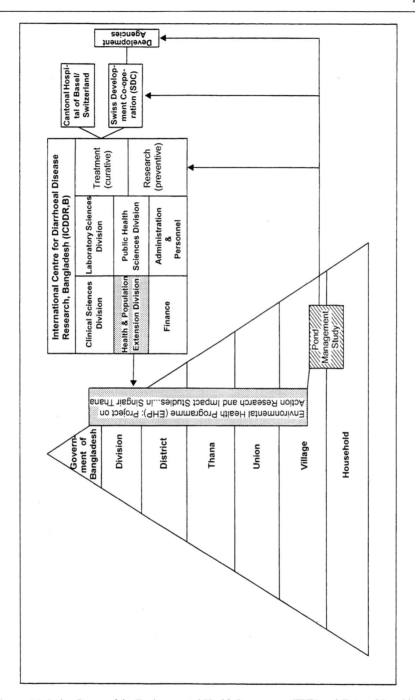

Figure 1.1 Action Range of the Environmental Health Programme (EHP) and External Providers within the International Centre for Diarrhoeal Disease Research (ICDDR,B) and the Administrative System of Bangladesh

village level due to the uneven distribution of hand tubewells as well as ecological problems because the water table started to decline due to the intensive groundwater irrigation by mechanised tubewells.

In addition to these problems, the contamination of the groundwater with arsenic has recently emerged as a major risk for the water supply in Bangladesh. Although there is no substantiation that excessive groundwater irrigation may be responsible for this, there is a concern that there is a relationship between the presence of arsenic and groundwater irrigation.

This study argues that ponds may be an alternative to tubewells and provide solution to these problems. It will be described how traditional pond management has changed due to the tubewells, which have altered the traditional function of the ponds. Before the introduction of tubewells, ponds were the main source of drinking water. The Government of Bangladesh has extensively promoted the use of tubewell water for drinking purposes. However, government policy on the use of tubewell water has met a number of obstacles. Firstly, it could not be proven that the consumption of tubewell water significantly reduced the incidence of diarrhoeal diseases. Secondly, groundwater consumption has recently become a health risk, which demands the provision of alternative water sources to provide for the needs of a growing population. It is in this context, that ponds are again becoming relevant for the supply of water in Bangladesh. For the rural population, ponds have always been a popular source of water. Although pond water is not used for drinking, it is used for different domestic purposes. It is generally agreed amongst the villagers who took part in the study, that pond water quality is not the same as it used to be. But it has not occurred to them that ponds are highly contaminated and, as such, represent a health risk when used for bathing, ablution, washing kitchen utensils and for cooking. Unsanitary conditions surrounding the ponds are seen as the main cause of pond contamination by the villagers. The study argues that inappropriate or irregular maintenance of the ponds has caused their deterioration and, as a consequence, has increased the contamination of pond water. Today, villagers disregard the importance of pond maintenance because they no longer use pond water for drinking purposes but use tubewell water instead. However, two important considerations justify the demand for the improvement of ponds as an alternative water source. These considerations include the fact that ponds are well accepted as a source of water for domestic purposes, and alternative water sources are required due to the severity of the groundwater situation in Bangladesh. Therefore, alternative methods have to be found for sustainable pond management. Pond management is sustainable if the ponds are regularly maintained to uphold the different functions and local forms of water supply, and to keep the water sufficiently safe for a determined purpose.

The problems associated with the use of tubewells for drinking water demonstrate the ecological and social imbalance introduced by development aid activities. One of the major reasons why development projects often fail at the village level is that there is insufficient consultation with the local community in the planning and implementation of a development project. Large-scale technocratic projects are limited in their transfer of technology and knowledge as they do not take into consideration the needs of the supposed beneficiaries of the project. In this situation, the motivation is usually profit-oriented and helps to increase the power and prestige of the companies and the élite of the village who are directly involved in the development project. As a result, development activities do not always reach the target groups for which they are intended. Although development theory and development practitioners have attempted to break the monopoly of the technocratic approaches they have encountered various problems. Some of the more appropriate approaches were:

- logic behaviour argument
- concept of appropriate technology
- basic needs approach
- self-reliance approach
- participatory development and community management
- concept of sustainable development

It is argued that only an actor-oriented, self-responsibility approach, which integrates the opinions and experiences of the people involved, guarantees the sustainability of a development project.

The study is not advocating a general endorsement of ponds as an alternative for tubewells, or for a traditional approach as opposed to modern technology, but rather would like to demonstrate that the specific locality of the water source has to be taken into consideration as well as the users' cultural and physical needs and their ability to be active participants in a decision-making process. Such considerations as these have often been ignored in the planning of projects directed at water supply, although local expertise in the management of water can be invaluable throughout the project cycle. In the section on pond management it will be shown that people's decisions are reasonable and realistic as they adapt to the environmental and cultural changes in order to cope with new situations. In this context, the contamination of a pond is generally accepted by the users because the pond is not used for drinking water anymore. Traditional concepts associated with pond management and water supply often conflict with western concepts which then creates tension between the initiators of a project and the beneficiaries. For example, local concepts of cleanliness and the quality and purity of the water supply ignore health awareness messages that are disseminated to rural areas in Bangladesh by non-government organizations and the government. But local indigenous knowledge can be invaluable in finding appropriate alternatives for improving the quality of pond water. The study integrates the people's views on the opportunities and the problems associated with pond management issues. These could make an effective contribution in future pond management projects. Finally, a community management approach will be presented and will focus on how such an approach could help to improve the situation of ponds within a village community.

In the past, the Bangladesh Water Policy has neglected ponds as an important water source. The policy clearly addresses and promotes water management projects that aim at increasing the output of food crops through irrigation, or of fish production in fishery projects. Ponds are only mentioned in the policy as a potential source for investment in fish production. Consequently, statistics on ponds as well as scientific studies have only considered the possibility of raising the status and potential of ponds for increasing fish production. This study looks at water policy and research on ponds that has been neglected up until now and focuses on the importance of ponds for domestic purposes. This use of ponds has been of little interest in the past because there was no profit associated with it. Moreover, the main actors who are responsible for ponds are women and they are not normally considered in development projects aimed at water supply.

1.4
Hypotheses

Given the circumstances outlined above, two main hypotheses are directing this study:

1. Pond management, defined as the use, maintenance and control mechanism of ponds, has changed, principally due to the external development intervention of the introduction of tubewells. The effects of the change are visible in two ways:

- Ecological aspects. Pond maintenance has deteriorated. In the past, ponds were used for drinking water purposes and protected by the local landlords. Today, hand tubewells have replaced the ponds for drinking purposes. Consequently, many ponds have become derelict and are not properly maintained. Contaminated water and the collapse of embankments pose major health risks.
- Social aspects. The original concept and function of the ponds have changed. Pond use is being commercialised: new forms of production, e.g. fish production, compete with traditional forms of consumption (cooking, bathing, washing). The domestic function of the pond is slowly undermined by a profit-oriented motive. This may increase the social imbalance and conflict between the different pond users.

2. Ponds may be a viable alternative for future water management in Bangladesh if their inherent problems are dealt with:

- Ponds, as a traditional water source, are still able to meet people's needs. Ponds are a popular and culturally accepted water source for various domestic purposes, for example bathing, washing clothes and utensils and cooking and ablution in Bangladesh. With regard to the high level of people's acceptance to the use of ponds and the urgent need for alternative water sources due to the arsenic contamination of the groundwater, it is reasonable to consider ponds as alternatives to tubewells. Therefore, the focus will be on the viability of ponds for domestic purposes because this aspect has been neglected in the field of research and policy on ponds.
- Local people can help themselves decide on appropriate measures because they think rationally and have local experience and knowledge. The study argues that people are aware of the changes and have acted accordingly. Rural people have their own knowledge about water treatment methods and pond maintenance techniques and they have their own institutions to handle village affairs. These facts should be considered when planning improvements to ponds. Taking into account local people's statements and opinions people-centred propositions can be identified.

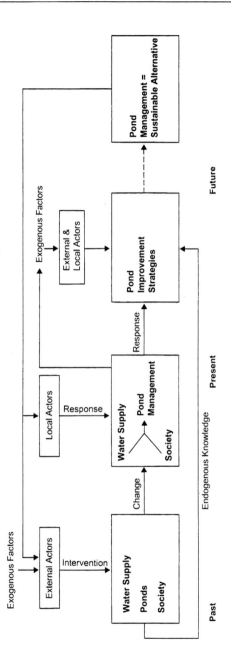

Figure 1.2 Development Aid, System Changes and Sustainability in a Rural Setting – The case of Tubewells and Pond Management in Bangladesh (I)

Figure 1.2 outlines in a simplified way the processes of change and the reactions of the actors in the case of the ponds influenced by external interventions.

1.5
Significance of the hypotheses

The hypotheses are relevant at two levels:

1. Significance of theory:

- The study on pond management attempts to fill a gap in the research on water management in Bangladesh. Until now, there has been no general study on ponds available although ponds were, and still are, an important water source. The only studies that were conducted investigated the economic aspects of ponds either for fish production or for irrigation purposes. These studies emphasised the business aspects and were aimed at increasing the production of fish or crops. Studies on the domestic function of ponds have not been conducted. Only some gender studies have emphasised the many uses of ponds for domestic purposes. Therefore, this study is the first to focus on the domestic use of ponds and the first to compile information on different aspects of ponds from a historical, socio-cultural, economic and ecological point of view.
- Moreover, this study on ponds defines and explains the integrative geographical approach. Pond management is seen as a complex system where historical, social and economical factors interrelate with epidemiological, technical and ecological factors. Because of its integrative and interdisciplinary nature the geographical approach is considered an appropriate method to investigate, understand and explain complex problems by interconnecting the physical and social aspects of a spatial system. The complex system analysis will be applied on a small scale utilising the instrument of a locality study and a variety of social science methods. Therefore, the study is a cognitive contribution to the theory of geography.

2. Significance of policy:

- The study focuses on the use of ponds for domestic purposes and stresses the importance of ponds as domestic water supply sources. The study presents an argument for an intensive discussion on gender topics in water management as women are the main actors in water supply for domestic purposes as they are responsible for collecting water on a daily basis for domestic use.
- The study argues that it is essential to know the views and opinions of the people before any project can be planned. Local knowledge and experience is important to integrate in the planning phase of a project in order to ensure the project's sustainability. This study is relevant in this respect as it provides basic information on ponds for development projects. In addition, the study attempts to discover what measures could be feasible for a sustainable pond management project. This implies that there is a need for discussion on the

difficulties of taking measures or action which result from the tensions that occur due to cultural transition in the society of Bangladesh.

- The study considers ponds in a broad perspective. It is impossible to cover all aspects of this topic in this dissertation. However, it is anticipated that perhaps the input given will motivate further and specific research on ponds.

1.6
Methodology

The complex topic of this research demands an appropriate research design. A dynamic research process was chosen that was flexible enough to integrate relevant questions that were forthcoming in the research process (see figure 1.3). This enabled me to study the topic in greater detail. To meet these requirements various methods, mainly qualitative but also quantitative, were considered appropriate. Among the qualitative methods were: semi-structured, expert and narrative interviews as well as a focus group discussion. Surveys, observations and water quality tests were the quantitative methods selected. The research was based primarily on one in-depth case-study in one locality. This represents a micro system where the structures and processes are easily detectable. In addition, a locality study shows on a small scale how the various elements of a system interact. Although the results are principally valid for the specific locality only, extrapolation can be made to other sites where selected variables are tested. This was done in two additional case studies in order to complement and round out the findings from the main investigation.

A link between the empirical findings and policy was constructed by a short evaluation of three local pond improvement projects according to the criterion of community management.

1.7
The structure of the study

The study is divided into two conceptual parts (chapters 2 to 4) and an empirical part (chapters 5 to 9). The final chapter presents the synthesis of this study.

Chapter 2 outlines why development projects often fail. A brief history of development theories over the previous 50 years is presented. This shows that the universal application of economic theories have contributed to an alienation of development from the beneficiaries. Old and new counter-approaches that criticise the conventional development paradigm are reviewed regarding their potential for overcoming the deficits of development programmes. The second part of the chapter introduces a methodological approach that is considered helpful for both development researchers and practitioners: the integrative system approach, characteristic for the discipline of geography, stresses the interaction of actors and locality. This approach corresponds with the community management approach which is currently the most appropriate way of bringing about sustainable development.

Chapter 3 describes the water sources, the water policy and the water crisis in Bangladesh. It shows that despite the multitude and availability of water sources

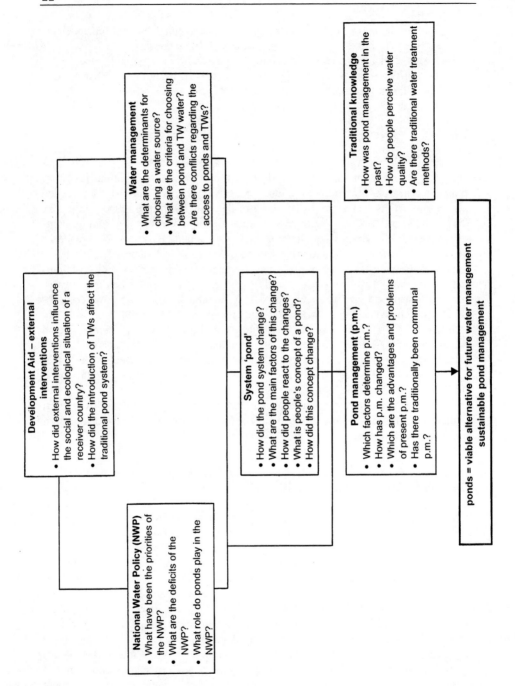

Development Aid – external interventions
- How did external interventions influence the social and ecological situation of a receiver country?
- How did the introduction of TWs affect the traditional pond system?

National Water Policy (NWP)
- Which have been the priorities of the NWP?
- What are the deficits of the NWP?
- What role do ponds play in the NWP?

Water management
- What are the determinants for choosing a water source?
- What are the criteria for choosing between pond and TW water?
- Are there conflicts regarding the access to ponds and TWs?

System 'pond'
- How did the pond system change?
- What are the main factors of this change?
- How did people react to the changes?
- What is people's concept of a pond?
- How did this concept change?

Pond management (p.m.)
- Which factors determine p.m.?
- How has p.m. changed?
- Which are the advantages and problems of present p.m.?
- Has there traditionally been communal p.m.?

Traditional knowledge
- How was pond management in the past?
- How do people perceive water quality?
- Are there traditional water treatment methods?

ponds = viable alternative for future water management sustainable pond management

Figure 1.3 Iterative Research Process: Research Questions

Bangladesh needs to reconsider its water policy that should also include the ponds.

Chapter 4 starts with the presentation of some sustainable water treatment methods that could be applicable for ponds. Then, the change of the pond concept is illustrated by describing historical, socio-cultural, economic and ecological aspects. This reveals that the cultural value attached to ponds has gradually shifted, which can explain the present situation of the ponds and of pond management.

Chapter 5 gives an overview of the research design in line with the integrative system approach and provides the research methodology. The selection of the study areas is outlined as well as considerations about social research in a foreign culture. Then the methods and problems that occurred during data collection and analysis are explained.

Chapter 6 first presents the socio-economic structure and processes of the village studied in depth, then the changes in the water supply are described. Finally, the factors that determine the villagers' choice of a water source for domestic purposes are outlined. This demonstrates the importance of various water sources in the village.

Chapter 7 deals with pond management in the village case-study. The use and the determinants of use, maintenance and its determinants, and the water quality and environment of twelve ponds in the village are investigated and described. The opportunities and problems of the ponds in serving domestic purposes are presented.

The importance of ponds in critical groundwater areas is explored in chapter 8. A comparative study of two additional villages investigates the role of pond maintenance and local water treatment methods in order to identify similarities and to draw general conclusions.

The relevance of the research findings for development policy to improve ponds are discussed in chapter 9. Institutional and technical considerations are relevant, the emphasis, however, is on institutional aspects. The findings support the community management approach as most appropriate to guarantee the sustainability of pond improvement projects.

The last chapter finally returns to the objectives and hypotheses of this study and evaluates them in view of the empirical findings. The relevance of the findings is summed up for the discipline of geography, development practice, and the project partners and donors.

2 Conceptual framework: economic development theories and the integrative system approach

For many years development was equated with economic growth and modernisation. Technological progress, industrialisation and urbanisation were the instruments promoted to achieve this goal. Development aid was therefore meant to increase the long term economic growth of low income countries. However, this developmental misconception of economic growth and a unilateral transfer of technology and know-how ignoring the differences of nations, local needs and peculiarities, resulted in limited benefits of development aid, even polarisation. An example is the Green Revolution and its positive contributions in securing the supply of food crops in developing countries. But the negative consequences of this approach cannot be denied and are well documented. Mechanisation of agricultural labour caused an increase in agricultural unemployment and resulted in massive rural-urban migration. Regional (class) disparities widened as favourable regions were preferred for investment. The intensive input of fertiliser and chemicals to highly sensitive ecosystems affected local biodiversity including resources such as water, fish and soil (CLEAVER 1972: 181-186; GLAESER 1987).

External intervention under modernisation policies took various forms: constructing infrastructure, linking a region with the market economy, changing the institutional decision-making patterns or providing technological input. These factors are mostly interrelated and contribute to a general change of the traditional system. Various studies have investigated such changes. JODHA (1989) and MOSSE (1997) for example, discuss the effects of privatisation and especially nationalisation of common property resources in India. EHLERS (1996) describes the destruction of the livelihood system of Iranian Highland nomads as part of an orchestrated regional change. APPADURAI (1990) focuses on the impact of new technology, in the form of motorised wells, on traditional agricultural systems in India. All the studies come to similar conclusions: external intervention has led to a mismanagement of local resources, a new stratification of the rural community and the loss of traditional knowledge. As a consequence, the vulnerability of the social and ecological system has increased.

This study supports these general findings by taking the example of a traditional water source: the pond in rural Bangladesh. It shows that the introduction of hand tubewells for disease prevention contributed to the deterioration in the management of ponds. This is all the more relevant because Bangladesh faces an acute groundwater deficit. Furthermore, the groundwater crisis might have been accelerated by the policy focus on tubewell irrigation.

This chapter provides the theoretical background of the study. It aims at

1. understanding and explaining the reasons for the failure of conventional development programmes;
2. presenting elements of an alternative approach to development.

The chapter commences with an overview of the economic development theories of the past 50 years that have determined development policies and programmes. Critical approaches that countered standard economic development theories are also included in this review. Two causes are held responsible for the limited success of development. They centre on the disjunction of development aid and beneficiaries, and on the presumption that economic principles are universally applicable and relevant to all problems and regions. Accordingly, some counter approaches are discussed that suggest a people-centred course of development. Being aware of the complexity and volume of literature on development economics, this chapter refers only to the most relevant theories and thoughts.

2.1
Pertinent economic development theories

The link between the terms 'economic' and 'development' and the term 'economic development' was not established before the 1940s (MEIER & SEERS 1984: 6). The term 'development' implies that a basis is given but has to be improved upon to reach a higher level. Development in this sense implies progress and growth (RUTZ-IMHOOF & TOCHTERMANN-PEDIO 1989: 4). Originally, the term was understood in the historical context of Western philosophy: The Judaeo-Christian linear conception of a beginning (creation of the World) to an end (judgement) which during the Period of Enlightenment introduced a new understanding of human consciousness and a turning away from religious dogmatism. The concept of evolution was increasingly influencing science and the general view of the world. GEORG W. F. HEGEL explained in his first work, *The Phenomenology of the Mind* (1809), that the history of human self-consciousness corresponds with the history of cultures in general and is structured according to stages striving towards absolute knowledge. But it was CHARLES DARWIN'S book, *The Origin of Species by Means of Natural Selection* (1895), that propagated the concept of evolution. According to DARWIN, the human species is the final stage in a sequence in the development of life. HERBERT SPENCER tried to extend Darwin's findings to science in general. For SPENCER the principle of evolution is able to structure all empirical data, as stages of development and transformation processes are visible in biological as well as social sciences. In his main work *System of Synthetical Philosophy* (1862-69) SPENCER describes the evolution of society and the way to social Darwinism. He declared that social change towards a functionally more complex and more differentiated society is the result of progress, which means adaptation to functional changes. VOLTAIRE (1694-1778) was interested in the stages of progress that human beings transcended, from barbarians to civilisation. VOLTAIRE considered development an eminent law that was guiding world history

(HELFERICH 1992: 213). As statesmen, VOLTAIRE and MONTESQUIEU (1689-1755), regarded the nation state as the main force and goal of progress (HERB et al. 1985: 56-59).

The economists of that time were concerned with the question as to how a nation may achieve economic progress. In his classical work *Inquiry into the Nature and Causes of the Wealth of Nations* (1776) ADAM SMITH identified capital accumulation as the source of growth. Opposing mercantilism, SMITH proclaimed an economic liberalism where the invisible hand of the market price automatically balances demand and supply. The division of labour, technological progress and foreign trade would accelerate the capital growth of a nation (MEIER 1989: 86). SMITH's contemporary colleague DAVID RICARDO (1772-1823) supported the idea of the *laissez faire* philosophy in his theory of comparative costs. Comparing the production costs of commodities between the United Kingdom and the USA, RICARDO concluded that each country should concentrate on its comparative advantage in production through specialisation and division of labour (DESOUZA & BRADY 1976: 8). The reverend and mathematician, but non-economist, THOMAS MALTHUS, expressed his doubts about unlimited economic growth in his *Essay on the Principle of Population* (1798). He postulated that population would grow at a geometric rate and therefore surpass food supplies, which can only increase at an arithmetic rate. Therefore, an agricultural society would not be able to supply the necessary amount of food, given limited land resources. Consequently, progress would be impossible, as *per capita* income would decline. MALTHUS is considered a representative of the classical economy. His theory was interpreted as a legitimisation of supply-side economics which promoted a cheap labour policy in the colonial empires (TODARO 1994: 191, 192; MEHMET 1995: 37, 38).

In the 19th century, Marxism vehemently opposed the classical economic growth theory. KARL MARX stated that economic growth was always unbalanced because competitive production created cyclical crisis. He included the colonial countries in his theories, interpreting them as extensions of the capitalist system. Later, these concepts were specified by the theory of imperialism. ROSA LUXEMBURG for example, noted that capital accumulation could only continue for the benefit of the capitalist societies if the underdeveloped countries were exploited (DESOUZA & BRADY 1976: 11, 12).

Nevertheless, the belief in the free market mechanism was held until the 1930s. Then, the world depression destroyed the existing assumption that capital accumulation always leads to full-employment. In this situation, JOHN MAYNARD KEYNES demanded an active fiscal policy of the government to overcome unemployment. KEYNES broke with the theory of an uncontrolled free market economy and introduced an alternative for socialism. It can be said that economic theories, including economic development theories, from the 1940s onwards have followed either the classical (conservative) ideas or the Keynesian (liberal) approach. Radical or Marxist ideas have played a marginal role. These three mainstream schools of economy and their derivatives are presented selectively in figure 2.1.

After World War II economics returned to growth theories. Many former colonial states, which had gained political independence in this period, requested participation in development. These former 'underdeveloped' countries became

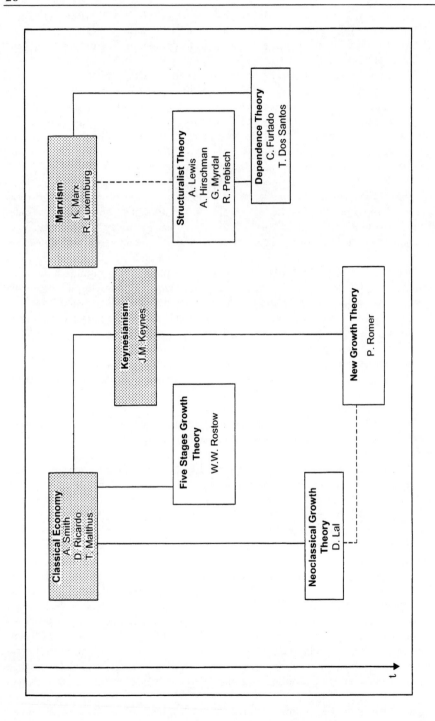

Figure 2.1 Selected Economic Development Theories and Their Representatives

'developing countries' (MEIER 1989: 82). Development economics were attributed two tasks: to find out the forces of development and to suggest policies to eradicate poverty (MEIER & SEERS 1984: 4, 6). Based on classical economic theory development meant growth of *per capita* real income. This period and also the interests of Western politicians and scientists were in favour of the linear growth model, which was the beginning of development economics in the 1950s and 1960s (SEERS 1979: 709). Two growth models were at the forefront of development economics: the five-stages growth model of WALT WHITMAN ROSTOW in 1960, and the dual sector model of ARTHUR LEWIS, published in 1954.

ROSTOW'S growth model is a theory of economic growth and of modern history. Taking a historical perspective, ROSTOW attributed to every society a certain stage of economic development. To become a capitalist society, every society has to undergo five stages of economic growth.[1] He considered the Newtonian principle, which stands for modern technology and science, as the main reason to emerge from the traditional stage. Risk taking, mobility of capital, technology and political will are among the most important conditions to prepare for this emergence. This 'take-off' is characterised by an expansion of industries and an increasing investment in the primary and secondary sector and hence self-sustained growth. Economic growth implies structural changes in the leading sectors of an economy and the stages of growth reflect the strategic choice of a society (ROSTOW 1960: 1-16).

In his dual sector model, ARTHUR LEWIS expands the classical model and views the unlimited supply of labour as the engine of growth. He argues that development occurs through the expansion of the capitalist sector, which attracts labour forces from the subsistence sector as long as wages in the capitalist sector exceed wages in the subsistence sector. However, the key for expansion is reinvestment of the capitalist surplus. Although modernisation of the subsistence sector is considered necessary to support the development of the capitalist sector only by capital accumulation and larger saving rates can investment be enhanced. LEWIS held the notion that countries are underdeveloped not because they are poor but because their capitalist sector is too small and does not provide profits for investment (LEWIS 1954: 141, 146-152, 157, 159). Therefore, "it is true to say that it is agriculture which finances industrialisation" if the capitalist sector is not self-contained (LEWIS 1954: 174). Capital formation and technological incentives also contribute to a rise in profits and stimulates investment (LEWIS 1954: 190). This urban and industry-biased linear growth model was criticised by THEODORE SCHULTZ in 1964. He stressed the importance of agricultural development and human investment. SCHULTZ denied the thesis of the inefficiency of traditional farmers and granted them reasonable behaviour (SCHULTZ 1964: 31, 37; see also chapter 2.3.1).

Criticism also was raised by the structuralists, who acknowledged that economic development was polarising and that equilibrium models had failed. ALBERT HIRSCHMAN, GUNNAR MYRDAL or RAUL PREBISCH for example, recognised that structural problems within developing countries impeded development. HIRSCHMAN did not accept a balanced, linear growth model and

---

[1] These five stages are: 1. The traditional society. 2. The preconditions for take-off. 3. The take-off. 4. The drive to maturity and 5. The age of high mass consumption (ROSTOW 1960).

presented a more complex and dynamic understanding of development processes. He stated that what "'leads away from equilibrium' is precisely an ideal pattern of development" (HIRSCHMAN 1958: 66). According to HIRSCHMAN, polarisation effects in the beginning of development are natural. He even considered growth points as positive because they create multiple effects, generate new demand and induce new investment (DESOUZA & BRADY 1976: 573, 574; HIRSCHMAN 1958: 70). Like HIRSCHMAN, GUNNAR MYRDAL offered an explanation for unbalanced growth. His model of cumulative upward causation demonstrated that change in one region creates further change there and in other regions. The expanding locations create backwash effects, as they extract capital, labour and skills from other locations and hence increase inequality between locations. But a growing location may also induce growth in another location through diffusion of technology or increase in demand. Only if these spread effects are greater than the negative backwash effects would equal development occur (DESOUZA & BRADY 1976: 572, 574). An attempt to explain inequalities was given by RAUL PREBISCH. In 1950, he introduced the centre-periphery concept. PREBISCH explained the disparities between 'centres' and 'peripheries' with unbalanced terms of trade between exporters of finished goods and exporters of primary goods. PREBISCH demonstrated in the context of Latin America that the industrialised countries, through their technological advantage, acted as the centres and profited from the peripheral exporters of raw materials. According to PREBISCH, the deterioration of the terms of trade, resulting from low-income elasticities of demand for imported primary goods in the centre and high-income elasticities of demand for imported manufactured goods in the periphery, could be solved by import substitution industrialisation. With the help of protectionist politics, production for the domestic market should be promoted (PREBISCH 1984: 178, 179). The structuralists clearly voted for government intervention in the case of unequal development. However, they also took into account that at the beginning of development distribution of income in the developing countries would be unequal but that, over time, through a process of trickling-down, less developed regions would disappear. As a result, structuralists accepted growth policies without distribution, at least for the time being (MEHMET 1995: 84-86; NOHLEN & NUSCHELER 1992: 135, 136). In this sense, the structuralists represent the liberal strain of economic development theorists.

The 'radical' perspective of development economics resulted from the structuralist approach and was represented by the dependency theory. Responding to the political instability in Latin America in the 1960s their common incentive was to explain the incapacity of Latin American economies to adapt to capitalist structures. Moreover, they referred to the imperialist theory of the Marxists, describing underdevelopment as a historical process. Only the following two representatives of the mainstream schools of economy, C. FURTADO and THEOTONIO DOS SANTOS, were focused. For FURTADO, the invasion of a capitalist structure in a pre-capitalist region is expressed in a dualistic economy, which manifests underdevelopment. The main problem is the balance of payment deficits, which results from a stagnant economic structure and increasing consumption of imported goods in the pre-capitalist country (FURTADO 1981: 34, 37, 38). DOS SANTOS extends the argument saying that import substitution industrialisation had made the situation even worse due to dependence on external suppliers of vital goods and the accompanying high prices. As a consequence, even with import substitution, industrialisation, foreign capital and technology increasingly gain control over a country, which the government is unable to counteract. Dependence then is a "conditioning situation", in which some countries are conditioned by the economies of other countries. Thus underdevelopment is nothing more than a consequence of capitalist development, and import substitution industrialisation is "dependent capitalism". The only solution would be to change the internal structure of developing countries. But this would create confrontation on an international level (DOS SANTOS 1981: 67, 68, 76, 79).

In the beginning of the 1970s, new development strategies emerged. Although many developing countries reported rapid GNP growth the rate of unemployment was steadily increasing and income distribution became more and more unequal. It was acknowledged that growth of the GNP should not be considered the aim of development but its result. Several schools offered explanations for the failure to reduce poverty (STEWART & STREETEN 1981: 148, 149).[2] Poverty remained a severe problem. It was acknowledged that the development problem was a distribution problem (DAG HAMMARSKJÖLD FOUNDATION 1975: 26). AMARTYA SEN for example, demonstrated that starvation and famines, like the Great Bengal Famine of 1943, could not be attributed to food scarcity or low agricultural productivity but to policy failure and deprivation of entitlements (SEN 1997). Moreover, unemployment in developing countries, particularly in the urban centres, was alarming. In 1969, the International Labour Office (ILO) launched an employment-oriented study to investigate the problem and structure of unemployment in several developing countries (INTERNATIONAL LABOUR OFFICE 1976: 2). The ILO report on *Employment, Income and Equality* in Kenya stated that unemployment was not the problem but that the disregard of what was believed to be unproductive employment, as in the informal sector economy, was responsible for poverty, reduced access to education and urban migration. The study considered far-reaching social and economic measures to tackle the employment problem. Among the major concepts were:

- economic growth - to raise the minimum level of income
- redistribution from growth - to reduce the large regional income disparities
- acknowledgement and support of the informal sector

The strategy of *redistribution with growth* intended to extract parts of the incremental labour income via taxation of the public and then distribute this income to the poor (INTERNATIONAL LABOUR OFFICE 1972). Unemployment in the metropolitan cities of developing countries also indicated that LEWIS' two sector-model had failed. The mass rural-urban migration had not increased economic growth but rather unemployment. MICHAEL TODARO developed a model that explained the rationale behind this apparent economic paradox. His main argument is that migration is determined by the expected, and not the real, income

---

[2] Price Theory blamed the price system which was incorrectly settled. Radicals asked for a structural reform in the developing countries, for a redistribution of the assets and equal access to resources. The technologist school believed innovative technology to be the appropriate strategy to eliminate poverty (STEWART & STREETEN 1981: 163-168).

differentials between rural and urban areas. Assuming a long-term goal on part of the migrant and the possibility of urban employment migration becomes justified. Thus, it would be wrong to create more urban jobs because the imbalance of economic opportunities between rural and urban areas was already the central problem. Therefore, TODARO voted for a policy focusing on rural and agricultural development (TODARO 1998: 280-87).

However, both objectives of reducing unemployment and inequality, could not be achieved. Increasing urban employment opportunities led to greater rural-urban migration. Moreover, the initial distributions of assets or available technology were not taken into consideration in this approach. Finally, reducing inequality appeared to be highly complex. Under these circumstances the basic needs approach offered a more concrete and realistic alternative (STREETEN 1981: 325- 329, GHAI 1978: 3). As STREETEN (1981: 332, 333) notes:

> "We are now back to where we started in the 1950s, when pioneers [...] told us that development must be concerned with meeting basic human needs [...]."

Statements about the basic needs approach were published in various international documents, such as the UNCTAD Cocoyot Declaration in 1974, the report of the Dag Hammarskjöld Foundation in 1975 and the ILO Report on *Employment, Growth and Basic Needs* in 1976. The basic needs approach has been generally considered to contribute to a fundamental change in many of the international development problems, like the deterioration of the terms of trade, migration and the transfer of technology (GHAI 1978: 4, 5) (see Chapter 2.3.3). Ideas and approaches, referring to the basic needs concept, determined development activities during the 1970s.

The general belief that economic development had aggravated economic disparities was extended by the fact that the increasing cultural and economic interdependence of the developing countries was not met by an effective international development co-operation. Moreover, the success of the OPEC[3] and the experience of the Vietnam War indicated that the old-world order was shaken. In 1975, the Dag Hammarskjöld Foundation submitted a report on behalf of the United Nations General Assembly that required another perspective on development and a new international order. Self-reliance, in a national and a collective manner, was the main driving force of the concept. The report clearly condemned the unequal economic relations and the exploitative power structures and asked for structural transformation (DAG HAMMARSKJÖLD FOUNDATION 1975: 6, 63, 64, 71). However, the New International Economic Order created confusion as it was interpreted in different ways. On one side, it was seen as the demand to release developing countries from the established rules. Whereas, on the other hand it was seen that more concessions on the part of the developed countries would be sought. A third strain wanted the international relations to be restructured in total (STREETEN 1981: 240, 241).

Economic growth not only failed to diminish poverty it also took a heavy toll on the natural resources pool. "Green movements" in industrialised countries

---

[3] OPEC stood for the example of a transnational organisation, representing the developing countries, which had achieved to determine the global market and hence the industrialised countries.

became active in the late 1960s. In 1972, the landmark publication of the Club of Rome (MEADOWS et al. 1972) demonstrated the physical limits of economic growth (see chapter 2.3.6). The consequences of exponential population growth on non-regenerative resources and food supply were described graphically. Measures against environmental pollution and supply constraints were mainly seen from a technological perspective. Moreover, ethical issues concerning the Western system were discussed by economists such as E.F. SCHUMACHER, as well as philosophers like HANS JONAS (see chapter 2.2).

In the 1980s, under the conservative governments of Britain and the United States, the neoclassical economy regained favour. Reasons for this shift were a general revival of the neo-classical theory, but also empirical evidence. On the one hand there were the success stories of some Southeast Asian countries following the example of free-market economy, on the other hand there were the negative outcomes of state intervention in Latin America and Africa. Underdevelopment was considered an internally induced phenomenon of developing countries, caused especially by state intervention and corruption. Therefore, the privatisation of public enterprises and a *laissez faire* economy with promotion of export and open markets were proclaimed (NOHLEN & NUSCHELER 1992: 152, 153; TODARO 1998: 86-89; MEHMET 1995: 128). One of the advocates of the neo-classical growth theory, DEEPAK LAL, accused the "dirigistes" for their disapproving attitude towards the poor as they deprived them of economic thinking. The dominance of state policy was responsible for the distortions in developing countries. LAL prefers imperfect markets to imperfect planning and was convinced of the power of growth to alleviate poverty (LAL 1997: 95, 103-106).

However, despite the liberalisation of trade and free-market reforms in the 1980s and 1990s, developing countries did not produce the expected growth rates. Indeed, major developing countries were facing a debt crisis. One reaction to the failure of neo-classical theory was the new growth theory, which states that the national growth depends on endogenous forces on a long-term basis. One of the main reasons for the developing countries to lag behind is their low investment in human capital, infrastructure and research and development (R&D). The new growth theory points out that growth is achieved in an endogenous deliberate way through investment in human capital and research and development. The role of the state is to support this policy actively (TODARO 1998: 90-93). PAUL ROMER, for example, stresses the importance of endogenous technological change for growth. Although technology itself is a non-rival input, it is partially excluded as the "ability to add" depends on human capital that reacts to market incentives. Therefore, investment in human capital is decisive to expand research and development and to increase the rate of growth. Integration into the world market is desirable because it further increases the pool of human capital (ROMER 1989: 3-6, 31).

In spite of changing paradigms, the development theories presented have the following points in common:

• Development has basically been identified with economic growth

- Over the past 50 years development theories have undergone a cyclical development where classical approaches alternated with more liberal and radical approaches
- Technology was always considered an important factor in modernising and developing traditional economies
- Economic development theories could not manage to reduce poverty and/or inequality in a sustainable way

2.2
Critique of economic development theories

The fact that growth was seen as the goal of development, not as the means, and that all economic development concepts were too abstract and disregarded the human factor impeded the sustainability of development attempts. Finally, social and ecological considerations became established in economic development. Current approaches in development cooperation try to combine economic growth with social and ecological components. But, in retrospective, one can see that critique of conventional economic theories is as old as the theories themselves. Drawing from the previous review of economic development theories, the two major arguments of these criticisms are disclosed in this chapter. They can be seen as the background on which an alternative development can be built upon. Elements of such a development will be itemised in the next chapter in the form of counter approaches.

The essence of a critique on economic development theories is based on the following two statements:

1. Development theories of the past 50 years contributed to an alienation of the human being from its natural habitat. The technical and scientific achievements have led to the impression that the human being is separated from the natural environment and from everything that she or he has not produced themselves. This attitude goes partly back to the interpretation of Protestant ethics and Enlightenment philosophy (SCHUMACHER 1973: 12).[4] On the one hand, a return to more humanistic forms of production is supported (SCHUMACHER 1973: 144). On the other hand, a revision of the ethical attitude towards nature and life is promoted. The German philosopher HANS JONAS (1984: 372, 392), for example, argues that we have to take responsibility for our actions by facing the future dangers of the planet. JONAS concludes that we need to regain reverence for life in order to overcome the feeling of alienation from nature. The school of ARNE NAESS represents a similar thinking. Their philosophy of Deep Ecology includes a respect for the diversity of human and non-human life, which has to be preserved for future generations. Striving for the goals and not for the means is considered the main aspiration in life (BODIAN 1995: 28, 29).

---

[4] SCHUMACHER (1973: 49, 51) compares Western and Buddhist economies. Taking the concept of work, he demonstrates that it is understood entirely different in Buddhist economy where the producer remains related to his or her product. Instead of accumulation of goods, Buddhist economy aims at simplicity and non-violence.

2. Universal validity of economics has dominated development theory and practise of all the social sciences in this century, economics has achieved an outstanding universal credibility. But economics has transformed from a developing to a defensive science. Whereas, in the beginning the science of economics was considered a means to achieve certain social goals, today it represents the means itself (HERB 1985: 65, 69). SCHULTZ (1964) already questioned the universal application of western economic principles as he recognised that non-western countries are differently constituted. SCHUMACHER (1973: 40, 42) believes that economists have a reductionist perspective, concentrating on the market only, and that this can be dangerous when they attempt to explain matters in different cultural and regional contexts. The critique may be extended to all sciences, which pursue a highly specialised direction but do not take into account the complex whole in its variations. MEHMET (1995: 6) vehemently refuses "the universality and scientific attributes of Western economics" which caused an eurocentric attitude of development.

This critique implies a return to an integrative thinking and to a broader understanding of development. Development is regarded as a complex field, which can not be managed by one discipline alone. But despite the complexity of taking the individual into account, people cannot be reduced to mere numbers in statistics. These two positions will be discussed in following chapters. Chapter 2.3 presents six counter approaches, which stress the involvement of people and the environment in development projects. Chapter 2.4 offers a broader methodological approach to handle complex problems, such as development problems. This is seen as a methodological alternative to the reductionist economic approaches.

2.3
Selected counter approaches

Some ideas behind the counter approaches can be traced back to the 1950s, or even before then. However, most counter approaches attained popularity in development discussion in the 1970s. The distinction between the different approaches, which will be explained in this chapter, is an artificial one, because every approach contains elements of other approaches. Therefore, one can say that it is the conglomerate of all approaches that constitutes 'another development'. The following approaches will be described:

- the logic behaviour argument
- the concept of appropriate technology
- the basic needs approach
- the self-reliance approach
- participatory development and community management
- the concept of sustainable development

2.3.1
The logic behaviour argument

In his book, *Transforming Traditional Agriculture*, ARTHUR SCHULTZ (1964) attempts to explore why traditional agriculture are not growing according to western economic principles. He argues that there is a logical reason why traditional farmers behave in the way they do. SCHULTZ proves with case studies that traditional agriculture is relatively efficient but that the communities involved in this agriculture are poor because the set of production factors remains static. SCHULTZ views this as a problem of investment. In contrast to the common opinion that investment should be made either in land, capital or labour, he demands investment in the farmers' capabilities and knowledge. He states that farmers are very much aware of their marginal rate of return to investment, but given the present circumstances farmers do not have the incentive to save money in order to invest more in new agricultural factors. Economic growth in traditional agriculture is possible through technological change and human resources development. SCHULTZ refers to the given "body of knowledge" on which to build upon.

Although SCHULTZ's argument is based on the principle of *homo oeconomicus* who tries to allocate his resources optimally, his explanation goes beyond the implication of the classical set of factors of production, land, capital and labour. He takes a more actor-focused perspective considering farmer's behaviour and given knowledge. Moreover, SCHULTZ argues that the existing conditions should be taken into account for a modernisation of the first sector in developing countries. One can say that he respected the farmer in his function as decision-maker.

2.3.2
The concept of appropriate technology

Technological change is regarded as a main contribution to modernisation of traditional economies. Technology can be defined as the "application of scientific principles toward solving problems within a particular cultural context" (MALIK & BHARDWAJ 1983: 2, 3). As the western scientific principles were taken for granted, the transfer of technology to non-western countries has always affected the cultural and ecological endowments of a particular society. To often large-scale, capital intensive technology was applied whilst at the same time the regional specificity was ignored. The example of the Green Revolution proved that the same technology is not universally applicable. Technology transfer also intensified the existing power structures in development countries at the cost of the poor. Therefore, developing countries have also demanded a change in the social arrangements that determine the access to and control of technology (CHATTERJI 1990: 131, 133).

A landmark publication on an alternative technology was ERNST FRIEDRICH SCHUMACHER's book, *Small is Beautiful* (SCHUMACHER 1977). He pleaded for a technology of human dimensions, which would facilitate labour but not deprive people of labour. In this sense, technology is not disregarded totally but recognised as an important tool of development. A so-called appropriate or intermediate technology should:

- be on a small-scale and provide for locally situated jobs
- consider local needs, skills and the factor endowment
- realise low investment costs per work place and low capital investment per unit of output
- consider local ideology and institutional framework
- be decentralised and accessible to all
- use natural resources sparingly
- be cheap (SCHUMACHER 1977: 140, 159; EVANS 1979: 42, 43; CARR 1985: 9)

There are no appropriate technologies, for industrialised countries or for developing countries, but technology always has to be modified to meet the given conditions (MALIK & BHARDWAJ 1983: 4).

2.3.3
The basic needs approach

When DUDLEY SEERS was reflecting on the *Meaning of Development* in 1969 he concluded that the universal goal of development was "the realization of the potential of human personality" (SEERS 1969: 2). Searching for a more adequate measure of development than the conventional national growth rate he listed certain "*absolute* necessities", such as food, clothing, shelter and a job.

In the early 1970s, several reports to the United Nations described a basic needs concept. The basic needs approach was a consequence of the dissatisfaction with previous unsuccessful approaches to alleviate the problem of poverty. The advantage of the approach lies in its emphasis on the concrete, not abstract, and on the ends, not the means (STREETEN 1982: 335) (see Chapter 2.1). The ILO report *Employment, Growth and Basic Needs* that was prepared for the World Employment Conference in 1976 was a directive for the basic needs approach. The report proposed that "development planning should include, as an explicit goal, the satisfaction of an absolute level of basic needs" (INTERNATIONAL LABOUR OFFICE 1976: 31). The concept of basic needs implied on the one hand the minimum private requirements, such as adequate food, shelter, clothing as well as household equipment, and on the other hand necessary public services such as safe water, sanitation, public transport, and health and educational facilities. Employment was considered a means and an end of the basic needs approach as it would provide an income and should also give a meaning to a person's life. Since the set of basic needs vary according to the economic development of a country the report stresses people's participation in the determination of their needs (INTERNATIONAL LABOUR OFFICE 1976: 32-35).

The basic needs approach can also be valued as the main step towards people's mobilisation and participation in the development process. Furthermore, it embraces several former development approaches, which have found a common roof within the basic needs concept (STREETEN 1981: 334, 335). Terms like *self-reliance* and *participation* are incorporated in the basic needs approach, they are instruments rather than objectives to poverty alleviation.

2.3.4
The self-reliance approach

The principle of self-reliance goes back to Mao Zedong who proclaimed regeneration through people's own efforts (GALTUNG 1988: 47), and Mahatma Gandhi's statement that not mass production but production for the masses (and by the masses) is needed (SCHUMACHER 1973: 139). The idea of self-reliance reappeared in the context of the basic needs approach of which it is a key element. The Dag Hammarskjöld report particularly emphasised self-reliance for development besides the satisfaction of needs and the eradication of poverty. A self-reliant, endogenous development is supposed to stimulate creativity for a more effective use of the production factors, which in turn reduces vulnerability and dependence. Self-reliance does not mean autarchy but "autonomous capacity to develop and to take decisions..." (DAG HAMMARSKJÖLD FOUNDATION 1975: 34, 35).

Self-reliance includes the concept that people should have confidence in their own capacities and rely on local resources. Self-reliance is supposed to mobilise people in order to return their self-determination and self-esteem which the economic development process deprived them of. This is particularly relevant for marginal segments of a community, women, children or the poor, who are often excluded from participation. These groups need empowerment first. It is the role of the target-group approach to strengthen these marginal groups and improve their self-determination (personal communication with CLAUDE ANDRE RIBAUX, consultant, St. Gallen).

> "People must feel and believe that it is their own efforts that are driving the development process. They must feel that they themselves are contributing the maximum of their own human, financial and material resources, and that assistance from outside is only for what they cannot yet manage themselves.[...]. People must have confidence in their own knowledge and skills, in their ability to identify problems and find solutions in order to make improvements in their own lives" (BURKEY 1993: 50).

The concept of self-reliance also has a political component. Strengthening individual and communal self-determination implies decentralisation and democratisation.[5] The vertical type of organisation, as given in industrialised countries, has to be transformed into a horizontal structure, as was the case in traditional communities (GALTUNG 1983: 28-30, 77, 78). This political aspect of self-reliance is also part of Political Ecology.[6] Although self-reliant development has to be rooted at the local level it is also valid on an international dimension. A third world collective self-reliance would mean, "co-operation against poverty and for development by groups of third world countries...", for example through trade unions to improve the position of developing countries in the international market (DAG HAMMARSKJÖLD FOUNDATION 1975: 35, 71).

The concept of self-reliance can be regarded as a course for an alternative development. In many ways it reverses classical development approaches which

---

[5] The Sarvodaya movement in Sri Lanka is a famous example where the community is the central decision making body (ARIYARATNE 1988).
[6] ATKINSON (1991: 182) for instance demands a "self-reliant regionalism" where the social and political structures are decentralised.

were centralised, technocratic and abstract. CHAMBERS (1985: 173) demonstrates this development bias in a list. Development programmes have mainly favoured the urban, industrialised and (male) educated side concentrating on large-scale, high cost and high prestige projects. The self-reliance concept however, puts people at the centre and transmits power and responsibility to local communities. Rural poor and women are addressed more and the projects should be conducted on a small scale with simple, low cost input and should consider local knowledge.

2.3.5
Participatory development and community management

Ideas to have the community participate in development go back to the 1950s and 1960s.[7] The basic goal of these approaches was community development, that is to say the improvement of the living conditions of a community. In Bangladesh, community management approaches have a long standing tradition. Initiatives started in the 1950s but remained of limited success. The Comilla Programme by the Bangladesh Academy of Rural Development (BARD) was initially very successful. It was declared to be *the* model to improve rural people's life for Bangladesh and for developing countries in general. But the fundamental mistake was that the programme did not aim at self-reliance (JESSEN 1990: 39-44).[8] Also, in the water management sector there have been numerous local initiatives in Bangladesh for a long time already. Unfortunately these community actions have been ignored by external agencies so far. Instead they introduced standardised models that did not bring the desired results (DUYNE 1998: 266).

To create a development from within, the members of the community have to participate actively in their decision-making processes. For this purpose, self-confidence is required and has to be built up through empowerment. According to RAHMAN (1993:116) people's demand should be: "We can produce all these things that we need; give us this power and opportunity." Self-determination and participation are prerequisites for community management. Therefore, participation has to be understood as a process, which passes through various stages. It starts with participation in the implementation of a project and moves towards participation in consultation and decision making until finally, self-reliance is achieved and the community is fully in charge of a project (MCCOMMON, WARNER & YOHALEM 1990: 10; personal communication with CLAUDE ANDRE RIBAUX).

Participation is an indispensable tool for self-reliant community management. The concept of participation reflects the belief today that development is considered a partnership, a cooperation between the leading agencies and donors and the beneficiaries. It is also recognised that development is a process of mutual

---

[7] In the aftermath of independence several countries fell back on traditional self-help concepts. The most famous community programme was started in India in 1952, relating to the principles of Gandhi. The goal was to develop the community which should be guided by village *panchayats* (CHAUKAN 1983: 10, 11).

[8] One main problem of the early approaches was that rich members of village society were the principal beneficiaries of communal development programmes. Grassroots organisations therefore started to shift their approach from "betting on the strong" to the target group. (BURKEY 1993: 43; RIBAUX, ISLAM & MOTALEB 1999: 1-2)).

40

exchange, based on ethical principles such as human dignity and self-esteem. The community management approach can be regarded as the end of a logical argument against conventional development theory. It entails all the elements that are part of development critique: consideration of local circumstances (resources, knowledge, technology, institutions etc.), people-centred development, integration of the natural environment, and self-reliance. Therefore, this approach seems appropriate to realise the requirements that were challenged by the development critique.

2.3.6
The concept of sustainable development

Participatory development that leads to self-reliance has been proven to markedly increase project effectiveness and efficiency (SCHNEIDER & LIBERCIER 1993: 11). In this sense, it may be interpreted as sustainable development. But the concept of sustainable development has a different interpretation. Again, the term is much older[9] but was revived in 1987 through the report of the World Commission on Environment and Development (WCED).[10] The report can be seen as a continuation of the publication of the Club of Rome in 1972, where the limits of natural resources were a major concern. Although the WCED report argues that the needs of the poor should be emphasised and that measures have to be taken on a global scale it remains conformist and technocratic, promoting economic growth but on an environmentally friendly basis.

> "The concept of sustainable development does imply limits - not absolute limits but limitations imposed by the present state of technology and social organization on environmental resources and by the ability of the biosphere to absorb the effects of human activities. But technology and social organization can be both managed and improved to make way for a new era of economic growth" (THE WORLD COMMISSION ON ENVIRONMENT AND DEVELOPMENT 1987: 8).

Nevertheless, the concept of sustainable development has contributed to an increased consideration of the ecological aspects of development. The World Bank, for example, has hired ecologists and anthropologists for Environmental Impact Assessments of their projects, and funds are increasingly used for ecological projects (MEHMET 1995: 125, 126). Furthermore, the Conference in Rio de Janeiro in 1992 proceeded towards a global coordination and cooperation for environmental preservation.

2.3.7
Conclusions

The central aspects of chapter 2.3 can be summarised as follows:

---

[9] Originally the term was utilised in forest management to stress the importance of natural resources balance.

[10] There, sustainable development is defined as: "[...] development that meets the needs of the present without compromising the ability of future generations to meet their own needs" (THE WORLD COMMISSION ON ENVIRONMENT AND DEVELOPMENT 1987: 43).

- Economic development theories of the past 50 years have followed a cyclical pattern. Conservative and liberal streams alternated. Apparently new ideas, such as basic needs or self-reliance, were known facts and were taken up again.
- Development is recognised as a complex field. Abstract economic models did not touch the root of the development problem — poverty. The beneficiaries of a development project were too often excluded from the development process.
- The critique, represented by the counter approaches, is a general critique of the classical economic growth theories. Growth as one aspect towards development is not strictly refused acknowledgement. But growth should emerge from the people and not be imposed on them from above.
- All counter approaches place people in the centre of development activities. First of all they are considered actors not receivers. The cultural and regional particularities are taken into account and are supposed to be integrated into development projects. Finally, people are given back their self-determination and their self-consciousness, which make them feel capable of helping themselves.
- Although the counter approaches are presented separately, in reality they form a complementary unity. The basic needs approach for example, also incorporates the ideas of appropriate technology, participatory development and self-reliance.
- The community management approach is considered the best approach for sustainable development projects because it entails all the elements of an alternative development: the consideration of local circumstances (resources, knowledge, technology, institutions etc.), a people-centred development, integration of the natural environment, etc. In fact, community management represents the end of a self-reliant development. The practical relevance of community management for this study will be outlined in Chapter 9.

It may be anticipated that the community management approach is the most practical instrument for sustainable development and one which is consistent with the integrative approach that is the subject of the following chapter.

2.4
An integrative concept for development research and practise

This chapter centres on a methodological dimension for an approach to deal with complex development problems. A system approach, integrating space, actors and the factors that interconnect them, will be outlined. It will be shown that this approach provides a methodological framework for research on development issues in general and on ponds in particular. Moreover, it also offers conceptual grounds for development projects, especially practical considerations.

The development approaches of the past decades were determined by two paradigms – modernisation and political economy. Today, the development debate is characterised by two tendencies which are a withdrawal from the field of action and a postmodern perspective. On the one hand the negative impacts that development projects had on the local level deter from local involvement, on the other hand it is acknowledged that only a multitude of strategies can help to overcome development problems (SIMON 1997: 184, 187, 192). The previous chapters have illustrated that the economic perspective is too reductionist and that only a broader view, including social and ecological components, enables us to grasp development issues in a comprehensive way. This chapter presents a methodological concept for the analysis of development issues and problems on the background of the past deficits.

The chapter propagates a combination of theory and practise in development, referring to the actors of development. This means to investigate the 'what' and 'why' in order to plan the 'how'. Firstly, a development issue has to be explored in order to understand the problem that it proposes to solve. A development project will commence on the basis of the given information. In either process, the multiple strategies of the actors and their institutional settings have to be taken into account. The question remains: which methodology would be most appropriate to analyse and explain development issues and problems? Past experiences indicate that the modernisation of traditional structures has created new structures that often represent a syncretism of different concepts (SIMON 1997: 191, 192). It is through field work that these new structures, manifested through people's livelihood strategies, can be investigated and explained. Therefore, field work becomes an essential instrument of development studies. Based on these considerations and on the findings of the counter approaches the following elements are seen as beneficial for a methodological concept of development issues:

- a holistic, integrative view
- a dynamic perspective
- an idiographic rather than a nomothetic approach
- a small scale rather than a large scale approach
- and an actor-oriented approach

It is argued that this methodology is considered useful and applicable for both researchers and practitioners in development. To ensure the sustainability of development projects it is therefore necessary for development researchers and practitioner to cooperate. Geography could make a valuable contribution mainly because of its field work tradition and its interdisciplinary character:

> "Development geography might be a useful discipline to overcome some of the difficulties in a further integration between theory and practice" (NARMANN 1997: 181).

2.4.1
System approach: integrative and dynamic

Development issues are complex as they deal with the entire spectrum of human and natural environment on different scales. Therefore, a mono-causal, nomothetic approach, as presented in economic theory, is too simplistic to appropriately understand development processes. GALTUNG (1986: 73, 74), for example, calls for holism and dynamism in development theories and stresses the importance of including the natural and the human space which have been left out.

It is argued in this paper that a system approach is appropriate to understand and explain complex problems. According to system theory, a system is defined as the sum of elements and relations that are interrelated and constitute the structure of the system. A system describes the structural and functional aspects of reality. It is the purpose of system analysis to investigate complex facts. System analysis can be defined as an interdisciplinary tool with which to describe the state of a system and its processes and the resulting changes after system modifications (LESER 1991: 55). KAMANN (1998: 280) uses the term 'network'. A network consists of a multitude of elements, which are interconnected with each other through relationships. Since the relations are changing as the elements change, the system is dynamic. In transferring the system approach to the field of development one can see that the natural environment and the social arrangement is a body of elements of one system which are interrelated with each other in a given space. Any disturbance of one element from within the natural or human spheres, or from outside the system, changes the relationships and produces a reaction, in either the human or the natural sphere which is reflected, for example, in conflict or natural disaster. This networking character of the system elements comes much closer to reality and is, therefore, considered valuable to describe and explain complex problems such as development problems. However, a system approach is restricted to problems of implementation. Modelling systems, that means compressing the complex structures and processes of reality, provide the best solution at the moment. An attempt to network modelling is given by KAMANN (1998: 286). He acknowledges four increasingly complex layers of a system after careful analysis of each layer. The first layer includes material relations, the second social interactions, the third the dynamics and the last layer the cultural and cognitive elements. Whereas all layers are interrelated and interact with each other, layer four is attributed an additional explanatory function. It explains why actors behave the way they do.

In this study, the pond constitutes a system which is characterised by the interrelation of social and physical elements. The change of the system pond is influenced by the man-environment interaction. This view of human ecology has a long tradition in social geography (BARROWS 1923). It also indicates that geography moves between two concepts, a cultural and a natural concept, each one taking its specific field as the basis of human adaptation to changes (EISEL 1992: 113).[11]

System changes always take place in a given space, which will be influenced by this change. KAMANN (1998: 280) calls this space 'milieu' which he defines as a 'constructed territory', a unity comprising social, economical and geographical structures of a culture. This construct and its dimensions are discussed next.

2.4.2
Small-scale approach: case-study and locality

Changes in the system affect its elements and, therefore, the space, which they construct. System disturbances in certain regions may have global effects. But it

---

[11] EISEL reproaches the disciplines of ecology and biology with natural determinism, and sociology and anthropology with cultural determinism.

would be quite ineffective to take global measures in changing the regional cause of disturbance. Therefore, solutions have to be found on small scale (LESER 1997: 535, 536). The focus on the specificity of a space is sufficiently relevant because the individual and specific is always a part of the general, despite the uniqueness of a particular place.[12] It is the perspective of the idiographic method, which enables the detection of differences.[13] Small-scale approaches have two advantages; they are closer to what BROWN (1988: 256) calls the "ground reality" and they are methodologically more feasible. The methodological approach of idiographic research is the case-study (see chapter 5.1). Accordingly, the decision for a case-study corresponds with the decision to investigate an individual situation, which embodies part of the entire system. The results of a case-study provide specific solutions. The small-scale is also the dimension for planning and implementation. For these reasons investigating the changes of the system pond started with a village case-study.

Any action or change is always expressed in space. This place of action can be called locality. Common experience, knowledge and a relationship of trust are the fundamentals on which coalitions and local interests are formed that characterise a specific locality (COX 1998: 20, 21). It is the ground level reality where the sense of place is defined by imprints of endogenous characteristics and exogenous forces (BROWN 1988: 256, 261, 270). This space is a social materialisation, created by forces of production, property relations and superstructures (LEFEBVRE 1997: 85). Thus, the local scale, identified by the locality, is the scale of action. These actions are manifested in the *life worlds*. As *life worlds* underlie exogenous forces, they change in time. As a consequence, a locality is also subject to changes, as it reacts dynamically. Thus, any change, from outside the system or from within, influences *life worlds* and action and, consequently, the locality. The empirical study will show that external interventions have influenced people's *life world,* and through this their concept of the pond has changed. Consequently, the locality – the system pond in its spatial context – has also altered which is expressed in the present pond management.

2.4.3
Actor-oriented approach: *life worlds* and strategic action

Life worlds are systems of meaning constructed and established by a community (COX 1998: 26). They enclose the physical (or natural) and the social world. A methodological approach to explore *life worlds* could be the concept of livelihood system as presented by the mandala of an Indo-Swiss research project.[14] The nine square mandala[15] puts the individual in the centre and surrounds it with all spheres

---

[12] EISEL (1992: 139, 140) uses the example of the landscape. Every landscape is unique but at the same time represents typical, general structures.

[13] A nomothetic approach, on the contrary, assumes an individual case to be generally representative.

[14] A study group of the NADEL in Zurich developed this mandala for their ongoing project on Rural Livelihood Systems in India (personal communication with Prof. Dr. RUDOLF BAUMGARTNER, NADEL, ETH Zurich).

[15] A mandala is a symbolic representation of the entire cosmos, illustrated by circles and squares. The concentric structure places the divine sphere in the middle and the different spheres of life

of his life, going from the outer reality (physical conditions) to the inner reality (emotions), from his tradition background (knowledge, experience) to his future orientation (personal aspirations, collective visions) (SWISS NATIONAL SCIENCE FOUNDATION 1998). This holistic perspective manifests a dialectic axis, going from the inner space towards the outer space, which corresponds with the emotional and the physical side of an individual *life world* (see chapter 4.2). An actor may act utilitaristic, according the understanding of the *homo oeconomicus*. But his action can also be normatively regulated as *life worlds* and include the normative and spiritual directives of a community on the basis of the action that occurs (SEUR 1992: 116). This means that the *life world* of a community determines their action and hence influences their place of living. Thus, on one side action by an individual or a community reflects and influences the *life world* of the actor(s), on the other side the *life world* composes the basis of action. Therefore, the most appropriate way to understand *life worlds* is to look at action. Consequently, a change of the *life world* has its impact on individual action and indirectly on the system as a whole.

As a result, the interrelation of actor and locality forms a system that is regulated by the *life world* and exogenous forces. When exogenous forces destabilise the system, there are generally two options: either the system will adapt or collapse. In both respects, it is subject to changes which will affect the given *life world*. Indeed, *life worlds* may only become visible when exogenous forces threaten them. Resistance or solidarity from part of the community are forms which manifest *life worlds* towards outside (COX 1998: 26). A transformation of a particular *life world* will produce imprints in the particular locality through the actor's reaction to the change (BROWN 1988: 267).[16] The system is more capable of adapting to changes if it has reached a certain maturity, which means it is more resilient to injuries. System resilience is enhanced by increased diversity. Integrating various possibilities, allowing synergy to emerge out of interactions is what makes a system stronger (GALTUNG 1988: 81, 83-85).[17] There has to be an either-and attitude instead of an either-or attitude. One can conclude that a more resilient system is more sustainable because it will be less vulnerable to injuries.

---

around, unifying the spiritual with the physical. Particularly in Buddhist societies mandalas serve as basis for meditation.

[16] APPADURAI (1990: 188-198) showed in the Western Ghats of India how the commercialisation of agriculture has affected agricultural knowledge. Whereas technical knowledge used to be integrated in a wider epistemological context, commercialisation created a separation and enhanced the value of technical knowledge. This has caused a secularisation of agriculture and increased the spatial social and ecological differentiation.

[17] GALTUNG (1988: 85) refers to all spaces of development: natural, human, social and world space. A human being, for example, is more resistant to diseases "letting the various homotopes in himself/herself play together." And a society which considers both market and planning mechanism is stronger and more flexible.

2.5
Conclusions of the system approach for development research and practise

According to the integrative system approach the pond is understood as a system containing social, economical, cultural and ecological factors. A pond is a product of human activities and external influences, which is expressed spatially in the pond locality. The pond as the smallest spatial unit changes if one factor of the system changes. The actors: pond owners and pond users, as the smallest non-spatial units, determine the pond locality through their actions. Action is a result of individual decision-making which is based on behavioural patterns. As every actor is a part of a social group his or her behaviour is dependent on the *life world* of this group. The *life world* consists of the totality of the physical endowments and the immaterial reality, such as culture, norms, language and social interactions. The *life world* influences individual needs and preferences and also the image of specific objects, such as the pond. A change in the *life world* induces a change in action and hence in a change of the locality pond. Therefore, to analyse the change of pond management implies an analysis of the human actions because space is manifested through action.

Reviewing the previous chapters, moreover, the integrative concept is congruent with the ideas of the counter approaches to economic development. The principles of appropriate technology, basic needs and the like correspond with a small-scale, actor-oriented and integrative approach. Development is a learning process. The situation has to be understood before incentives for change can be provided. Out of these considerations four steps are proposed to approach development research and practise:

1. Understanding the structures and the processes of change: an investigation should start with the actor and his or her actions because actions manifest the changes of the *life world*, which are caused by external interventions (LONG 1992: 20). When access to the *life world* is established its characteristics can be explored: the physical endowments, the social arrangements, the knowledge, experience and norms that serve the actor in his or her decisions. Thus, the actor's decisions are accepted to be in his or her own way, logical. Becoming familiar with these characteristics is starting to understand the processes and the existing problems. This situation requires an attitude of tolerance and respect towards the other on the part of the outsider, according to the requirements of basic human needs - self-esteem and human dignity.
2. Identifying existing knowledge and resources: the next step would be to build on the existing knowledge and resources. This does not mean to glorify all the given characteristics but to apply an either-and strategy: to select the appropriate methods and instruments to develop what is already existing. It would be suitable to refer to the concepts of local knowledge and appropriate technology.
3. Aspiring self-reliance: during the entire process the holistic perspective should be kept in mind, that locality does not mean autarky and that an actor is part of a community. If self-determination is granted then self-reliance and

participatory approaches are to be realised to achieve development in order to solve problems.

4. Keeping a broad perspective: finally, the more diverse the approaches from within and from outside that actors and the community can make use of, the better prepared they will be to react to changes.

The integrative system approach serves as an analytical tool to explore the problems and opportunities of a specific development issue. The ultimate implementing approach is the community management approach.

2.6
Consequences for this study

After these more general conclusions for development research and practise, the consequences of the theoretical considerations for the research study on pond management are examined. This research is based on the integrative concept, developed in chapter 2.4. In other words, it follows a system approach with reference to a small-scale and actor orientation. Figure 2.2 illustrates the main elements of the study that are the following:

- A pond is considered a system that consists of social, cultural, economical and ecological components, which interrelate with each other. These components are described in chapter 4.2. As a system-construct, a pond also manifests a particular *life world* and specific locality.
- System changes are reflected in action and locality. On the one hand the shift in pond management is expressed in people's action, in the way they use, maintain and control ponds. The pond as a locality has changed, which is also expressed in the physical structure and the environment of the ponds. These processes of change are described.
- Pond management is an expression of system changes. Disturbances inducing change can occur from external actors (for example development agencies) but also from internal actors (pond owners, villagers) through a change of their *life world*. Thus, pond management reflects individual action and changes of the *life world*. The empirical study will also show that today, *life world* is determined more by outer space leading to a concept of the pond which is determined by productive and secular values. Moreover, the contamination of pond water can partly be explained rationally due to the changed concept of the pond.
- The study follows an idiographic method, using case studies to explore on a small-scale the structure and the function of pond management and its processes of change. However, the case of pond management is of general relevance as it describes the impact of exogenous forces and their endogenous reactions in a system. The study does not claim to be representative of rural Bangladesh but certain findings are also relevant for other parts of the country.

Before the change of the system 'pond' through the empirical investigation of pond management is addressed, the subject 'pond' is embedded in the broader context of water management policy in Bangladesh. The next chapter commences with a description of the country's water sources, the water policy and the present water supply problems. It will be shown that national water policy is partly responsible for the acute water crisis in Bangladesh. Among the alternatives for a future water management the ponds should be included. Chapter 4 then demonstrates that technical options for treating pond water exist but that the changed attitude towards the ponds has to be taken into account.

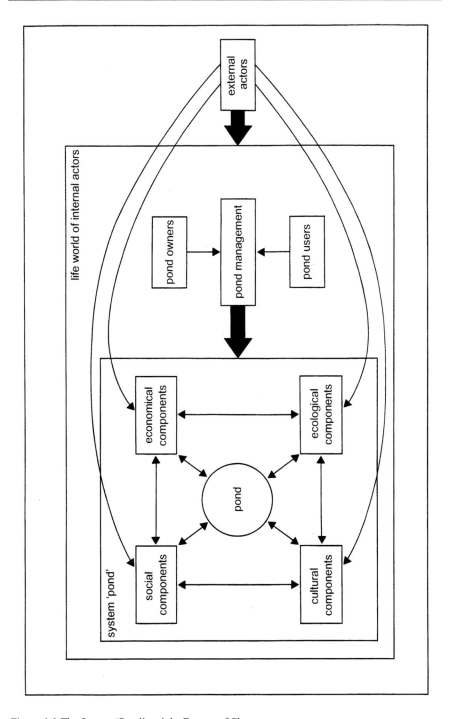

Figure 2.2 The System 'Pond' and the Factors of Change

PART II: WATER AND WATER MANAGEMENT IN BANGLADESH

3 Water sources, water crisis and water policy in Bangladesh

"Water is not only the font of life in Bangladesh. It is the means" (NOVAK 1994: 28). Water is a blessing and a curse at the same time. These extremes are closely related in Bangladesh: the land is flooded during the monsoon period and is then confronted with water scarcity before the monsoon sets in again. The often-hazardous climatic effects are intensified by human activity. Water is a highly political topic. Sector programmes have reacted to the requirements of a growing population. This, however, has led to a pressure on the physical endowment and the water resources, enhancing the potential for conflicts. Therefore, a sustainable management of water resources is needed taking into account the physical constraints as well as the social needs.

The first subchapter provides an insight into the variety of water sources found in Bangladesh. Yet, these have become increasingly vulnerable: today, Bangladesh is confronted with an immense water supply crisis. The second subchapter describes this crisis' form and extent. It is argued that short-term economic water policy has partly been responsible for it. Technical and political considerations have been prioritised and the local actors and ecological factors neglected. Subchapter three illustrates this policy with two examples, the Flood Action Plan (FAP) and the introduction of tubewells for irrigation and drinking water supply. Bangladesh has extended agricultural productivity and provided access to safe drinking water, but social polarisation and ecological deterioration has become a serious reality. Given the fact that Bangladesh has a population of 120 million and the annual growth rate is above 2 percent, urgent measures are needed to find solutions for the critical water supply issue.

3.1 Water sources in Bangladesh

Bangladesh is a country that is situated on a delta. Three large rivers, the Padma, the Jamuna[18] and the Meghna and their tributaries and numerous smaller rivers form the alluvial plain. 50 percent of the country lies less than 12.5 metres above sea level (PITMAN 1993: 34). 90 percent of the water flow comes from the neighbouring Himalayan countries. The precipitation in these areas determines the water flow through Bangladesh. The outflow of water into the Bay of Bengal is the second largest in the world after that of the Amazon system (RASHID 1991:

---

[18] In Bangladesh the Ganges is called Padma and the Brahmaputra Jamuna.

44). The tropical climate characterised by hot and humid summers and dry and cool winters, governs the hydrological system of the country. The main precipitation falls during the monsoon season from the end of May to mid October. Agricultural production relies very much on these south-west trade winds (RASHID 1991: 79, 81)[19].

3.1.1
Groundwater

According to the hydrological cycle the groundwater level is also subject to seasonal variations. The monsoon rains fully recharge the groundwater reservoir. Groundwater levels in general are close to the surface during this period and can drop 15 metres or more in the dry season depending on the area (RASHID 1991: 69). As the contour map (map 3.1) of the lowest groundwater levels shows, the seasonal variations are less in the coastal districts but marked in the central northern and the north-western districts. The extremes are between 2 and 11 metres below the surface for the highest groundwater level, and 5 and 25 metres below the surface for the lowest groundwater level in the *thanas* of Patuakhali on the coast and Nachole in the High Barind respectively (personal communications with BODUR RAHMAN, DPHE Patuakhali and AMJAD HOSSEIN, BMDA Rajshahi). A study conducted by UNICEF and DPHE in 1994 confirmed that during the dry season the groundwater level has been declining over the past few years. A major reason is the excessive abstraction of groundwater by mechanised tubewells for irrigation to sustain the country's food crops (SADEQUE 1996: 11; DPHE & UNICEF 1994). The consequences are obvious: during the dry season the suction mode hand pumps, which are used to draw drinking water, become inoperable in many parts of the country. They have to be replaced by more expensive pumps, such as Mini Tara and Tara pumps. DPHE & UNICEF (1994) have elaborated a list of hand tubewell requirements for all *thanas* of Bangladesh beyond the year 2010. The problem is not merely technical but will become political in the future. The first priority of the government and the World Bank continues to be an increase in food grain production, which can only be achieved by exploring the groundwater resources for irrigation (PITMAN 1993: 31, 34). The National Water Policy has focused totally on groundwater availability for irrigation and has neglected the domestic use requirements.

3.1.2
Surface water

Surface water may be classified as open surface water (rivers, canals) or closed surface water (*beel, haor*, pond etc.). Closed surface water sources are subdivided into natural and man-made water bodies and will be described in more detail.

The river network is Bangladesh's lifeline. Together rivers and canals total more than 24,000 kilometres (RASHID 1991: 44). About 85 percent of the total volume of water is transported by the three major rivers, the Padma, Jamuna and

---

[19] If the monsoon starts too early the *aus* rice crop is endangered, if the monsoon delays the *aman* rice crop may be destroyed.

Meghna. Rivers are the main method of transportation and a principal source of fish, which is one of the staple foods of Bangladesh. Although flooding during the monsoon is important for agricultural production there is also the danger of loss of life and crops in years of major floods. Flood protection measures would be required to minimise the damage but they also imply social and ecological problems (chapter 3.3.1).

3.1.2.1 Natural surface water bodies: lake, beel, baor, haor

There are three lakes in Bangladesh. Two are located in the Hill Tracts south-east of the country, and one in the Eastern Barind. More numerous are *beels* which RASHID (1991: 67) defines as "saucer-like depressions, of a marshy character." During the rainy season, *beels* look like lakes but transform into marshes during the dry season. *Beels* are used for fishing, as water reservoirs for irrigation and domestic purposes, for flood-recession agriculture and transportation (BANGLADESH WATER DEVELOPMENT BOARD et al. 1997: 40). The largest *beels* are located in the districts of Dinajpur, Rangpur and Bogra. *Baors* are old, dried up river courses in oxbow shape. They can be found in the Moribund Delta.[20] Although the boars are more stagnant than the *beels* they are permanently filled with water (RASHID 1991: 68). The *haor* is also characteristic of an entire area around Sylhet. It is a bowl-shaped basin in the Sylhet depression that covers 6,000 square kilometres (BANGLADESH WATER DEVELOPMENT BOARD et al. 1997: 42). In this *haor* basin there are over 400 *haors* and *beels* (RASHID 1991: 68) which are used for fishing, transportation and irrigation. Besides the productive and domestic use of these natural water bodies they also serve as natural water storage for excessive rainfall. This is also the case with man-made surface water bodies, which are described in the following section.

3.1.2.2 Man-made surface water bodies: pond, tank, ditch, dighi

In the literature there is hardly any clear definition or distinction between the terms 'tank' and 'pond'. In general, the term pond includes a variety of small water bodies and often taken as a synonym for tank or ditch. The common definitions for pond indicate that the most important criteria are the size and the use of a pond. In their last pond survey, the Bangladesh Bureau of Statistics for example defined ponds as "...an area of water body covering at least 0.01 acre and it contains water for at least three months of a year. It includes tanks, ditches etc." In addition, they refer to the fitness of a pond to serve for fish production when they distinguish between derelict and non-derelict ponds (1994: 6).[21] KHAN (1990: 166) equals pond and tank and subordinates ditches: "Ponds are small water bodies, less than 0.20 acre on an average, and sometimes are very tiny ditches, about 0.05 acres in size". Another source (SPARSSO 1984: 1) distinguishes between smaller water areas called ponds and larger water areas known as *dighis*.

---

[20] The Moribund Delta is the delta of the Ganges - Brahmaputra rivers, enclosing the districts of Jessore and Kushtia.

[21] A derelict pond is defined as a pond "[...] which cannot be used for fishing without expensive re-excavation (digging), repair of embankments (bounds) or other measures" (BBS 1994: 6).

Ponds "are natural, partly excavated or wholly artificial reservoirs charged by stream, rain or floodwater or all three and used for irrigation, fisheries and domestic purposes". Thus, a pond can be defined as an artificial water body of more than 0.01 acre size (more than 40 square metres)[22] that is mainly charged by rainwater and underground water.

Historians tell us that *dighi* is the oldest and first word for pond. It already had appeared in the 7th century. With the presence of the Muslims in Bengal the terms *pukur* and *pushkurni* were introduced from the Persian language, and the term *dighi* was consequently used for large ponds linked to a famous place or story (personal communication with SAIDUR RAHMAN, former Bangla Academy). The term 'tank' supposedly originated from the Sanskrit word *tagada* and was then adopted by the Portuguese who transformed it into *tanque*.

Apparently there is no single definition for pond but each definition implies the purpose of use. Therefore, it is important to be clear about the specific definition from the beginning in order to understand and react to people's views and needs. For this study a definition of pond from the people's perspective was attempted. It revealed that villagers clearly distinguish between different water bodies and know how to separate a ditch from a pond. The villagers in Dokkhin Garadia defined a pond as follows:

> "A pond is a well-maintained, big and deep water body with four embankments and a bathing site, situated close to the home. Its water and environment is clean. The pond is used for fish cultivation and domestic purposes such as bathing, cooking and washing clothes and utensils" (own interviews in Dokkhin Garadia, December 1996).

But apart from this definition, field work in Dokkhin Garadia indicated that beside the common term for pond (*pukur/pushkurni* or *talab*) other terms such as *maital*, *danga* and *doba* were used. Whereas *doba* corresponds to a ditch, a *maital* is considered to be a small pond and a *danga* a pond which is situated in the fields.[23] This specific distinction between different terms was only observed in Dokkhin Garadia.[24]

Compared with natural surface water bodies ponds are man-made water bodies that originate from excavating soil mainly to build homestead mounds (*bhithi*).[25] Therefore, their number must be much higher than the number of *haors*, *baors* or *beels*. However, few statistics exist on pond coverage in the country. The Agricultural Census in 1960 counted 43,370 ponds (SIDDIQUI 1976: 109), whereas the survey of the Land Revenue Department in 1961 came to 70,000 ponds

---

[22] The Bangladesh Bureau of Statistics has stratified the ponds in three different categories: (1) ponds between 0.01 and 0.10 acres (2) ponds between 0.11 and 0.30 acres and (3) ponds above 0.31 acres (BBS 1994: 2).

[23] Chapter 6.3 discusses the use of different water sources by women. Women clearly distinguish between the use of a *doba*, a *pukur* or a *danga*. Dobas are generally not used because they are perceived dirty. A *pukur* though, like a *maital*, is used for all kinds of domestic purposes. Dangas are only rarely frequented, mainly for bathing, because they are located in the fields.

[24] It remains unknown whether clear distinctions are also made in other parts of the country and why they are made in some parts and not in others. An anthropological investigation might be useful to explore this issue.

[25] Ponds may be as old as the construction of *bhithis*. The original inhabitants of the Bengal delta, the *Bengala*, were said to live on mounds throughout the year because of the floods (NOVAK 1994: 69).

(personal communication with MAHBUBAR RAHMAN, Rajshahi University). In 1984, the Bangladesh Space Research and Remote Sensing Organisation (SPARSSO) mapped all water bodies of 40 selected *thanas* for a joint project between the government and FAO/UNDP. Based on the number of ponds in these 40 *thanas*, the total number of ponds in Bangladesh was estimated to be 13.43 *lakh* (1.34 million) (SPARSSO 1984: iii). The most recent survey, conducted by the Bangladesh Bureau of Statistics in 1989, estimates the total number of ponds in the country to be 1.949 million, which corresponds to a rise of five percent compared with the previous survey results of 1982 (BBS 1994: 9, 11).

These surveys show that the number of ponds has increased over the previous years. It may be assumed that this is linked to the increasing importance of fish production and a corresponding promotion policy. The National Water Policy has stressed that the gap between the potential and the production of fishery resources has to be closed by "scientific management". "Pond culture fishery is expected to play an important role in satisfying the demand for fish in the domestic market" (MINISTRY OF IRRIGATION, WATER DEVELOPMENT AND FLOOD CONTROL, UNDP & WORLD BANK 1991: 5-6; 5-9). Pond definitions reflect this profit-oriented approach. Pond use is officially limited to productive purposes such as fishing and irrigation (see chapter 4.2.3).

3.2
The water crisis in Bangladesh

Despite the apparent variety and abundance of water sources, water supply problems have been increasing over the past years and today present a major burden for the economic and social future of Bangladesh. As early as in 1989 DANIDA predicted several negative environmental effects affecting the future water supply in Bangladesh:

- due to an increasing extraction of groundwater for irrigation there are indications that the water table was lowering
- flood control, drainage and irrigation structures contribute to a siltation of the rivers, affecting navigation and fish supply
- due to prolonged periods of surface water shortage the salinity of the ground- and surface water was increasing
- water pollution: faecal, industrial and agro-chemical, is intensifying (DANIDA 1989: 8)

In the meantime all these concerns have been confirmed and substantiated by various studies. The principal problems are summarised as follows:

Decline of water table

In 1994 DPHE and UNICEF published a study affirming that the water table had been constantly declining in an increasing number of districts of Bangladesh. During the dry season hand tubewells and shallow tubewells for drinking purpose

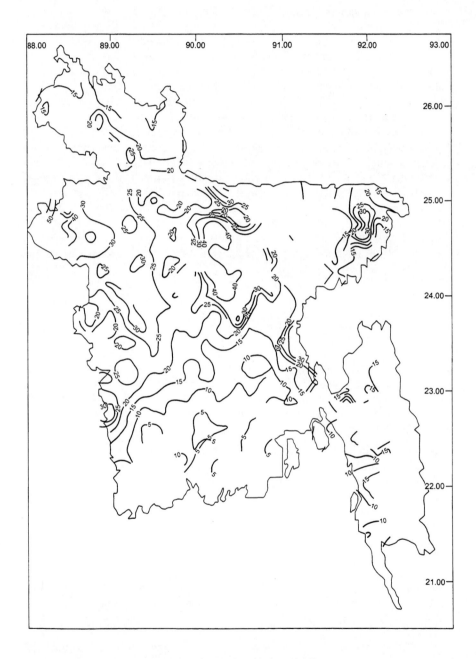

Map 3.1 Bangladesh: Lowest Groundwater Level Contour Map 1996
Source: Department of Public Health Engineering (DPHE), Dhaka

run dry in various parts of the country (DPHE & UNICEF 1994; KHAN, L.R. 1990: 142). Map 3.1 shows the groundwater levels of Bangladesh in 1996.

Decline of surface water

Surface water sources, mainly rivers, tend to silt up. The processes considered responsible are principally the large flood control, drainage and irrigation structures in the country as well as the Farakka barrage[26] in West Bengal (KHAN & HOSSAIN 1994: 105, 109). Moreover, navigation on the rivers is also affected, and fish supply has drastically declined. In addition both processes, excessive abstraction of surface and groundwater, reinforce one another as they are linked in the hydrological system.

Contamination of surface and groundwater

- Uncontrolled industrial waste effluents cause serious pollution of the rivers as well as a decimation of the fish population. The most polluting industries are textile mills, tanneries, pharmaceutical and jute manufacturers.
- Highly toxic fertilisers[27] slowly poison the soil and the farmers and are also washed off into the waterbodies (GAIN 1998: 59, 60, 167).
- Because of the very high population density faecal waste deposit is an obvious problem and faecal pollution of waterbodies is apparent.
- Finally, in the second half of 1996, an additional problem emerged which has taken on alarming proportions – the arsenic contamination of the groundwater.[28] 50-80 million people are supposedly affected in Bangladesh (STEINBERGER 1998: 44). The cause of the arsenic contamination is not yet known for certain. However, it has been proved that arsenic is naturally present

---

[26] The Farakka barrage has posed a major political obstacle between India and Bangladesh for years. The dam was constructed in 1975 to divert water from the Ganges to the Bhagirathi-Hooghly river system in order to preserve the port of Caluctta. Consequently the flow of the Ganges into Bangladesh declined alarmingly: in March 1993 only 9,218 cusec were measured compared with 64,430 cusec before the dam was built (KHONDER 1996: 381, 382). The Governments of India and Bangladesh managed to sign a treaty in December 1996 which agreed on a mutual share of the Ganges water. However, the point of argument has not disappeared as again in August 1997 the Minister of Forest and Environment blamed the barrage for creating droughts in the North of Bangladesh (THE INDEPENDENT 12.12.1996:1; 19.8.1997: 2).

[27] One example is the Zinc Oxysulfate fertiliser, imported from the US, that contains highly toxic liead and cadmium. In addition this fertiliser, which is locally known as *zip*, is also very cheap (GAIN 1998: 59, 60).

[28] Arsenic was detected in the groundwater for the first time in West Bengal in 1978 (QUAIYUM 1997: 13). In Bangladesh it was discovered for the first time in 1993 (ITN NEWSLETTER BANGLADESH 2.7.1997: 2) but a first report was only published in 1994 by Jadavpur University in Calcutta to WHO and UNICEF. This university finally disclosed the topic to the public in 1995 and consequently stimulated further actions in Bangladesh (KHAN 1997: 13). Several governmental and international organisations started to undertake investigations from late 1996 onwards to detect the extend of the arsenic contamination and its cause. In February 1998 an international conference was held in Dhaka to discuss the problem and possible measures. 42 out of 64 districts of Bangladesh are supposedly affected with a concentration of arsenic in the groundwater that surpasses the WHO standard of 0.05 mg per litre (MAJUMDER 1998: 17). The World Bank provided 150 million US$ to combat the arsenic disaster (ISLAM 1997: 1).

in the geology of the Ganges delta. One theory assumes that arsenic has always been present in the groundwater, but only due to the increasing tubewell water consumption over the past 20 years, related health problems have now emerged in the population. Another theory states that arsenic was released by reductive dissolution of iron oxyhydroxides. The intensive input of fertiliser in agriculture and the excessive withdrawal of groundwater by deep tubewells for irrigation may have accelerated the microbiological and chemical processes and hence the natural mobility of arsenic (ACHARYYA et al. 1999: 545). Today it is acknowledged that the country faces a major disaster whose extent cannot be estimated yet as it will have long lasting implications for the health[29] of the working forces and for the social structure and the political stability in general. The arsenic contamination of the groundwater also poses a political challenge: for 25 years the government has propagated the idea of substituting groundwater for surface water for drinking purposes because of health risks. The tubewell programme has achieved that: today 96 percent of the population drink groundwater from tubewells. Now, as arsenic has been discovered in the groundwater, tubewells are sealed up in the villages, and their use is strictly forbidden. It is obvious that the confidence of the people in their government is profoundly shaken.

Social conflicts

The increasing scarcity of water in general and of unpolluted water in particular will create more conflict between the different users, the farmers on one side who need groundwater for irrigation, and the rural dwellers on the other side who require drinking water (KHAN, L.R. 1990: 143). In such a conflict the poor will be even more disadvantaged as they do not have any property rights on tubewells.

3.3
Two cases of water policy in Bangladesh

From its beginnings water policy in Bangladesh was dependent on external support. Several donor agencies helped the government in extending the irrigation area to meet the supply of food crops for the growing population. Furthermore, combating the disastrous floods and endemic diarrhoeal diseases were important goals of the National Water Policy. In this context two projects will be presented which are characteristic in lacking sensibility of water sector programmes: the Flood Action Plan (FAP), a large-scale flood control, drainage and irrigation project, partly responsible for the growing ecological imbalance, and the tubewell programme which is closely linked to some water supply problems in general and to pond deterioration in particular.

---

[29] Chronic arsenic poisoning affects human health in various forms. Arsenic patients may suffer from weakness, nausea, diarrhoea and chronic bronchitis. Melanosis, the alteration in skin pigmentation, is the first clinical symptom of arsenicosis. At a later stage, hands and feet become swollen, and finally keratosis, the hardening of the skin, sets in. Internal organs are also affected. Depending on the concentration of arsenic input it is assumed that after 10-20 years of exposure cancer, in particular skin and liver cancer, will occur (Bangladesh Environmental Newsletter 1997: 1;7).

3.3.1
The Flood Action Plan (FAP)

The Flood Action Plan (FAP) was initiated jointly by the Government of Bangladesh and the World Bank in 1989 in response to the 1988 floods. During the 1988 flood, which was the worst flood in recorded history, approximately 60 percent of the land was immersed in water. The economic loss incurred by the flood was 1.2 billion US$ (ISLAM & KAMAL 1993: 666, 667). The idea behind the FAP was to construct thousands of kilometres of embankments along the major rivers to protect the land from flooding. At the same time drainage and irrigation systems were to be constructed to modernise agriculture.[30] Since 1990, sixteen bilateral and multilateral donor agencies have become active in 26 different projects under the control of the World Bank. However, this large-scale project has come under attack. Critics point out that the project disturbs the ecological balance and, therefore, the livelihood of the population. Floods are a natural occurrence in Bangladesh and they can be beneficial for agricultural production. Controlling the rivers however may be dangerous as unforeseeable structural changes in the water resource system and the environment can occur. The FAP is scheduled to continue to the year 2015. More than 5 billion US$ have been spent so far (GAIN 1998: 35, 36).

The FAP has been determined by the following characteristics:

- although it is a water management project it is based on an agricultural policy aimed to increase food grain production
- it has been widely directed and implemented by external agencies
- technology and know-how have been imported
- social and need assessment studies have not been seriously undertaken until recently
- the approach has been a centralist one, without taking into consideration participatory or actor-oriented components

One can conclude that the FAP is a typical example of a development project that was driven by conventional economic principles: supporting the import of high technology and know-how and conducting a large-scale project without the people's consideration or involvement. The World Bank has confirmed that large-scale flood control, drainage and irrigation projects often produced adverse effects and low profit for the farmers because they were often ill considered (THE WORLD BANK 1990: 70-72).

3.3.2
The introduction of tubewells: promotion of safe water supply and irrigation

This chapter introduces a time horizon for the development of the tubewell policy in Bangladesh and indicates the achievements and problems that have occurred

---

[30] Protection from flood allows the cultivation of high yielding varieties (HYVs) (KHAN & HOSSAIN 1994: 110).

Photo 3.1 STW irrigation with groundwater during the dry season in Singar *thana*

Photo 3.2 Pond water irrigation by Low Lift Pump in the High Barind area

due to this policy. For this discussion it is important to distinguish between manually operated hand tubewells for domestic purposes and mechanised tubewells for irrigation.[31]

The first incentive to sink hand tubewells was in the 1920s when the Provincial Government of Bengal asked the Government of India for measures to eradicate the regularly occurring cholera epidemics. Local landlords haphazardly dug wells for the people but due to an inadequate communication system at that time, tubewell technology could hardly enter the rural areas of East Bengal. The first tubewells in rural areas were sunk in the hinterland of Calcutta in 1928. In the 1930s, the Government of India provided subsidies and entrusted the District Board with the responsibility of supplying drinking water. However, the distribution of tubewells progressed more in the towns for the purpose of civil defence than in rural areas. After World War II, rural water supply achieved top priority. The government established the goal of providing one tubewell per four hundred people. In 1947, when East Bengal came under the jurisdiction of Pakistan, the Pakistani Government inherited 50,000 tubewells. 12,000 of these tubewells were clogged (SALAM 1963: 2, 3). In 1954, a severe cholera epidemic in the south of Bengal resulted in the government requesting the help of the World Health Organisation (WHO). The causes of cholera were investigated. The former implementing body of the government for rural water supply, the Department of Public Health (DPH), conducted a vaccination campaign. In 1956, this Department was restructured and renamed the Department of Public Health Engineering (DPHE) (personal communication with ABDUL RAHMAN, formerly of DPHE Dhaka). In 1960, the Pakistani Government introduced the Basic Democracies Scheme. The idea was to include elected representatives of the community in the water supply procedure. The government provided loans for tubewell installation and local governments were charged to entrust the chairmen of the Union and District Councils to manage and implement the works with the community. The goal was to sink 20,000 tubewells per year. The attempt failed, however, because of the lack of education which hampered the cooperation between the different parties, and also because of corruption and lack of technical supervision. Consequently, the responsibility was directed to the *thana* level, and training of technicians was given priority (SALAM 1963: 5-10). Up until 1972, 18,500 tubewells were sunk. Since the independence of Bangladesh in 1972, UNICEF has assisted DPHE in the rural water supply programme (DANIDA 1979:

---

[31] Because of different hydrological conditions in Bangladesh various types of tubewells are in use:
- Shallow tubewells (STW): They are operable down to 7 metres and are not very costly to install and maintain. The prototype and most widely used hand pump in the country is the Number 6 handpump.
- Deepset tubewells: Based on a similar technology these pumps can lift water from more than 8 metres. With the invention of the Tara pump deepset tubewells also became cheaper and easier to operate. Compared to the shallow tubewells,which are often private, Tara pumps are always public because they are very expensive.
- Deep tubewells (DTW): They are utilised in low water table areas (150-300m) and are very expensive. Therefore, the number of users per tubewell is higher than in shallow water table areas.
- Very shallow shrouded tubewells: They serve to draw water from pockets close to the surface in the saline coastal areas. They are rather cheap (MLG,RD&C et al. 1992: 12, 13).

7). UNICEF stopped the importation of technical parts from India in favour of other export countries such as Japan, Germany or the US for reasons of international compatibility (personal communication with ABDUL RAHMAN). In 1975, the financial and technical support was extended by the Danish International Development Agency (DANIDA) and the Swiss Development Cooperation (SDC) (SDC 1995: 47). DPHE remained responsible for the implementation of the Rural Water Supply (RWS) programme.[32] The programme included the resinking of previously dug wells, the construction of shallow and deep tubewells and the reconstruction of township supplies. The target was set to increase the tubewell coverage from 200 people per tubewell (1963) to 125 in 1980 and 70 people per shallow tubewell by 1995 (DANIDA 1979: 8, 11, 12). During the International Drinking Water Supply and Sanitation Decade 1980-1990 Bangladesh notched up enormous success. In rural areas access to safe water increased from 37 to 96 percent. In 1991 there were approximately 2.45 million hand pumps installed in rural Bangladesh (MINISTRY OF LOCAL GOVERNMENT... et al. 1992: 5, 11). By 1996 tubewell coverage for high water tables was around 75 people per tubewell and for low water tables and coastal areas around 150 people per tubewell. The target for 2000 is 50 respectively 75 people per tubewell (personal communication with BODUR RAHMAN, DPHE Patuakhali).

The history of the tubewell programme is accompanied by a changing policy. Although the responsibility for safe water supply has always remained with the government and was highly subsidised for many years it recently started to decentralise by reducing the amount of subsidies for tubewells. The privatisation of the tubewell production and sales has an economic as well as a psychological profit. The sector is donor driven and the centralised structure of DPHE hampers local involvement (UNDP & WORLD BANK 1996: 13, 14). In 1994 the government launched the Social Mobilisation (SOC-MOB) programme, supported by donors and international organisations.[33] The programme includes local people in every stage of a project and tries to improve the vertical communication of the partners – from grassroots to the government level.

From the very beginning of external assistance in the water management of Bangladesh the first priority was to increase the area of irrigated land to raise the agricultural output. According to the World Bank's food supply policy the cultivation of high yielding varieties (HYVs), requiring irrigation, would solve the food supply problem for the growing population of Bangladesh. Therefore, water control projects and the extensive distribution of mechanised tubewells for

---

[32] "The statuary responsibility for the water supply and sanitation (WSS) sector is vested in the Ministry of Local Government, Rural Development and Cooperatives (MLGRD&C) (...). The functional responsibility is delegated to the Department of Public Health Engineering (DPHE) in all rural and urban areas except Dhaka and Chittagong (...). DPHE is responsible for planning, designing and implementing water supply and sanitation services in rural areas, thana towns and pourashavas." There is one executive engineer for each district office, and on thana level DPHE is represented by sub-assistant engineers (Ministry of local government... 1992: 28).

[33] The objectives of the programme were "to improve safe disposal of excreta, promote personal hygiene, and increase the use of safe water for all domestic purposes, thereby improving the quality of life of the rural people" (HOQUE et al. 19997:6)

groundwater irrigation were heavily promoted. Groundwater extraction by tubewells only started in 1972. Due to declining surface water supply for irrigation groundwater utilisation increased rapidly using the new technology (KHAN, L.R. 1990: 140). From 1973 to 1987 193,400 shallow tubewells were sold and 19,100 deep tubewells installed for irrigation purpose (PITMAN 1993: 33). In the period of 1994 -1995 8,126,000 acres of different crops were under irrigation, 80 percent were in rice cultivation alone (BBS 1997: 195). The government planned to expand the irrigated area to 88 percent of the potential area by 1990 (KHAN, L.R. 1990: 140). When reviewing the policy of the 1980s, the World Bank admits in a report the mistake of government agencies in Bangladesh promoting high-cost technology. The government actively discouraged low-cost (irrigation) technology in favour of DTWs which were heavily subsidised to irrigate large areas. In the long term they were not profitable.

> "The experience points to the pitfalls of decisions taken centrally and without adequate testing, and suggests that selection of equipment better be left to the end user to reflect individual agronomic, hydrological and economic circumstances [...]. In the first place, farmers are in a better position than government officials to determine what type of equipment are suitable to meet their needs, including the organizational form to operate such equipment" (THE WORLD BANK 1990: 69).

As a consequence the World Bank started to alter their policy, promoting the elimination of subsidies for DTWs and strengthening the private sector.

"The STW programme has been the major groundwater development mode in this country" (KHAN, L.R. 1990: 147). The popularity of the programme made them forget its missing coordination and assessment. Therefore, despite numerous achievements of the tubewell programme the introduction of tubewells also created several environmental and social problems:

- Groundwater irrigation with deep tubewells has contributed to a decline of the water table in many parts of the country.
- Village society polarised because influential villagers were the main beneficiaries of tubewell technology whereas the small farmers had to pay for the water (ERLER 1994: 11, 12; HOERING 1988: 95-97). And as groundwater for drinking purpose is becoming scarce during the dry season social conflicts around hand pumps are likely to occur (SADEQUE & TURNQUIST 1995).
- The health improving effect of tubewell coverage has also been doubted. A study in 1976 discovered that tubewell users had as many or even more cholera attacks than non-tubewell users (LEVINE et al. 1976). There was no evidence that the use of safe water reduced the diarrhoeal incidence rate.[34]

These problems induced by the introduction of tubewells are linked to political measures in the water sector. The water sector policy was supply driven and strongly linked to the agricultural policy. In the beginning external technical support and political assistance were uncritically accepted. Moreover, the centralised and bureaucratic structure of the responsible government agencies often hampered an effective and efficient implementation of the programme. In the 1980s important donor agencies, like the World Bank, realised that water

---

[34] Besides the provision of hardware, health and hygiene education has been increasingly given priority in water supply and sanitation.projects (see for example ZEITLYN & BRAHMAN 1994).

management had to become demand driven and people oriented (MCCOMMON, WARNER & YOHALEM 1990). Facing the serious situation in Bangladesh today, it is important to implement these new approaches quickly and seriously.

3.4
Outlook: Coping strategies for the water sector in Bangladesh

Being aware of the multitude of problems, fighting the shortage of water for drinking and domestic purposes which results from the decline and contamination of the water table will be of utmost importance. The current most common coping strategies are listed below:

- Improvement of tubewell technology. It is assumed that by the year 2000, 50 percent of the conventional hand pumps will become inoperable due to the constant decline of the water table. Continuous development of tubewell technology and large financial inputs will be necessary to sink appropriate pumps (UNDP & WORLD BANK 1996: 15).
- Ganges barrage. In response to the Farakka barrage, the project of a Ganges barrage, which was already conceptualised in the 1960s, is taken up again. This project should maximise the benefits from the Ganges water in Bangladesh and help to reverse the negative environmental effects (QADER MIRZA 1998: 8).
- Strategies combating the arsenic threat. Huge efforts are being undertaken to remove arsenic from the groundwater. One promising technique seems to be solar oxidation, making use of the common occurrence of iron in the groundwater for arsenic oxidation, based on solar exposition (EAWAG 1998). Purification of surface water, especially pond water, is another accounted strategy. In general there are two types of water treatment methods: treatment of surface water at the household level, for example by potash alum, boiling or chlorination, filtering or solar water disinfection; or treatment at the source, for example by slow sand filters, as in the case of pond sand filters (AHMED 1998: 12), or eventually by duckweed. Finally, other alternative water supply techniques are reconsidered, such as rainwater harvesting.

The problem of the future water provision is not merely technical but also political. The first priority of the government and the World Bank continues to be an increase in food grain production which can only be achieved by exploring the groundwater resources for irrigation (PITMAN 1993: 31, 34). National Water Policy has focused completely on groundwater availability for irrigation and has neglected the domestic use requirements. Conflicts of interest are inevitable taking into account the fact that Bangladesh has no well-defined regulations concerning groundwater (SADEQUE 1996: 6, 7).

In the context of this complex and urgent water supply problem ponds may offer a useful alternative. Ponds have traditionally been used in a multipurpose manner. They provided water for drinking and have also served as fish reservoirs. Traditional methods are known to clean pond water for use. To this day, ponds are highly acknowledged for domestic and productive purposes all over the country. The next chapter focuses on the ponds, their multipurpose aspects and their possibilities as alternative water source.

4 Pond: Sustainable resource and changing concept

Bangladesh faces severe water supply problems in the future. Some of the coping strategies presented here, such as the Ganges barrage and the replacement of tubewells, require great technical skill and financial inputs and therefore may raise the dependency of the country on external providers. Moreover, they are also questionable from an environmental point of view. Sustainable alternatives are required.

Water management projects are considered sustainable if:

- They can be handled by the people themselves: development practitioners have learned from past experiences. The World Bank clearly promotes community management approaches, as this is the case with the arsenic programme of the World Bank in Dhaka (personal communication with BABAR N. KABIR, World Bank Dhaka).
- Their technology is simple, cheap and easy to operate and manage.

This chapter argues that ponds represent a valuable alternative for domestic purposes as sustainable water treatment methods already exist. The first subchapter presents three pond water treatment methods which are considered sustainable. Two of them are based on traditional knowledge. However, this knowledge is neglected today which is somewhat due to the general system changes which include: the provision of safe tubewell water, the decay of the traditional authoritarian system and the rise of fish production are some events that have altered people's *life world* and, consequently, influenced their concept of the pond and pond management.

The second subchapter demonstrates the previous concept of the pond which was rooted in spirituality and religion. It also shows that the present concept of the pond is economically oriented. As the pond is a system designed for a multipurpose use, productive and domestic uses often compete. In any case, the health aspect of pond water should be given priority.

4.1
Traditional and sustainable pond water purifying methods

The discussion in the following chapter presents three methods which would be appropriate for the treatment of pond water: potash alum, pond sand filters and solar water disinfection (SODIS). The advantage of these methods is that they are technically relatively simple and can easily be managed by the users themselves. In addition, the biological treatment method with duckweed will be presented because of its amazing potential for water purification.

4.1.1
Potash alum

Potash alum is a whitish transparent mineral salt. Chemically it is a double sulphate of aluminium and potassium, $AlK (SO_4)_2$. Due to its astringent character potash alum is used in the dyeing industry and in medicine. The local expression in Bangladesh is *fitkiri*, and it is easily available everywhere in the local markets and is rather cheap. It was traditional in rural households to use *fitkiri* to treat surface water before consumption. A piece of the mineral was tied around a bamboo stick and swirled in the water for a couple of minutes. After eight to twelve hours storage time the water was consumed. Some women in the coastal district of Patuakhali stated that today they still apply *fitkiri* to clean very turbid pond water before using it for cooking (see chapter 8). Potash alum is not a water disinfectant as such but enhances the process of sedimentation as it binds bacteria and particles. However, studies reveal that it is an effective method of remarkably reducing the number of bacteria in water. AHMAD & JAHAN (1984) recommend the use of potash alum to prepare oral rehydration solutions (ORS)[35] in Bangladesh. Their analysis showed that pond water, treated with 500mg/ml alum, had a total bacterial count of 1.0×10^2, compared with 2.0×10^3 of untreated pond water. *Vibrio cholerae* and *E. coli* bacteria were killed within one hour in a solution of 1 gram alum per litre (AHMAD & JAHAN 1984: 56). Another study (KHIN et al. 1994) reconfirmed the effectiveness of alum for household water decontamination but stressed that "large scale studies are needed on highly contaminated water to determine the effectiveness, acceptability, safety and long term effects of potash alum" (KHIN et al. 1994: 174). Chlorination or boiling are much safer methods for water disinfection, because they also kill viruses. But they are less often applied in rural sites because of lack of money or cultural acceptability.

4.1.2
Pond sand filters

Slow sand filters are traditionally in use at the household level in Bangladesh. The large-scale application of this method was introduced in 1984 by DPHE and UNICEF. They jointly launched the pond sand filter (PSF) project with the objectives of providing safe drinking water to the districts along the coast of Bangladesh where the saline content of the groundwater is too high for

---

[35] The Oral Rehydration Solution (ORS) is a mixture of salt and sugar in water that was clinically produced for the first time by the International Centre of Diarrhoeal Disease Research, Bangladesh (ICDDR,B) in 1968. The simple technique avoids dehydration of patients suffering from diarrhoea and cholera. It was successfully applied in many epidemics, for example during the Bangladesh Liberation War in 1971 or in Rwanda in 1994, and saved millions of lives (ICDDR,B 1994: 3).

consumption. In those areas treated pond water is the only source of drinking water (DPHE & UNICEF 1989: 2). The PSF project was interesting for two reasons:
1. The traditional sand filter method was combined with the traditional water source pond. Filtered pond water is safe drinking water as tests confirmed in the beginning of the project.
2. The idea of having the community participate in the project was a reaction to the fact that community participation enhances project sustainability.

On average there are 300 to 500 people per PSF according the type of PSF (DPHE & UNICEF 1989: 8). A PSF consists of a tank beside a pond which is connected with the pond by a pipe system. The tank is equipped with a handpump to draw the water from the pond into the tank. There, pumped water has to flow through three different chambers. The pre-filter chamber is filled with coconut fibre which reduces the turbidity of the water. Then the water trickles down the main filter chamber. The slower this process the better its purification effect. The main filter chamber contains sands in the upper layer and coarse bricks in the lower layer. Finally the water is led into the storage tank. The users can draw water by operating a tap (DPHE & UNICEF 1989: 8). The quality of the filtered water is acceptable for drinking purpose.[36] Women in the field stated that they appreciate PSFs because they can save time, that would be needed for treatment and storage, and the costs of buying fuel.

Although the technique is simple there are some limiting conditions:

- Regular maintenance of the tank and the filters is essential. Rotting of coconut fibres, breeding of insects and clogging of sands are the most serious problems which hamper the function of a PSF (DPHE & UNICEF 1989: 17-19; WHO, DPHE & UNICEF 1990: 3).
- PSFs normally are installed by a team of DPHE. They are heavily subsidised because a PSF costs around 50,000 Taka (1,163 US$) (personal communication with MONOAR HOSSEIN, DPHE Barguna). The caretakers have to pay around 4,500 Taka (105 US$) contribution fee to DPHE for construction.

The PSF project has not been very successful. An evaluation report in 1990 concluded that 18 percent of the 153 PSFs checked were abandoned, and 41 percent of the households used untreated pond water supplementary to water from the PSF (WHO, DPHE & UNICEF 1990: 2, 3). Although the report did not analyse the community approach it is an unwritten fact that DPHE had dropped the project because they considered it unfeasible (personal communication with AZAD, formerly of UNICEF Dhaka). This might have been the reason that the project was set on ice during the past years and has only recently been reconsidered due to the arsenic contamination of the groundwater.[37]

---

[36] In two cases coliform bacteria counts were reduced from 42 to 2 and from 39 to 0 units/100 ml (DPHE & UNICEF 1989: 9).

[37] To evaluate the present situation a short check up of PSFs in Patharghata (Barguna district) was conducted. Three PSFs in the surroundings of Patharghata town were visited. Two of three were out of service. Two PSFs were private, one public. Access to the PSFs is free, and the owner of the pond does not charge any maintenance costs from the users. It turned out that the community is rather dependant on the owners of a PSF and helpless in the case of a broken

4.1.3
Solar water disinfection

The American University of Beirut started experiments with solar disinfection of water in the late 1970s. In their study (ACRA et al. 1980) they assessed the influence of solar radiation on Oral Rehydration Solution (ORS). The objective was to obtain safe water to prepare ORS for treatement. The field tests revealed that after one hour of exposure to sunlight, in the range of 300-400 nm UV light and a constant temperature of 5 °C, the *E. coli* bacteria units reduced from 71/100ml to 0/100ml. In addition the $NaHCO_3$ concentration remained unchanged and the microorganisms did not start to reproduce after one hour due to the constant temperature. For this reason storage of the solution is possible.

In 1991 the Swiss Federal Institute for Environmental Science and Technology (EAWAG) continued and intensified research on solar water disinfection. Solar water disinfection (SODIS) was considered a cheap, simple and easy manageable method to purify surface water for drinking purpose at the household level in developing countries (WEGELIN et al. 1994).

EAWAG especially focused on the impact of temperature on the process of water disinfection. First findings (WEGELIN et al. 1994) showed that a combination of two processes – solar radiation and thermal exposure – produce the best results. At a temperature of 50 °C and UV-A light of 320-400 nm inactivation of bacteria and viruses is best achieved. *E. coli* bacteria and bacteriophage were found valid indicators for effective inactivation of bacteria and viruses. For application a PET bottle is filled with surface water and put on a piece or roof of corrugated iron. The purification process, called batch process, can be intensified when one side of a plastic bottle is coloured black. Then inactivation of microorganisms is achieved within five hours. EAWAG furthermore tried to achieve the same effectiveness taking an increased volume of water. However, this SODIS reactor, containing 30 litres of water, is still in a phase of experimentation (SOMMER et al. 1997).

EAWAG has already successfully applied the batch system in several communities of developing countries such as in Togo, Vietnam, China and Bolivia (WEGELIN & SOMMER 1998). Due to the arsenic problem first field trials are being conducted in Bangladesh with assistance of the Swiss Development Co-operation (SDC) (personal communication with CLAUDE ANDRE RIBAUX).

PSF. In the case of the chairman's broken PSF the users have not complained for the last three years because he continuously pretends to repair it. One man started an initiative and wanted to form a group of people in order to purchase a PSF. He failed because the people were poor and not sufficiently conscious of clean water, he stated. The school PSF, donated by the commissioner of Khulna, has already broken several times, and the caretaker, the school headmaster, is not willing to repeatedly bear all the costs as he is not the owner of the PSF. A user argued that the community twice supported the caretaker financially but now they refuse to provide money anymore.

4.1.4
Duckweed

Duckweed is a tiny floating water plant which belongs to the family of *Lemnaceae* and occurs naturally in Bangladesh. However, duckweed, locally known as *kutipana,* is not traditionally known as a useful water plant.

The microphyte is highly tolerant to saline water and common in eutrophied water bodies. The plant is astonishing for the following reasons:

- Spectacular growth rate: given ideal conditions duckweed can double its weight within two to four days (IQBAL 1995: 4).
- High nutritional value: duckweed has little wooden texture and a high protein content. For these reasons it is a perfect fodder for fish, poultry and cattle (personal communication with MD. IKRAMULLAH, PRISM Dhaka; HILLMAN & CULLEY 1978: 444, 445).
- Effective biological water treatment method: duckweed rapidly extracts nutrients from eutrophied water bodies and thus has a purifying effect. PRISM, a national NGO, constructed a lagoon system to treat wastewater from the Hospital of Mirzapur. A study of this system showed that plant production was highest in the first three phases of the lagoon system which corresponded with the complete extraction of phosphate and nitrate (ALAERTS, MAHBUBAR & KELDERMAN 1996). In fact, duckweed can extract 42-47 percent of the total nitrogen and phosphorus, and in the wet season the removal rate increases to 68-80 percent (ALAERTS, MAHBUBAR & KELDERMAN 1996: 850). A running study at ICDDR,B (ISLAM et al. 1996b) is investigating the concentrations of pathogens, principally faecal coliform, in water, duckweed and fish in wastewater and non-wastewater at Mirzapur. To date it is known that faecal coliform count was reduced from $4.57\text{x}10^4$/ml in raw wastewater to $< 10^2$/ml after treatment with duckweed.

The question is whether duckweed can also present a water treatment method for improving the quality of pond water for domestic purposes. Apparently this research question has not yet been closely investigated. However, PRISM is conducting a project where duckweed is produced in derelict ponds for fish fodder. In this sense, derelict ponds are made usable and communities should profit economically from fish production.

The discussion revealed that there are sustainable methods to treat pond water in Bangladesh. These are considered sustainable because:

- the material is locally or naturally available
- operation and maintenance of the technique does not require much know-how
- costs are low, except in the case of PSFs

However, all techniques still require more research studies in order to explore the range of effectiveness of each method as well as its practical applicability and cultural acceptability. Beside the technical obstacles effective institutional mechanism are needed for successful implementation. Potash alum and SODIS are both techniques for treating pond water at the individual consumption level whereas PSFs are designed to treat the water at the source. In order to obtain a drinking water-quality pond, regular maintenance and strict control of the pond will be just as important as an effective purification technique. Therefore, it may be useful to consider a community management approach to guarantee safe pond water for everyone. Moreover, the way people perceive ponds today has also to be taken into account when planning pond improvement (see chapter 9).

The next sub-chapter reveals that the concept of the pond has changed over time: the economic importance of the pond has surpassed the socio-cultural importance. In addition, scientific findings in pond ecology have drawn attention to the effects of contaminated pond water on health. In fact, the concept of the pond has been modernised – it has generally shifted orientation from spiritual to secular, from domestic to production-oriented and from communal to individual.

4.2
The changing concept of the pond

4.2.1
Historical accounts of ponds in Bengal

In many cultures of South and Southeast Asia, ponds are indispensable water sources. They are found close to religious sites in Buddhist as well as Hindu and Muslim cultures. Originally special professional groups were in charge of digging ponds (see chapter 4.2.2.1). However, it is difficult to find historical accounts of pond management in the region of Bengal. Intensive research of English literature revealed that there is plenty of material on traditional tank irrigation in India and Sri Lanka. These studies often describe the transformation of the traditional system through external interventions and indicate the social and ecological damage that these changes induced.[38] Historical accounts in English mostly originate from colonial times when British Commissioners were in charge of reporting from the various regions. It can be assumed that records of drinking water ponds were neglected because these ponds did not contribute to economic development of the region as irrigation tanks did.[39] Furthermore, a pond was not seen as a separate property resource but a construction on a plot of land, hence, considered land property (see chapter 9).

Historical accounts mostly refer to the term 'tank'. In India, tanks have been known for at least two thousand years. "In south India chieftains promoted the construction of tens of thousands of village tanks in the medieval period" (GADGIL 1995: 17). These tanks were mainly dammed rivers and took the shape of an oxbow lake. They were principally used for irrigation but also as water reservoirs. Various authors have described traditional small-scale tank irrigation schemes in India and Sri Lanka.[40]

---

[38] Examples can be found in the studies of JODHA (1989) and MOSSE (1997).

[39] Evidence of this is found in a letter to the British Board of Revenue in 1792 written by two commissioners who recommend the re-excavation and repair of tanks for irrigation purposes. This was to promote grain production in order to avoid regular famines (CHAKRABORTY & NOMA 1989: 40-43).

[40] MOSSE (1997) for Tamil Nadu; GADGIL (1995) for south India; HARDIMAN (1996) for west India; GEISER (1993) and KANTOWSKY (1980) for Sri Lanka.

In the following section, a description of historical pond management in Bengal[41] is outlined. It appears that original pond management in Bengal was based on the *zamindar* system.[42] Local *zamindars* of the dukedom of Varendra introduced a taxation system that was used by the British (NOVAK 1993: 68). In 1750, the East India Company commissioned Hindu *zamindars* tax collectors. In the Permanent Settlement Act of 1793 the *zamindar* tax collectors received all rights to cultivate land. The intention of the British was to secure revenue and to improve the productivity of agriculture (CHOWDHURY, HAKIM & RASHID 1989:21). The *zamindars*, eager to increase their power, created a hierarchical system of land tenancy and developed a low-rent land strategy.[43] They reduced the rental of land for a peasant if the peasant managed to increase the revenue of his land. Equally, anyone who converted land into a tank was exempted from land rent because it was regarded a productive investment when the tank was used for irrigation of the fields, for stocking fish and planting valuable trees (MCLANE 1993: 103-105). However, the right to dig a pond remained an exclusive right of the *zamindar* until independence in 1947. Following the settlement strategy of the British, many *zamindars* had ponds dug that provided water for the various domestic purposes required by the villagers. The maintenance of these ponds was the responsibility of the *zamindars* (personal communication with MAHBUBAR RAHMAN).[44] Interviews confirm that *zamindar* ponds were principally dug and used for the purpose of drinking water supply (see Chapter 8.4).

The only written evidence of drinking water ponds was found in Hunter's account of Bengal.[45] In the Bardwan Division of West Bengal, ponds, known as tanks, dominated the towns. The following excerpts illustrate the former situation of tanks in Birbhum District:

> "The town (Dubrajpur, I.K.) is surrounded on all sides by numerous large tanks, the banks of which are generally planted with tal, or fan-leaved palm trees [...]. These trees yield a considerable excise revenue to government, their juice forming a powerful spirit, which is largely consumed by almost all classes. The tanks surrounding the town contain abundance of fish, which are brought from the Bhagirathi river. Great attention is paid to the rearing and breeding of these fish, and, as they increase in size and number, they are transferred from tank to tank, according to their ages. These tanks are either the property of zamindars, or of mahajans who farm the fishings, or they are public property. Those that are private property, and are preserved, produce fish of great size and delicacy: those

---

[41] Geographically the former Bengal covered today's Bangladesh as well as the Indian States of West Bengal, Assam, Bihar and Orissa and western parts of Burma.

[42] The *zamindar* system emerged under the Sena, a Hindu dynasty that originated from southern India. Under the Sena empire several mini-dukedoms, so called *rajadoms*, covered Bengal. They were ruled by feudal lords (*zamindars*) or kings (*rajas*).

[43] RAHMAN (1988) discusses in detail the land relations between *zamindars* and various levels of tenants in colonial Rangpur district.

[44] In 1885 the District Board was established that transferred public maintenance tasks to the government, such as road construction and pond maintenance. But as the officials of the Board were mainly *zamindars* the responsibility remained with the same people.

[45] The East India Company commissioned the accounts of District Gazetteers of Bengal. But these Gazetteers were revised during the Pakistan Period and reprinted in 1976. Therefore, the most authentic historical documents are probably Hunter's statistical account of Bengal. Hunter was Director General of Statistics to the Government of India and compiled information from all districts of Bengal which were published in 20 volumes between 1875-77.

that are public property are so constantly disturbed, by being dragged with small hand and casting nets of the poor, as to produce no fish of any large size" (HUNTER 1973: 337).

"Near the town of Bishnupur [...] are several picturesque tanks or small artificial lakes, constructed by the ancient rajas, who, taking advantage of natural hollows, threw embankments across them to confine the surface drainage. These tanks of lakes served to supply the city and fort with an abundance of good water and also to fill the fort moat" (HUNTER 1973: 210).

India's independence in 1947 caused a major migration which also affected the pond system. The Hindus left East Bengal, which was transformed into East Pakistan, to settle in India, and the Muslims emigrated from West Bengal to the new Islamic State. Many *zamindars* left without selling their property. In 1950, the Pakistani Government abolished the *zamindar* system. The Land Revenue Department consequently transferred all the land property, that was not yet sold to the respective cultivators. But as ponds did not come under this law they became government property, so called *khas* property. There were cases of wealthy peasants bribing the government to prove ownership of a former *zamindar* pond that they had appropriated. Others bought land adjacent to a *khas* pond. According to the law they were then allowed to lease the pond. When the pond turned derelict it was used for crop cultivation (personal communication with MAHBUBAR RAHMAN). As the Pakistani Government was not interested in the re-excavation of the *zamindar* ponds many of them silted up, and their numbers declined.[46]

The historical accounts lead to the following conclusions:

- Ponds were principally a public water source, located in the centre of a settlement, of a religious site or a mansion, and used for ritual and domestic purposes.
- The expansive settlement and agricultural policy of the British favoured the digging of ponds through *zamindars* for productive purposes such as irrigation, fishing and tree cultivation.
- Ponds have never been counted as an independent entity or as water source but were always considered part of the land. Therefore, records on ponds are integrated in land records and surveys, and there have not been any particular laws regarding ponds. This may explain the low priority that ponds have in water development projects. Institutions, for example the Bangladesh Water Development Board (BWDB), have never had ponds on their agenda of action.
- During the *zamindar* period the majority of the (Muslim) farmers did not have any land property but were tenants. They did not have any rights over the pond and therefore did not have any responsibility to maintain them. Therefore, it may be assumed that there is very little traditional knowledge on the part of the

---

[46] In seven *mouzas* of Bogra District the distribution of land on the basis of use was recorded in three different periods. The statistics revealed that ponds counted for 5.8 percent of the total land in use between 1923-29. During the time of state acquisition (1956-62) this percentage fell to 5.1 percent and rose up again to 7.3 percent in the Revisional Survey of 1986-87 (CHOWDHURY, HAKIM & RASHID 1989: 37).

peasant population in Bangladesh concerning the maintenance of ponds for drinking purposes.

4.2.2
Socio-cultural perspective[47]

tumi khaw bhare jol, ami khay ghate
(You drink water from the pot, I drink it from the bathing site)

Ponds are not only a popular source of water but they have had a deeper meaning to the people. Ponds appear in legends, poems, folk theatre, riddles and mystery stories. Many people are still able to tell a story about a pond but the inner meaning of such a story has fallen into oblivion. The spiritual meaning of ponds goes back to Hindu religion where water plays a major role. In this context, ponds were regarded as a *pars pro toto* for the element water and as a symbol of life. Rituals and myths around ponds reflect the close connection of man with nature. Later, during the Muslim period, ponds were linked to stories of local saints and heroes, they are central to folk songs and dramas and they appear in riddles and proverbs. Slowly the meaning of ponds shifted from a spiritual to a secular level. This chapter gives insight into some aspects of pond mythology and folklore.

4.2.2.1 Rituals and myths

Since the 7th century, professional groups were in charge of digging ponds and *dighis*. These *dighi* digging communities were mostly of tribal or Hindu origin. Digging of a *dighi* required careful preparation. The right location had to be found, and there were various beliefs and restrictions on this.[48] Furthermore, the auspicious time for the excavation was calculated according to the position of the stars. All communities sacrificed an animal before they started excavation. The excavation was executed following different rituals and prayers to gods and goddesses. Before taking water for the first time, offerings and prayers again had to be made. Today, the *maital* community of Jamalpur is the last pond-digging community in Bangladesh.

Many pond stories that were collected are rather mysterious and seem inexplicable. Three typical stories are depicted to give an impression (see boxes 1 and 2). In general, three motives appear and can be interpreted as follows:[49]

1. Ponds are locations for hidden treasure, which are guarded by a snake. The treasure consists mostly of gold, which is seen as the purest metal in Asian culture. The snake (*naga* or cobra) is a very important animal all over Asia and is considered a spirit that symbolises the protection of purity. Snakes are often related to water and the underworld, expressed by ponds, roots of trees and the

---

[47] Most of the information in this chapter was collected with the help of Saidur Rahman, formerly working at the Bangla Academy in Dhaka.

[48] For example: a pond should not be dug on the north side of the house. Otherwise the water does not emerge, or someone may drown in the pond; or: a pond should never stretch in an east-west direction because this will bring bad luck.

[49] For interpretations of the pond stories merit goes to Prof. Dr. Suzanne Hanchett.

like (HANCHETT 1988: 232). In the story about the chain (see box 1), the chain may stand for the snake that reminds people of the mysterious power of the pond. Thus, a pond represents a highly valued, pure and protected place.

2. Ponds often require a sacrifice. The pond invokes a respectful reciprocity of man towards nature: to receive good water, the source of life, man has to contribute an equal share. In stories, this often happens through human sacrifices. In the most extreme form the only child or the wife, who is considered the carrier of offspring, are demanded as a sacrifice (see box 2).

3. The pond is an autonomous body, an animated place that links the surface with the underworld and human beings with spirits. The ponds are often inhabited by a crocodile or big turtles, which are transformed spirits that remind people to respect the water. The pond can offer objects and the water can change colour or boil. These are indicators that a pond is an autonomous body (see box 1).

Box 1

The chain in the pond

There was once a pond in Bogra, called taltaly dighi (pond under the palm trees). One day the villagers discovered the end of a chain coming out of the pond and lying on the embankment. Being curious they organised elephants and started to pull the chain out of the pond. At the end of the day a huge pile of chain was in front of them. They left the place. When they returned the next morning they saw that the chain had disappeared in the pond again, only its end lying on the embankment. Again the villagers pulled the chain out of the pond, and again the next day the chain remained in its old position...

The provider of kitchen pots

There is another story about the same pond. It was said that any one, who did not have the amount of kitchen utensils needed for wedding ceremonies, could go to the pond and request it. The next day big pots would be on the embankment, so that people could use them for the required purpose. However, they had to bring the utensils back after use. For many years it went well. But suddenly people did not find it necessary to return the borrowed pots anymore, and kept them at home. From this time on the pond did not provide any utensils anymore (MD. MOBARAK ALI, Dokkhin Garadia, 28.11.1996).

The most attractive ponds that are frequently visited in Bangladesh today are those inhabited by big turtles or crocodiles, for example the Bajasid Bustani *dighi* in Chittagong or the Khan Jahan Ali *dighi* in Bagherhat (Khulna). These ponds go back to historically and religiously important persons, for example to *pirs* (local saints) whose life stories are repeatedly told. However, people visit these ponds more for curiosity than for spiritual reasons. In India however, the sprit of the crocodile in the pond is still alive. In Karnataka there is a pond where today around 40 devotees daily present offerings to Babya, the temple crocodile, in order to receive its blessings (DAVID 1997: 10).

Box 2

The pond of King Bebuid

This is the story of a large and deep pond belonging to King Bebuid and was located in Agarosindhu village in Kishorganj district. King Bebuid was a feudal lord in the ninth to tenth century.

One night in a dream the queen of King Bebuid was ordered by a goddess to have a large and deep pond dug. At that time the subjects of the king were complaining because there was a scarcity of drinking water in the area. When the king got to know about the dream he immediately employed thousands of labourers, and they dug for one day and one night. But they could not find any water emerging from the ground. At night the king dreamt that water would appear if the queen descended into the pond with a cup of milk and flowers to worship the water god. The next day, after having told his wife about the dream, the queen took all that was required and descended into the pond. Shortly after she had started to worship the water god, water started to come into the pond from all sides, and within a brief moment the queen was engulfed and drowned (personal communication with SAIDUR RAHMAN).

4.2.2.2 Legends and folklore

During the Muslim period of Bengal, the idea of an animated world faded and religious leaders, *pirs*, gained importance. One of the most famous heroes was Hazrat Khan Jahan Ali, a preacher of Islam and general benefactor to the people in the southwest Bengal in the 16th century. On his travels through the Sundarbans he had many ponds dug for the people who were lacking drinking water. Khan Jahan Ali was also respected by the Hindu community. Beside the burial place of the *pir* is the Khanjeli *dighi* where two crocodiles live. At the time of Khan Jahan Ali the crocodiles came from the jungle, followed the hero as disciples and settled in the pond. Today, they are considered *jins* (ghosts). Therefore, Khan Jahan Ali can be seen as a unifying personality who was respected equally by the natural and the supernatural world.

Ponds and dighis are also represented in songs, poems and theatre. There is a narrative opera called Bhelua which lasts for seven days and nights. The beautiful woman Bhelua, courted by a man, agrees to marry him if he excavates a tank with a paved floor in front of the house. Ponds often appear in love stories and ballads where they provide meeting points for the young couple. Finally, ponds form riddles and proverbs, for example:

> There is a small pond
> where water blinks.
> What is this?
> (Answer: The eye)

Photo 4.1 *Zamindar* ponds were highly appreciated for their beauty and good drinking water quality.

Photo 4.2 Duckweed covering a former *zamindar* pond. Today it is used for fish production.

4.2.2.3 Muslim water laws

The Muslim religion follows a clear cultural code, which is written down in the Holy Koran. The *Sunna* contains the basis of Islamic water regulations, as they were preached by the Prophet Mohammed. Water is valued as an element of purification for the Muslims and therefore access to water should be free for the entire Muslim community. Water is a "common entitlement of all Moslems" (CAPONERA 1973: 10, 13). The water allocation rights cover regulations regarding access to drinking water, rules for irrigation as well as water protection measures. They can be summarised as follows:

- It is sinful to store and refuse (surplus) water to someone who is in need of (drinking) water. Allah will punish this person. On the other hand, to limit one's own water use for others is a virtue and will be rewarded (CAPONERA 1973: 11; AL-SAFADI 1992: 39).
- The right for irrigation cannot be sold independently from the attached land. The owners of water constructions are responsible for the use and maintenance of the infrastructure (AL-SAFADI 1992: 37, 42).
- Water is a public good (*res nullius* or *mubah*). It is prohibited to consider water as a commercial matter. There is no tax on investigation and use of water but only agricultural crop output (AL-SAFADI 1992: 39).
- Water should not be wasted but carefully used. It is prohibited to pollute drinking water. Any violation of this law has to be rebuked by the community and the authority. Therefore, protection areas should be defined (AL-SAFADI 1992: 39).

The Islamic water laws demand a sustainable use of water. From a historical background, these laws were important and relevant for the Arabic cultures living in arid and semi-arid regions where water allocation was originally based on the law of force (CAPONERA 1973: 10). But for the Muslim society in Bangladesh these regulations are also binding in the daily context as the case-study of Dokkhin Garadia will highlight. Furthermore, these regulations could also serve to enforce responsibility in water management, a cultural factor which may become more important in the context of the serious water crisis in Bangladesh.

4.2.3
Economic perspective

Ek Takay pukur niye tin Takay katay
(buy a pond for one Taka, then spend three digging it)

According to the latest pond survey, the majority of the ponds in Bangladesh are used for bathing and washing (39.1 percent). 20.8 percent are exclusively used for fish production and 37.1 percent combine both uses. Only 2 percent are dedicated to irrigation and 1 percent to other purposes (BBS 1994: 14). Evidently ponds are used in multipurpose ways, and domestic purposes remain the most important. Nevertheless, the economic importance of ponds has grown over the years as attested by a large amount of studies on pond fishery. Increased fish production has become an important economic goal of the national policy. In this context, ponds are considered to increase the output, either of fish through pond fishery or of crops through pond irrigation.

This chapter points out why ponds have become more important for economic purposes and what the advantages and inconveniences of such a development may be, looking both at pond fish production and irrigation.

4.2.3.1 Fish production in ponds

Two major reasons can be outlined that justify the growing importance of fish production in general:[50]

1. Fish supply in floodplains and open water has been drastically reduced. This process, which started in the previous century, has been accelerating due to flood protection, drainage and irrigation projects (GAIN 1998: 96). These projects have contributed to a drying up of water bodies (NURUZZAMAN 1990: 2). Moreover, industrial and agro-chemical waste is polluting the water. A decline in fish supply stimulates over-fishing, which is further boosted by an increase in the demand for fish (BHUIYAN 1994: 11,12).

Massive population growth is another major reason to prioritise fish production.[51] The per capita consumption of fish has declined constantly in the past ten years, although fish provides 80 percent of the animal protein input in Bangladeshi diet (HOQ CHOWDHURY & AZAD 1991: 97). Consumption of fish, therefore, contributes to a healthy nutritious balance. Last but not least, fish is also a culturally important food item. To meet demand by the year 2010, 1.14 to 1.79 million metric tons of fish would be required (MINISTRY OF IRRIGATION et al. 1991: 5-7).

Given this background, several studies have investigated the potential of pond fish production and the problems that have hampered productivity so far. Various advantages favour fish production in ponds:

- Bangladesh has one of the highest man-water ratios in the world (ULLAH 1983: 319).[52] Regarding inland fishery resources Bangladesh ranks third in the world after China and India (BHUIYAN 1994: 1).
- The cost-return ratio for a pond is much better than for the corresponding amount of land. This means that fish production in a pond results in more productivity than crop cultivation (KHAN 1985: 265).
- Fishery is a traditional activity in Bangladesh. For centuries fish have been cultivated in ponds, although it was an extensive cultivation lacking scientific

---

[50] One distinguishes between inland fishery and marine fishery. Inland fishery is again classified into open water capture fishery, i.e. fishery in *beels, haors* and floodplains, and closed water culture fishery, i.e. fishery in ponds, tanks, *baors* and brackish water shrimp farms (BHUIYAN 1994: 7).

[51] In 1951 the population of Bangladesh was 44.1 million, in 1997 124.3 million. This means that population has almost tripled within 46 years (BBS 1997b).

[52] In 1977 this ration was 7:1, indicating that "for every seven persons there is an acre of water" (ULLAH 1983: 319).

management (NURUZZAMAN 1990: 3).[53] In addition, there were professional fishing groups, mainly Hindu communities, who belonged to a particular caste (ULLAH 1983: 324).

- Ponds can be considered an integrated production unit as they can serve multiple purposes. However, the different purposes may be incompatible with each other, for example fish production and irrigation (WALTER 1987: 33).
- The output of inland fresh fish has increased by 41 percent between 1990 and 1995 (BBS 1997: 203). 3.5 percent of the inland fish output today results from production in ponds (GAIN 1998: 95). Pond culture had a growth rate of 8.48 percent between 1985 and 1989. Nevertheless, the productivity of fish pond culture is still low when compared with other countries (BHUIYAN 1994: 10, 11, 34).[54]

Studies assess the inherent problems of improving productivity of fish production in ponds. The major problems are briefly:

- the number of derelict ponds has halved between 1982 and 1989. Of all non-derelict ponds almost one fifth, or 309,648 ponds, are not used but would be usable (BBS 1994: 11, 12)
- one third of fish cultivation in ponds is on a traditional basis and, therefore, of low profitability (HOQ CHOWDHURY & AZAD 1991: 101)
- social factors, such as joint ownership of ponds, jealousy and indecision impede investment in pond fishery (ULLAH 1983: 353; KHAN 1985: 268; HOQ CHOWDHURY & AZAD 1991: 107)

The request from researchers for scientific management techniques, training programmes, financial support by the government and the like has already introduced a shift of a traditional non-economic pond use to a market-oriented fish production. Fish production in ponds will generate employment, promote the industry and may even become a promising national export (BHUIYAN 1994: 39).[55]

4.2.3.2 Pond irrigation

The use of ponds for crop irrigation is considered less of a development strategy in comparison to fish production. Today, only 2 percent of the ponds are used for irrigation in combination with fishing (BBS 1994: 14). Two studies were conducted to test the efficiency of ponds for supplementary irrigation. The objective behind pond use for irrigation is to increase the irrigated area and expand agricultural production. One study tested the capacity of ponds as a buffer

---

[53] ULLAH (1983: 324) argues that previously intensive fish production was not necessary because fish was abundantly available in the open water and consequently not a scarce resource.

[54] Whereas in Bangladesh the average production in pond fish culture is 0.716 tons per hectare China has an average production of 2.5 tons per hectare and Indonesia 2.25 tons per hectare (CHOWDHURY & AZAD 1991: 109).

[55] In 1995 the entire fishery sector account for 3.5 percent of the Gross Domestic Product (GDP) and 9 percent of the national exports (TOUFIQUE 1997: 458).

storage (RASHID et al. 1992).[56] The advantages of supplementary pond irrigation besides tubewell irrigation are the following:

- Ponds represent an alternative to tubewells in case of electrical and mechanical failures
- Pond water is more nutritious for plants and, hence, less fertiliser needs to be applied to the crops
- Ponds are more easily available and accessible to smaller farmers, and furthermore, ponds do not depend on electricity and spare parts (Walter 1987: 2)
- Pond productivity can be increased: a one acre pond is able to irrigate five acres of dry season crop

However, it is acknowledged that "the potential of using pond water for irrigation is very limited in comparison to groundwater" (WALTER 1987: 13). Therefore, pond irrigation is only promoted on a micro level. The local circumstances, the type of crop and the time factor should be considered in order to optimise pond use for irrigation.

This chapter has shown that the economic relevance of ponds is more in the field of fish than irrigation. To value a pond as an economic resource has its advantages and disadvantages: the recent focus on the economic aspects of ponds has generally raised the awareness that ponds are an important water source; fishery in ponds is expected to contribute to the GDP, employment and a well balanced diet. However, pond improvement strategies have always been related to agricultural policy that focuses on increasing crop productivity. As ponds remain an essential water source for domestic use, conflict between economic and non-economic uses can arise. Therefore, need-assessment as well as comparative studies regarding the various purposes a pond is used for, are essential for successful pond management. As WALTER (1987: 7) states: "Any other use of the ponds that would seriously jeopardise access for washing and bathing should be promoted with extreme caution."

4.2.4
Pond ecology and its impact on health

Ga noshto kanay, pukur noshto panay
(a village is ruined by too many blind people, a pond is ruined by too many water plants)

Pond use influences pond ecology which, in turn, can impede domestic and non-domestic uses of a pond. It seems that multipurpose ponds are more able to uphold an ecological balance.

"The multipurpose nature of most ponds in Bangladesh indicate that they are ecological systems that are in equilibrium. If the multi uses of water are not helpful to one another they are at least not too harmful" (WALTER 1987: 33).

---

[56] The idea is to pump tubewell water during the night into the pond for irrigation during the day. This method reduces conveyance loss and increases the reliability of the water supply. The vicinity of an irrigation tubewell is a prerequisite though (RASHID et al. 1992: 2, 35).

But the equilibrium of a pond can easily be disturbed, for example through human activities. This has two major consequences: an impact on the type of pond use and on the health of the pond users. This subchapter describes:

- the ecological processes of ponds that lead to disturbance
- the health consequences of the ecological disequilibrium and counter measure.

4.2.4.1 Eutrophication and harmful water plants

From an ecological point of view a pond contributes to the regulation of the hydrological cycle. Seepage of pond water underground improves the groundwater reservoir, in this way ponds can be seen as a water storage facility. Further, pond water evaporates to its environment, which benefits precipitation. Pond water hydraulics varies greatly locally. Various factors determine pond water loss, for example the soil condition and the depth of the pond (RASHID et al. 1992: 1). A pond also has to be considered as a special eco-tope, which offers the necessary living conditions for certain plants and animals, in and around the water source.

Several factors can impair this ecological balance, such as eutrophication, excessive growth of water plants, lack of maintenance or population pressure. In the following section, euthrophication and excessive growth of a specific water plant are discussed.

The physical and chemical relations in a pond are complex. In general, one can say that the content of dissolved oxygen (DO_2) is lower in tropical water bodies than in the water bodies of temperate zones. As ponds are closed water bodies, water is not flowing like the water in a lake with an in- and an outlet. This impedes vertical mixing and slowly creates anaerobic conditions in the bottom water layer. This induces plant decomposition and sedimentation, which may be supported by natural silting of the water body. The natural process of eutrophication[57] will accelerate through external inputs in the form of fertiliser. As a consequence, plant growth is further enhanced and the organism and water quality start to alter (SAKAMOTO 1996: 300, 308). Indicators of eutrophic water bodies, observed in Lake Victoria in Kenya, are for example fish dying and the spreading of water plants such as the water hyacinth and the blue-green algae (BARG 1996: 451).

The water hyacinth (*Eichhornia crassipes*) is widely found in surface water bodies in Bangladesh. This extremely harmful aquatic weed was imported from South America and the good conditions found in Asia meant that it started to spread profusely. It creates various problems, for example it:

- affects navigation and recreation
- blocks up pumps, filters and irrigation systems
- increases the loss of water through evaporation
- represents an appropriate habitat for disease-spreading insects

---

[57] Eutrophication is "the process by which an aquatic ecosystem increases in productivity as a result of an increase in the rate of nutrient input" (FREEDMAN 1995: 552).

- promotes de-oxygenation (BARRETT 1996: 479-481)[58]

The only limnological study available for ponds in Bangladesh reveals that phytoplankton is highest in ponds from March to July and during November/December. In these periods, the pH was high, as was the DO_2 concentration and the turbidity of the water. These are the seasons when toxic algae blooms, which affects fish and people equally, and when the major outbreaks of cholera occur (OPPENHEIMER 1976: 26). Today, it is proven that the classical cholera pathogen, the *Vibrio cholerae 01*, survives, in the sheath of blue-green algae (*Anabaena variabilis*) and that during the blooming season the algae dies and releases the pathogen into the environment (ISLAM & BATEMAN 1994: 20). But the *Vibrio cholerae* also attaches itself to water hyacinths and crustacea such as crabs and shrimps. Given appropriate conditions, warm water and low salinity, the pathogen can multiply. Sources of reproduction can be storage water, food and also shellfish (STOREY 1994: 5-7).

The ecological value of ponds as eco-tope and as balance for local climatic and hydrological conditions is indisputable. But ponds are also notorious for being among the most contaminated water sources and therefore present a major health risk.[59] Natural processes such as eutrophication are accelerated today by human interference.

4.2.4.2 Water related diseases

40 of 50 common diseases in Bangladesh are transmitted principally via water and human excreta (MINISTRY OF LOCAL GOVERNMENT...et al. 1994: 4). Diarrhoeal diseases are the major cause of morbidity among children below the age of 5 in Bangladesh and world wide. In Bangladesh 250,000 children below 5 die annually of gastroenteritis and diarrhoea (NASH 1993: 25). It is in this context that ponds have to be addressed because they are contaminated water sources that carry pathogens and cause water related diseases.

WHITE, BRADELY & WHITE (1972) established a typology of water related diseases according to the transmission routes. They distinguished four classes of water related diseases:

1. Water-borne diseases: Different types of diarrhoea, dysentery, cholera, typhoid and hepatitis A are some of the diseases which are caused by ingestion of contaminated water. The route of transmission is faecal-oral. Either contaminated water is consumed directly or indirectly, for example via utensils washed with polluted water. In addition contaminated fingers and hands can also contaminate water or food.
2. Water-washed diseases: Several skin and eye infections, for example scabies and trachoma, result from an insufficient amount of water used for personal hygiene. The route of transmission is also faecal-oral.

---

[58] Due to the fact that it is impossible to eradicate this weed several studies tried to find ways to make use of it. Water hyacinths can serve various purposes: as manure, as fodder for cattle and fish, as raw material for paper and as ingredient for biogas production (BARRETT 1996: 522, 523; REZA 1990: 173-176).

[59] However, detailed epidemiological studies are lacking on this issue.

3. Water-based diseases: These diseases are transmitted by an intermediate host that lives in the water. The most famous example is schistosomiasis where the pathogenic helminth develops in a snail and then penetrates the skin.
4. Water-related insect vector diseases: This category includes sleeping sickness, malaria, dengue fever or yellow fever, diseases which are transmitted by insects breeding in the water (BATEMAN et al. 1995: 27-34; AZIZ et al. 1990: 3).

The major problem in Bangladesh regarding pond water contamination is water-borne diseases which are all intestinal diseases. The two most common diseases in this category, which are endemic in Bangladesh, are cholera and diarrhoea.[60]

4.2.4.3 Measures for improving pond ecology and health

Re-establishing the ecological equilibrium of the pond would also mean reducing the incidence of water related diseases. As ponds are closed water bodies and located in a tropical climatic zone they need special care because they are more susceptible to eutrophication. On one side avoiding the input of waste and manure is essential, on the other hand it would be necessary to increase the oxygen transportation, for example by mixing of the water and regular removal of aquatic weeds. Of course, technical measures to treat pond water are also useful to improve the water quality (see chapter 4.1).

Furthermore, water quality control, referring to given water quality standards, would reduce the health risk. But there are two points to consider: Firstly, the WHO drinking water standards[61] cannot be taken as the overall standard for water, especially not for untreated surface water. Every country has to set up its own standards which should be compatible with the user patterns in rural areas and the health requirements. This also implies that safe[62] water does not necessarily mean water that is culturally perceived as good.[63] Secondly, it is not

---

[60] The pathogenic organism that causes cholera is the bacteria *Vibrio cholerae* which consists of different subgroups. To become reactive the bacteria has to produce the toxin CT (*choleragenic toxin*) (STOREY 1994: 4). In the past the *V. cholerae 01*, either the 'Classical' or the 'El Tor' biotype, was responsible for cholera epidemics. However a new strain, the *V. cholerae 0139* Bengal appeared in 1992/93 in India and Bangladesh (ISLAM & BATEMAN 1994: 20). Cholera outbreaks coincide with the reproduction of certain water plants. Consumption of infected water or fish transmits the disease. Diarrhoeal diseases always result from faecal contamination of water. Although diarrhoea can be caused by various pathogenic bacteria the common indicator bacteria, which is also used for water analysis, is the *Escherichia coli* (*E. coli*). Not all *E. coli* are pathogenic but some strains are responsible for childhood diarrhoea worldwide (CAIRNCROSS & FEACHEM 1983: 28, 29).
[61] The WHO drinking water standards require no *E. coli* in 100ml and a maximum of 10 coliform organisms per 100ml (ENVIRONMENTAL SANITATION INFORMATION CENTRE 1982: 4).
[62] Safe water can be defined as "[...]be free of pathogenic organisms, toxic substances and an overdose of minerals and organic materials; it should be pleasant, i.e., free of colour, turbidity, taste and odour; it should contain a high enough oxygen content; and it should have a suitable temperature" (ENVIRONMENTAL SANITATION INFORMATION CENTRE 1982: 3).
[63] In Bangladesh groundwater has a high iron content which does not present any health hazard but is not appreciated by the consumers. People prefer pond water for cooking, bathing and washing despite the high bacterial content (see Chapter 6.3).

sufficient just to have standards, they also need to be enforced (CAIRNCROSS & FEACHEM 1983: 31, 35, 40). In Bangladesh water quality standards for various purposes exist but enforcement lags behind. The bacterial standards for inland surface water are as follows:

- water for recreational use should not contain more than 200 total coliform units (cfu) per 100 ml
- water for fishing purpose is allowed to contain up to 5,000 cfu/100 ml
- water which can be used for domestic purposes but which must be treated beforehand can contain up to 5,000 cfu/100 ml (GOVERNMENT OF BANGLADESH & MINISTRY OF ENVIRONMENT AND FORESTRY 1997: 3124)
- drinking water should contain no faecal cfu/100 ml and not more than 2 cfu/100ml (JAPANESE ENVIRONMENT CORPORATION 1996)

Finally, improving the health-prevention methods of the users is another measure. The promotion of safe water for drinking has been linked with the tubewell distribution policy of the government. Unfortunately, tubewell water is no longer absolutely safe everywhere. Health education campaigns intend to raise the awareness of health risks and of hygiene behaviour. For this purpose knowledge about folk-disease taxonomies, cultural beliefs and restrictions and about the role of social mobility in disease transmission has to be gained.[64] It is acknowledged that treatment and proper management of the physical structures are one thing, but that sustainable success in the reduction of water related diseases is only attained if people are made to change their hygiene behaviour (AZIZ et al. 1990; ZEITLYN & BRAHMAN 1994).

4.3
Conclusions

A pond is a system that entails various aspects – socio-cultural, economic, ecological – and serves multipurpose uses. This chapter revealed that the concept of the pond has changed. Whereas, during the Hindu period in Bengal a pond was an animated water body that symbolised the close relationship of man with nature, the pond became an economic good due to the influence of Islam and British rule. Thus, the relevance of the pond shifted from the spiritual to the secular. Maybe the increasing ignorance of inner values, as in the case of the ponds, has contributed to a distortion in the relationship between man and his environment. "The location of a ritual site and the definition of space are important ways of controlling the relation between the human and spirit domains" (HANCHETT 1988: 38). External circumstances in recent time, for instance the shortage of fish supply and population growth, have increased the demand for pond fish production. Thus, the commercial importance of the pond has been augmented at the cost of domestic uses. Finally, improved health consciousness induced people

---

[64] CHOWDHURY & KABIR (1991) discovered that rural Bangladeshis distinguish four different types of diarrhoea. ROUNDY (1978) provides an interesting attempt to assess disease hazards in a village. He studies the role of human behaviour in disease diffusion according to different geographical zones of human activity.

to consume more tubewell water. Consequently, the quality of drinking water ponds has become less important. When possible a pond owner tries to transform his pond into a fish pond because it is more profitable. Therefore, ponds increasingly become profitable resources for private persons.

This new concept of the pond also manifests in pond locality: pond management has altered, and many ponds have deteriorated physically. This will be the subject of the following empirical chapters. Finally, if ponds are to be reconsidered in the context of the water crisis in Bangladesh they need to be improved. This chapter has shown that sustainable methods for pond water treatment are available. However, successful pond improvement does not only depend on technical but also institutional aspects which will be discussed in chapter 9. The present problems and opportunities of pond management, as described in the chapters to come, provide the necessary information to build upon.

PART III POND MANAGEMENT: REACTION TO SYSTEM CHANGES

5 RESEARCH DESIGN, DATA AND METHODS

5.1
General considerations

Chapter 1 explained why pond management is an important research topic. Any initiative to improve ponds and pond water requires the compiling of basic data on ponds, for example, how ponds are used and why they are still used today; the extent of their contamination and the reasons why they are contaminated. It is also important to include a historical perspective that could explain the reason for the changes in pond management and which may offer solutions as to how to improve ponds, based on local knowledge and traditional methods. To date, no research study on the general aspects of pond management has been carried out in Bangladesh. This study will attempt to cover some of these gaps in pond management research.

The integrative system approach that was established in chapter 2.4 requires an actor-oriented, idiographic and dynamic methodology for the research of complex issues such as development. To fulfil these requirements three elements of the system approach determined and guided the research process:

- Actor-oriented approach: An actor-oriented approach was regarded the most suitable because action, expressed in pond management, reflects people's life world and their concept of the pond.
- Dynamic, process-oriented approach: On one hand a process-oriented approach includes historical accounts about pond management in order to compare past with presents structures and to detect the processes of change. On the other hand it is meant to remain flexible during the research process in order to take into account emerging relevant questions. During the period of the case-study new research questions arose, for example: Do poor people rely more on pond water because they are unable to use tubewells during the dry season? Do people in other areas, where tubewell coverage is not as high, manage ponds differently? Are there traditional water treatment and maintenance techniques that could be used to improve the present situation of the ponds? This implied a circular proceeding was preferable to a linear research process. The research on pond management provided information of past and present structures and of the processes of change. The second main objective of the study was to search for measures to improve ponds, respectively pond management for domestic purposes. This posed two more questions: Which was the most suitable approach for implementation? Were

there already approaches to improve ponds for the use of domestic purposes and could they provide useful ideas for future pond management?

- Idiographic, small-scale approach: The case-study is the instrument that focuses on the specificity of a place and, as such, permits to "identify and elucidate different social forms and processes" (LONG & LONG 1992: 136). The case-study also corresponds well with the two above mentioned approaches as it identifies new aspects of the problem and may generate new hypotheses, which can be integrated into the research process and followed through. This may also produce valuable contributions to theory (LONG & LONG 1992: 60, 136). Despite the contextual and a specific validity the case-study generates general questions and findings which can be applied to other places as was shown by a comparative study. As the case-study area did not represent an area with a high pond density it was considered invaluable to select a further two areas where problems with groundwater supply meant that ponds are used more regularly than in other parts of the country. The parameters which were considered most relevant for the comparison were selected from the first village case-study and applied to two villages from different regions. This process resembles what FLICK (1995: 255) calls the 'method of constant comparison'. This method is characterised by a continuous circular process where the former levels of analysis transform into new levels. Some levels remain constant throughout the entire research period to enable the development process to be examined (refer to figure 5.1). A constant comparison provided new insights into pond management and, in addition, enriched the findings for potential measures to be taken and also enhanced the validity of the study. Finally, three pond projects[65], which were presumed to contribute to the improvement of ponds were briefly evaluated according to the community management approach (chapter 9).

The research design and the methods were chosen accordingly. The two subchapters cover:

1. The research design, organisation and the process of the research are described. The resources available for the empirical study and the study area are presented. Finally, general considerations of field work in Bangladesh and the specifics of the study areas are explained.
2. Different types of qualitative and quantitative methods that were applied during the research process are discussed, as well as their appropriateness given the complex topic and external circumstances.

---

65 The three respective projects were initiated by an NGO, a semi-government organisation and the government. Two projects were aimed at increasing the profitability of the ponds through fish production and the third project aimed at improving the quality of pond water for drinking . purposes through a water filter technique.

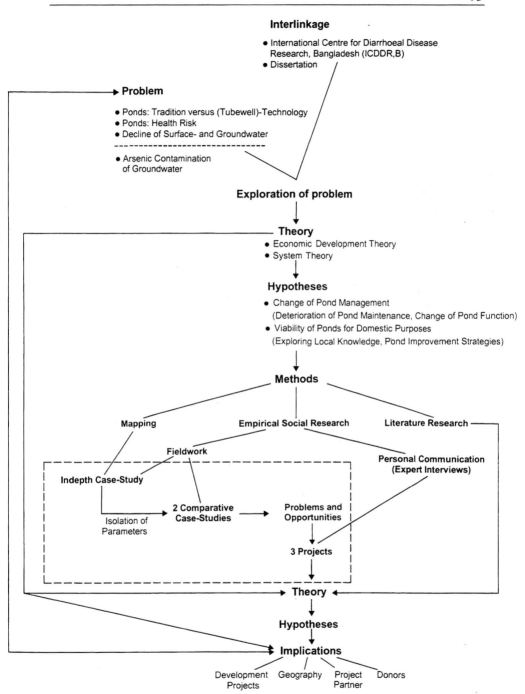

Figure 5.1 Research Overview

5.2
Research design

5.2.1
Resources and organisation of the research

The decision to go to Bangladesh for a PhD research project was initiated by an interlinkage programme between the University of Basel/Basel Cantonal Hospital/Swiss Development Cooperation (SDC) and the International Centre for Diarrhoeal Disease Research, Bangladesh (ICDDR,B). At the latter the research fellowship was affiliated to the Environmental Health Programme (EHP) of ICDDR,B. At the beginning of the fellowship period, it was planned to assist in an EHP project on water and sanitation but later the conditions changed, and it was requested to conduct an independent research for a PhD (refer to chapter 1 figure 1.1). EHP provided the necessary support with regard to the logistics for the study, transport facilities, personnel and technical assistance. Besides the personnel support of EHP, a female Bangladeshi assistant was hired for the field work. The research assistant, Shehla Parvin, who has a Master's degree in Social Anthropology from Jahangirnagar University Bangladesh, established a rapport with the people during the field work. The duration of the Bangladesh research component was for a period of over two years, January 1996 until March 1998. The identification of the research problem and the research design took eight months, field work, analysis and literature research were alternated over a period of 16 months.

5.2.2
Bangladesh: the research area

Bangladesh is one of the poorest countries in the world. It is known for its natural disasters such as floods and cyclones. Reports on such disasters are usually the only news transmitted by the media to the Western world. Unequal access to resources, political instability or poverty are rarely a subject of discussion abroad although such problems are relevant to the welfare of the people as a whole.

To conduct field work in Bangladesh meant living with, and adapting to, different cultural conditions. It also meant remaining open and reactive to the living conditions of a country where the following points often influenced the research process:

- In the beginning and towards the end of the field work period, the political situation of the country hampered field work activities. Days and weeks of strikes (*hartals*) throughout the country paralysed the entire transport system and the supply situation.

- Poor infrastructure in rural areas determined the selection of the study areas. Transport facilities, distance, safety[66] and a minimum of comfort for the researchers had to be taken into consideration.
- Bureaucracy is not unique to Bangladesh, but the country's special and lengthy procedures had to be followed with patience and persistence to achieve the goals of the study.
- Finally, the seasonal climatic variations in Bangladesh determined the research process considerably. The hydrological cycle, depending on the monsoon rains, regulates the agricultural production and the social life in the villages. The effect of the seasonal availability of water in ponds became an important factor to consider. Field work was planned accordingly: data, without a seasonal bias, was collected during the post-monsoon season (October to January). But data that was to show a considerable seasonal variation, for example water analysis test and pond use, was collected in the three main seasons - post-monsoon, dry season and monsoon season. Finally, information which was subject to a specific season was collected in that particular season. This was the case when information on disputes over access to tubewells during the dry season had to be collected.

These external factors cannot be influenced by the researcher as they are due to the physical and socio-political structure of the country where the research took place. But the researcher had to react to them according to the objectives of the study. The given time frame of the research demanded constant decisions on what to add or omit and this requires a general understanding of the basic conditions of the country. Meeting the people offered a challenge to the researcher as she interacted with them as a person with her own identity, which demanded constant reflections on the research topic, on the research process and about her role in it. The difficulties that a researcher had to negotiate during field work in a totally different culture is described in the next chapter.

5.2.3
Field work in a foreign culture and environment

What are the difficulties of undertaking field work in a foreign culture? What are the implications for the research process and data collection? The field of ethnography relates the description of a particular group to a specific context and to the researcher's own cultural background, which introduces cross-cultural comparisons (SANJEK 1996: 193). Negotiating within an unfamiliar context a researcher is challenged, through constant comparisons on two different levels, on an abstract/conceptual level and on a concrete/pragmatic level.

On the conceptual level, the researcher has to be aware of the distinction between the emic and the etic perspective of any construct.[67] This distinction, for

---

[66] Safety was an important consideration. To avoid health problems, careful handling of water and food was essential. Using a water filter and the researcher's own cooking facilities reduced this risk considerably. Safety also encompassed safe transport and lockable accommodation. Public transport could not be avoided even though it was considered dangerous and local buses, tempos and rickshaws were the daily mode of transport to and from the working areas.

example, became relevant when the boundaries of Dokkhin Garadia had to be drawn. Where and how did the villagers demarcate their village? It was obvious that the term *para* was important, but the term itself posed a problem. *Para* is a neighbourhood and a village may have several *paras*. The term has no administrative significance but is an instrument of orientation for the villagers. Therefore, *para* names differ as do the *para* boundaries. After various villager's opinions were identified five *paras* were determined and the village mapped accordingly. A similar situation arose when the households had be chosen for the survey. The question of household definition is not new.[68] Generally, the best operative definition is given by the term *chula*, meaning the fireplace, which constitutes the smallest social and economic unit. This unit can be a nuclear or an extended family, or even an incomplete family. Therefore, for the purpose of the survey a household corresponded to a fireplace in a homestead. Finally, it was not always apparent what villagers understood by a pond. The term *pukur* (pond) includes a particular concept. In Dokkhin Garadia it was observed that during the household survey the respondents referred to other terms for ponds such as *talab*, *danga*, *maital* and *doba*. Therefore, the villagers were asked to explain their concept of other terms for water bodies in comparison to a *pukur*. It is neither possible, nor desirable, to avoid the distinction between emic and etic and for research in a foreign culture it is important to remain conscious of these distinctions, for example when preparing, conducting and analysing interviews.

How does one interact with people from a different culture in order to acquire the necessary information but without compromising them, was a question that needed to be addressed. It was important to define a personal position within the given context and attempt to maintain a balance between two different cultural perspectives. It was not possible to undertake field work in the traditional anthropological sense due to the research design.[69] But as field work was the most important element of the research it was necessary to study Bangla for two months. For a more comprehensive understanding a Bangladeshi woman was employed to accompany the researcher during the field work to act in the capacity

---

[67] These terms are derived from the linguistic terms 'phonetic' and 'phonemic' and became important for models in cognitive anthropology. According to BARHARD & SPENCER (1996: 180) an emic model is "one which explains the ideology or behaviour of members of a culture according to indigenous definitions. An etic model is one which is based on criteria from outside a particular culture." In other words, an emic view refers to an approach which stems from within a specific culture, an etic view is the analytic interpretation of cultural phenomena from outside this culture (SICH et al. 1993: 177).

[68] See JANSEN, JAHANGIR & MAAL (1983). They point out that too little attention has been paid to defining household units in studies of rural Bangladesh. This can lead to serious distortions regarding land ownership distributions within a village. They distinguish between four terms: *ghor* (the house itself), *chula* (the fireplace), *bari* (a conglomerate of houses) and *gusti* (the patrilinear family). *Ghor* and *chula* are the smallest units but whereas *ghor* only implies a social unit, a *chula* contains a social and an economic unit.

[69] This study did not make use of participant observation as during the field work period accommodation was outside the village. The approach taken was that the research topic was the central focus and additional information was collected around the basis of this topic, whereas anthropologists normally collect information the other way round, that is, through direct observation (see SANJEK 1996: 196, 197).

of a linguistic and cultural translator.[70] This situation was an acceptable compromise and allowed the villagers to become familiar with the researchers who visited the village on a daily basis but stayed overnight in the nearby *thana* township. This facilitated an overall view of the village and an opportunity to assimilate information objectively. A cultural compromise with regard to appearances was also maintained. The researcher's hair was kept short, ears were not pierced and there was no pretence with regard to marital status. However, the researcher was not spared comments from women such as: "Why don't you pierce your ears? Why don't you put oil in your hair?" This meant that the researcher was accepted more for the fact that she was different and there was never a full acceptance in the context of the village society.[71] Doing field work was sometimes an awkward balancing act because people's association often did not fit with the investigator's behaviour. The material or financial expectations of the villagers were not met; instead information was demanded which would not provide any direct benefit to them.

5.2.4
Selection of the field areas

Field work was the main method used for this study. Map 5.1 shows the three villages and the three different project sites that were selected for investigation.

The empirical work started with a case-study in Dokkhin Garadia of Singair *thana* (maps 6.1 and 6.2) in order to describe and analyse the use, maintenance and control of ponds with a special focus on domestic purposes. The village was selected according to the following criteria:

- rural area
- high variety of ponds, with respect to the age of the pond, its size, use and ownership pattern
- representativeness of the village with regard to the rural character and to their religious affiliation
- accessibility to the village

The selection process required a careful screening at first. Data from the *thana* Fishery Office in Singair indicated the villages with the most ponds.[72] Four

---

[70] LEWIS (1991b: 48) also confirms the advantages of having an assistant but also points out that this requires the need to constantly filter the information obtained.

[71] KOTALOVA (1996: 30) and GARDNER (1991: 17, 18) who both did anthropological field work in rural Bangladesh, wrote about their experiences in the village where they were looked upon as babies who had to be taught everything, for example how to dress in a sari, how to talk Bangla and how to walk in public.

[72] In Singair *thana* there are not as many ponds as in other regions of the country because the area is a low-lying area. According to the *thana* Fishery Officer the reason for this is that fish production is less profitable because during the rainy season the floods release the fish in the ponds, which means a financial loss for the owner (Personal communication with Mr. FEDAS, *thana* Fishery Office, Singair). The statistical data on ponds thus imply that ponds are principally used for fish production. However, in the villages visited many more ponds were identified that were used for domestic purposes and not recorded by official statistics. Furthermore, not all ponds that were for fish production were utilised for professional fish production.

villages in Singair *thana* were then visited over a one-week period. Pond owners were interviewed using specific guidelines and the physical aspects of the ponds were examined. The findings of the inventory were then placed in a pond chart for ease of comparison. Two villages were eliminated from the sample, one because of its low number of ponds, the other because of difficulty of access and specific soil conditions. The two remaining villages were compared according to their household size and their representation of rural Bangladesh. The representative sample size was fixed at 250-350 households. However, obtaining information on the number of households proved difficult. Reliable statistics or household surveys were rarely available.[73] Furthermore, villages are generally divided into neighbourhoods (*paras*) with boundaries defined by the villagers and often are not well defined (refer to chapter 5.2.3). The village of Garadia posed the least number of problems. It was decided to consider only the southern part of the village, which was said to consist of about 300 households and had more ponds that were used for domestic purposes than the northern part. In addition, Garadia seemed to be more representative of Bangladesh because it is a Muslim village, whereas the alternative village consisted of a Hindu majority. Therefore, Dokkhin Garadia was chosen for the in-depth case-study.

In the second stage of the research, two additional village case studies were undertaken. The main selection criterion for these case studies was the hydrogeological situation, which was responsible for the poor quality and low availability of groundwater in these villages. In both areas tubewell coverage is lower and pond coverage higher than the national average. An area with poor quality groundwater is the coastal belt of Bangladesh where the groundwater is saline down to 200-300 meters (700-1,000 feet) (WHO, DPHE & UNICEF 1990: 1). Only deep tubewells provide good drinking water but in certain locations even deep tubewells fail to supply water. Patuakhali *thana* is one of these.[74] The other area where groundwater is insufficient in terms of availability is the Barind Tract in the north of Bangladesh. In this area, the water table is very low because of the geological formation and tara pumps are mainly used for groundwater. Nachole *thana* was selected because it belongs to the High Barind Tract. When selecting the village, the main criteria was accessibility to the field site from the town by either public transport or by rickshaw. Sehakati village, about 12 kilometers south of Patuakhali town, and Madhabpur village, about five kilometers from Nachole town, were chosen for field work. Rickshaw was the only mode of transport to these villages.

In the third stage of the research process three projects, which try to improve derelict ponds, were detected and chosen for investigation assuming that this would assist in proposing practical measures for future pond management. Due to their marginal relevance for policy they are briefly mentioned only.

---

[73] Three different statistical sources were consulted – the 1993 survey of children from the Garadia primary school, unofficial statistics from ICDDR,B and the Union Parishad statistics of 1995.

[74] In addition, the Environmental Health Programme had a project in Patuakhali and the researchers could expect some support from their presence in the research area.

99

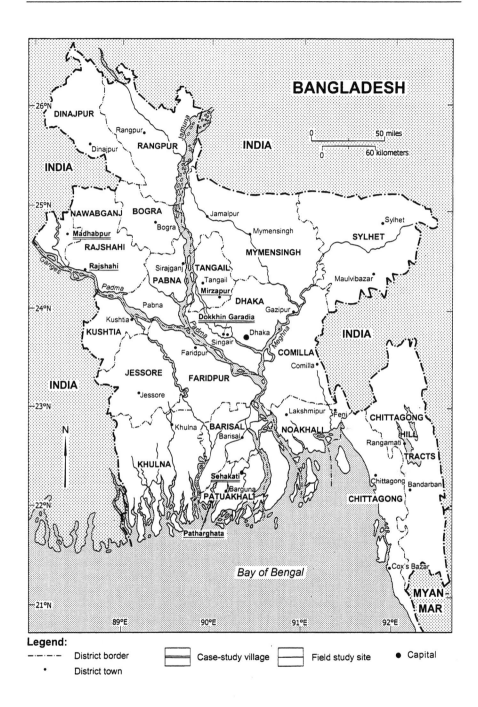

Map 5.1 Bangladesh: Locations of Field Work
Source: NOVAK (1993), changed by L. Baumann

Geographisches Institut
der Universität Kiel

Two of the selected projects: on the coast and in the High Barind, are situated in areas with groundwater deficits. The project on the coast was launched by the Department of Public Health Engineering (DPHE) with UNICEF and intended to construct pond sand filters because tubewells were inoperable. The idea was to treat pond water by sand filter for domestic use, including drinking purposes (see chapter 4.1). Patharghata (Barguna District) was chosen because pond sand filters are the only way of providing safe drinking water in this area. The second project, located in the High Barind, is part of a regional development programme that was initiated by the Barind Multipurpose Development Authority in Rajshahi. This autonomous organisation began excavating derelict government ponds. Excavation of derelict ponds was considered a direct pond improvement strategy. Finally, a third project was of interest. PRISM, a local NGO, had constructed a waste water treatment plant based on duckweed. As duckweed can be produced in derelict ponds it enhances fish production, but it also has water purifying characteristics. The projects were visited and briefly evaluated according the community management approach.

5.3
Research methods

The choice for certain methods is always one that reflects the researcher's view of the world and his or her way explaining given structures (HELBRECHT & MEIER 1998: 87). During the research process, the investigator was confronted with various realities while talking to villagers and to experts of development or research organisations both in the city and in the field. Being aware of different views and their implications is one thing but in the end it was necessary to decide on the limits of the study and whom and what to include or exclude. Therefore, the study represents one possible reality and does not pretend to be objective or representative, but only to demonstrate a partial truth.[75]

The fact that the research was actor- and process-oriented and took place in an unfamiliar environment and culture required a variety of methods. As every method selected only investigates a partial problem of the whole research question, various methods are needed to build up a systematic picture. Qualitative methods were principally selected for this study, which were completed and extended by quantitative data. A combination of different methods was applied as a form to increase the depth of the methodological procedure. This can enhance the validity of the findings (FLICK 1995: 249, 251). Besides primary data collection, mainly through field work, literature research and statistics provided background information and was partly useful in integrating the research process. In the following section, each method applied will be described and why it was chosen to explore a specific question. The inherent problems of a particular method will also be addressed.

---

[75] MEIER (1998: 109) regards social research as the practice of careful positioning: "Anders gesagt: sie (die Sozialforschung, I.K.) mischt sich ein, sie mischt mit im Kontext alltäglicher gesellschaftlicher Positionierungen, sie ermöglicht Begegnungen und schliesst andere aus, sie trägt zum Verbreiten der einen Weisheiten bei und lässt andere ungehört."

5.3.1
Surveys

The survey method was applied because quantitative data on the opinion of a certain group of people should be obtained. During the entire research period, three surveys were conducted: a household survey of 312 households in Dokkhin Garadia, a survey of fifty poorer women in Dokkhin Garadia and two short surveys of pond owners in the comparative studies of the villages of Sehakati and Madhabpur.

5.3.1.1 Household survey in Dokkhin Garadia

The first and largest survey was the household survey in Dokkhin Garadia undertaken to obtain basic information on the socio-economic structure of the village and on water supply focusing on tubewells and ponds. In September of 1996, a questionnaire was designed in English and revised several times. It was necessary to translate the questionnaire into Bangla because four field workers of EHP were assigned to conduct the survey. The findings of the pretest and advice from Bangladeshi friends and colleagues were taken into account before the questionnaire was finalised. A consent form was also developed to inform every respondent about the purpose of the inquiry and to promise confidentiality for individual data protection. The survey was undertaken over three weeks in November of 1996. 312 out of 315 households were covered. In the interviews, the male head of the household answered questions on land ownership and crop production, both of which belong to the male domain of knowledge.[76] The interviews were numbered and coded according to the neighbourhoods (*para*) and the location on either the right or left-hand side of the road. No one refused to be interviewed but the researchers were sometimes uncertain about the validity of the statements given. Although explanations were given many villagers did not understand the purpose of the survey as they had their own expectations and suspicions about the survey.[77] They expected at least a hand tubewell or a fish pond from the researchers.[78]

The analysis of the survey commenced in January 1997. As the questionnaire contained many open-ended questions they needed to be stratified for coding. The research assistant was trained in coding and data entry and coded all questionnaires. After setting up a field plan of all variables for a computer programme, two computer experts of EHP prepared the data entry programme in FoxPro and further analysed the data with SPSS 7.5. Analysis was completed by March 1997. Only descriptive statistics were applied, calculating frequencies and

---

[76] Where no male head of the household was available, the interview was conducted with a representative, his wife or a male relative.

[77] The researchers stressed at various times that they did not come from any organisation or NGO. However, they were met with a mixture of respect, fear and suspicion. The following anecdote illustrates this: With the woman's permission the researcher took her picture when she was washing clothes at the pond. Later the woman expressed her fear that her picture would be shown to the Prime Minister!

[78] The same experiences were also felt by LEWIS (1991: 53) during his field work. He was suspected of buying people's land for a multinational enterprise.

cross tables. Coding and analysis of the survey revealed some problems from which lessons were drawn for further surveys. The survey was too complex and complicated and contained too many variables, open-ended questions and tables and therefore was difficult not only to implement but to code and analyse. Although there was training given in data collection and coding, and despite the control over this, missing information was unavoidable. After familiarisation with the village conditions and the topic, it was apparent that several questions were inappropriate for the survey.[79]

5.3.1.2 Survey on seasonal water use in Dokkhin Garadia

The second survey focused on the water supply situation for the poor of Dokkhin Garadia. The objective of this survey was to clarify seasonal water use in the village and to examine whether the poor are given access to tubewells and ponds throughout the year, including during the dry season.[80] The survey was therefore conducted during the dry season, in April of 1997. The questionnaire was written in English and conducted by the researchers. 50 poorer households were selected after the socio-economic condition of each of the households was mapped. The villagers were familiar with the presence of the researchers, which facilitated the rapport with the respondents. Some women wondered why the researchers asked them questions as they assumed that the researchers knew everything and they knew nothing. Furthermore, the women sometimes did not consider the researchers' work as a real work.[81] When it became difficult to get reliable answers, for example because the respondent was surrounded by her neighbours and their children who commented on everything she said, the researchers separated the respondent from the others or suggested that she continued with her housework while she was asked the questions. This permitted the woman to have the feeling that her responses were considered important. The survey was analysed with the aid of written checklists.

5.3.1.3 Pond owner surveys in Sehakati (Patuakhali thana) and Madhabpur (Nachole thana)

The third survey aimed at detecting differences and congruences of pond management in another context. Information about pond management could be extended and data validity enhanced.[82] This also provided stimulation for the development of the theoretical and practical components of the research process. Certain parameters from Dokkhin Garadia were isolated and the questionnaire was shortened and adapted slightly to the local situation. As knowledge about

---

[79] Maybe it would have been more appropriate to collect more qualitative data first before implementing the questionnaire.

[80] This hypothesis was based on the findings of a study by SADEQUE & TURNQUIST (1995).

[81] The researchers sometimes overheard a woman tell another women: "They are walking all day around the village, while we are working."

[82] The transferability of the findings from one context to another and the degree of comparability, indicated by the appropriateness of the findings, can be seen as a criteria for generalisation (FLICK 1995: 254). Although this study was not aimed at generalisations, the method chosen for the study allowed validity of the data to be enhanced.

maintenance of the ponds was among the main parameters isolated, the survey was carried out with the pond owners only. This resulted in the sample size being reduced even more. 29 pond owners in Sehakati (Patuakhali *thana*) and 21 pond owners in Madhabpur (Nachole *thana*) were systematically selected and interviewed. Each survey lasted for approximately one week in October/November 1997. Data was entered and analysed for frequencies and cross-tables by SPSS 7.5.

5.3.2
Village mapping

Dokkhin Garadia was chosen to enable the researchers to investigate the structures and processes of water management, especially pond management. A village map was used for orientation during the research and to document the patterns of distribution of wealth and water supply, the latter in static and dynamic form (refer to maps 6.2 to 6.4 in chapter 6). The baseline map was established with the help of an agricultural engineer in October 1996. All roads were measured and their alignment noted by compass. This information was then transmitted by a goniometer onto graph paper. This baseline map was used to map all the households who were interviewed. The socio-economic situation of every household was added at a later date with the construction material of each house taken as an indicator of the socio-economic situation.[83] After the survey in April the findings about women's use of water and the distance to access the water were drawn onto the map showing their mobility for water over the year.

5.3.3
Water quality tests

The leading questions were: How much are ponds really contaminated as they are used all over Bangladesh for various purposes? Are there seasonal variations of pond water contamination? Water quality tests were considered an important method because it is a prerequisite to have data on water quality to start any discussion as to whether ponds should be improved.[84] For the analysis of water quality faecal coliform bacteria counts were chosen because they are most relevant and effective indicator for human health risk.[85]

Water sampling was only conducted in 12 ponds of Dokkhin Garadia.[86] The samples were taken during three different seasons – post-monsoon (October 1996), dry season (March 1997) and rainy season (July/August 1997) by a field

---

[83] Five categories were chosen, according to EHP classification: 1. Low class (L): jute stalk wall, straw roof; 2. Low medium class (LM): bamboo wall, straw roof; 3. Medium class (M): bamboo wall, tin roof; 4. High medium class (HM): tin wall, tin roof; 5. Rich class (R): brick wall, tin or concrete roof. These categories are based on personal communication with SHAFIUL AHMED, formerly of EHP.

[84] Chapter 4.2.4.3 referred to the discussion of specific water quality standards.

[85] The category of total coliform bacteria includes seven to eight different types of bacteria. Faecal coliform bacteria are a sub-category, including four to five different types of bacteria (personal communication with BILQIS AMIN HOQUE, Head EHP).

[86] In the other two villages it was impossible to analyse pond water quality for technical reasons.

worker from EHP at the main bathing sites of each pond under study. In big ponds two samples were taken from opposite banks and the mean value calculated. Each plastic water-container was given the number of the respective pond. To avoid the growth of bacteria it was important to keep the containers cool and to treat the samples within a few hours. Therefore, EHP transport took the samples back to Dhaka the same day. At the International Centre for Diarrhoeal Disease Research in Dhaka, staff of EHP laboratory immediately prepared the samples, about 20 each time, for analysis.[87]

The results of the October sample showed remarkable differences in the number of coliform counts, reaching from 30 to 10,500 cfu/100ml. It is well known that surface water analysis is prone to extreme fluctuations. The results of a sample taken in the morning can differ greatly from one taken in the afternoon after rainfall. Despite this fact, the fluctuations of the October measurement are not justified. It is possible that a technical problem caused this distortion. Unfortunately, a second sampling during the season was missed, which reduces the validity of the October results. Due to this experience, the mean value of two samples, taken within an interval of ten days, was calculated for the following samplings in the dry and monsoon periods. When discussing the health risk and the surface water contamination, the high susceptibility of surface water to climatic changes has to be kept in mind.

5.3.4
Observation

5.3.4.1 Observation of pond use

Pond use observation was included to cross-check the survey information[88] and to obtain quantitative data on pond use, frequency and duration. Since the seasonal pattern of pond use was also of interest, the twelve ponds were observed during post-monsoon, dry season and monsoon season. Two field workers of EHP were trained in observation. In groups of three[89] each pond was observed for one day from 9am to 5pm, and the activities observed were listed on an observation form. The observations were entirely open,[90] but reactivity of the people was not

---

[87] The procedure was as follows: From each sample two dilutions were taken, one of 1 ml and one of 10 ml. As surface water is generally highly contaminated it was not reasonable to take the common dilution of 100 ml. The 1 ml respectively 10 ml of the sample was filtered on mFC filter paper (.45 pore size) and afterwards put on a mFC media plate (based on broth base, Agar and Rosolic acid). All the plates were put in the incubator for 18-24 hours under 44.5°C. For analysis the blue colonies of the faecal coliforms were counted and the number calculated according to the standard of coliform units (cfu) per 100ml. For example, when 30 coliform units were counted in a 1 ml dilution this corresponded to 3,000 coliform units per 100 ml.

[88] Verbal information is often biased because the respondents have certain interests and expectations on the topic and therefore tend to manipulate their answers. For this reason observation is a better tool to find out what is actually happening (BOOT & CAIRNCROSS 1993: 50).

[89] Mainly the research assistant, one EHP field worker and the principal investigator.

[90] Visibly sitting beside the pond the observers were often involved in a conversation with the villagers.

considered to be a problem. Only during the first observation period was a slight distrust towards the observation activities. It is difficult to estimate to what extent the researchers might have influenced pond use through their presence. The researchers tried to minimise this factor by changing the observation site after half a day.

5.3.4.2 Observation of the pond environment

The observation of the pond environment will assist in finding a possible answer to the question of which factors contribute to pond water contamination. This observation took place during pond use observation and was recorded by spot checks.[91] The observer had to walk around the pond and collect information about latrines and waste around the pond, drainage, water plants and cultivation on the pond embankment.

5.3.5
Interviews

Different interview techniques were applied at every stage of the research process.

5.3.5.1 Expert interviews

Interviews with experts were helpful in exploring the research problem during the first stage, to obtain in-depth information during the next stage and to clarify issues in the last stage. Experts included university professors, consultants and officers of national and international organisations and research institutes, NGOs and different government departments in Dhaka and the field sites. The interviews followed an ad-hoc checklist. Field notes were taken.

5.3.5.2 Structured interviews

At the beginning of the field work in Dokkhin Garadia, structured interviews with the pond owners with the aid of a checklist, provided baseline data for pond selection and the household survey.

5.3.5.3 Semi-structured interviews

Semi-structured interviews were conducted in Dokkhin Garadia to complement the household survey information and to clarify upcoming questions. Of particular interest were the power structures and the institutional and religious situations in the village. For semi-structured interviews, the researchers addressed villagers holding a particular position in the village, for example the imam, a member of a village institution or a village leader. Two students proved to be helpful and

---

[91] BOOT & CAIRNCROSS (1993: 59) defined spot check as: "...a particular type of structured observation, whereby the observer records the presence or absence of a behaviour or physical characteristic of interest at the first moment of observation."

provided useful inside information. Later semi-structured interviews were used to find out about the different terms for water sources and to investigate conflict situations regarding access to ponds and tubewells. Women were mainly interviewed during these semi-structured interviews. The interviews followed a series of predetermined questions with sufficient space for open-ended answers.[92] Most interviews were recorded by taking field notes or were taped and then transcribed. In the case of field notes it was important to go through the notes the same day in order to guarantee the accuracy of the information (BERNARD 1994: 191). The field notes led to lively and interesting discussions.

The interview method implies a general communication problem.[93] In the transmission of a message from the sender to the receiver, information is always filtered. This is not only a matter of language but of different cognitive concepts and of different patterns of reaction. Translation from one language into another again filters information and sometimes even transforms the original meaning. Such difficulties are always a problem and the only way to overcome them is to be aware of them and to try to minimise them. Careful listening and probing is necessary during field work. The knowledge of some Bangla was useful when reviewing the translations in the field and also during the transcriptions. When there were no English words equivalent to the Bangla terms, they either were not translated or the term was explained.

5.3.6
Narrative interviews

Besides data collection of present pond management, there was still the question of how ponds were used and maintained in the past and especially before hand tubewells were introduced. It was assumed that traditional indigenous knowledge of pond management existed but had become lost over a period of time and that it might be useful to reactivate this knowledge in face of the present problems in pond management. As no literature could be found on this topic, oral history provided information on a small scale and could be linked to the specific context of the villages studied. Oral history can be defined as contemporary narratives, reminiscences of eyewitnesses about events and situations that occurred during their lifetime (VANSINA 1985: 12). For the purpose of this research it may be more appropriate to use the term narrative interview as pond management was the main subject of the eyewitness accounts. To go back as far as possible in terms of history, eyewitness accounts of the British period were sought. This is not easy in Bangladesh where life expectancy is still low.[94] In all three field areas, men and women, aged between 55 and 90, were interviewed: 13 in Dokkhin Garadia, seven in Patuakhali and eight in Nachole. Guidelines of topics for the interviews were decided upon but it was important to allow the person being interviewed to talk and for the interviewer to listen attentively and probe carefully.[95] The interviews were taped and transcribed in English. Transcriptions were completed word for

[92] BOOT & CAIRNCROSS (1993: 77) provide guidelines for semi-structured interviews.

[93] KROMREY (1995: 267-269) summarises the problems of interview situations and surveys.

[94] 58.7 years for both sexes in 1995 (BBS 1997: 145).

[95] BERNARD (1994: 215-218) provides excellent examples of different probing techniques.

word, except for very repetitive statements. For a recorded interview of one hour the researchers needed between three to six hours for the transcriptions. Narrative interviews always express a personal experience and are shaped by the emotions of the respondent and are therefore subject to a particular reality (VANSINA 1985: 4, 13). For the purpose of this study however, eyewitness accounts proved to be a useful method of discovering processes and of obtaining an idea of the past pond management situation.

5.3.7
Focus group discussion

At the end of the case-study in Dokkhin Garadia, the researchers invited a group of villagers to discuss the problems of pond management and their opinion on how ponds could be improved. A focus group discussion with knowledgeable village elders of Dokkhin Garadia seemed the appropriate method based on the definition of BOOT & CAIRNCROSS (1993: 74).[96] A focus group should comprise six to twelve participants who know each other and the subject in question, and it should last for about one to two hours (BOOT & CAIRNCROSS 1993: 74). From the eight villagers invited, only five accepted the invitation. Field work results were presented first and the participants were then asked to express their views on the problems. Controversial issues were cross-checked and certain issues explored in greater depth. This resulted in a stimulating process of exchange of opinions which aimed at formulating propositions for problem resolution. The two hour discussion took place in a religious school. It was taped and then transcribed into English.

5.3.8
Personal records

Three books, a diary, a log book and a field notebook, accompanied the investigator during all of the field work.[97] The diary consisted of a written record of each day in the field. It was important to remain conscious of personal feelings in order to be aware of the cultural differences and problems and thus balance them for personal stability whilst living and working in unfamiliar surroundings. In this sense, the diary afforded an excellent opportunity for a perspective to be maintained on relationships and surroundings from the field. The log helped to have a control over the field activities where comparisons could be made between the daily activities planned with the daily activities undertaken. It was a useful instrument for undertaking the field work efficiently and was always at hand during field trips. It was essential during field work to write everything down because the days were long, the impressions were many and the recall of details limited. The field notebook was used for a variety of purposes, for instance all

---

[96] They define focus group discussion as a "powerful method to explore subjects of interest and to gain a deeper understanding of attitudes, perceptions, beliefs and wishes of the group participants."

[97] BERNARD (1994: 182-191) suggests the use of these records to organise field work and to digest the experiences.

kinds of notes, ranging from notes on observations to interviews, plans, sketches of maps and brainstorming ideas.

5.3.9
Research of literature and statistics

Empirical research on the one hand and research in libraries and administrations on the other hand proved to be very stimulating. As field work inspired the research for written documents, texts provided new insights on certain issues. Literature research also provided the theoretical background. Different libraries in Switzerland and Bangladesh were visited over the period of the research process. The libraries visited in Dhaka were partly affiliated to international organisations (UNICEF, UNDP/World Bank, SDC), and partly to national organisations (ICDDR,B, Bangladesh Centre for Advanced Studies BCAS, Bangladesh Institute of Development Studies BIDS, Bangladesh Agricultural Research Council BARC) and to Dhaka University (Centre for Social Studies). Libraries of international organisations were frequented for consultancy reports and country programme reports on water supply and sanitation, national libraries and the university for scientific papers on water supply in Bangladesh, hydrogeography and health related and social issues.

Statistical material was mainly collected from the Bangladesh Bureau of Statistics (BBS). Three statistics provided the major sources of information: the Pond Survey, the Population Census for each *zila* (district) and the Census of Agriculture and Livestock. Certain recent statistics could be drawn from the Department of Public Health Engineering (DPHE) or from published reports by international organisations.

Accurate mapping material was difficult to obtain. Local Government (LGED) provided mediocre *thana* maps (scale 1:50.000). DPHE printouts of maps representing tubewell coverage, tubewell type and water table for Bangladesh could be obtained. The most accurate maps were probably the pond maps produced by the Bangladesh Space Research and Remote Sensing Organisation (SPARSSO). Unfortunately, these maps were already out-of-date. SPARSSO developed this set of maps (scale 1:50.000) for FAO/UNDP with the purpose of identifying suitable ponds for fish production (refer to chapter 4.2.3.1).

Chapter 5 laid down the methodological fundament for the empirical study to come. An actor-oriented, dynamic and idiographic research process in combination with a mixture of different methods was chosen for the operationalisation of the hypotheses. Chapters 6 and 7 deal with the indepth case-study of the village of Dokkhin Garadia. Chapter 6 presents the structures and processes of change from past to present water supply whereas chapter 7 looks into pond management as reaction to these changing conditions. Chapter 8 will refer to two additional village studies comparing the situation of pond management with Dokkhin Garadia.

6 Domestic water supply, ponds and hand tubewells in Dokkhin Garadia: structures and processes of change

This chapter will show the processes of change in Dokkhin Garadia with regard to the water supply, particularly the ponds, from the past to the present and the villagers' reactions to these changes. The first subchapter introduces the study area, in its physical, socio-economic, institutional and religious context. Data from the household survey and semi-structured interviews were utilised. The second subchapter recalls the past situation with regard to water supply and pond management through narrative interviews with older villagers. It indicates the change in the concept of the ponds and of pond management that was due to external influences. The third subchapter investigates domestic water supply and its determinants, drawing information from literature and the researcher's own survey data.

6.1
Dokkhin Garadia: the village

6.1.1
Physical aspects of the village

The study area is situated in Singair *thana*, one of the seven *thana*s of the Manikganj District. Singair *thana* consists of 11 unions, of which one union is the urban headquarters. Dokkhin Garadia, the study village, is part of Baira union on the western border with Manikganj *thana* (map 6.1).[98] In 1985, Singair *thana* was connected with Dhaka by a main road. A ferry is needed to cross the Daleswari River, although a bridge is being constructed. In 1993, a road was built connecting the district town Manikganj with Baira and Singair. In Singair, electricity was introduced in 1977/78, in Baira in 1984 (personal communication with DEWAN MD. ALI, chairman of Baira union).

Singair *thana* is a low-lying area, geologically belonging to the Young Brahmaputra flood-plain, providing shallow soils that are silted (BRAMMER 1996: 61). The water table is rather high, ranging from 3.5 to 4.5 metres during the rainy

---

[98] In 1991, the population of Singair *thana* was about 230,000 people, 1066 people per square kilometre. The average population of a village is 981, the average household size is 5.3 persons. The population of Baira union is about 20,000 people (BBS, 1996a: 31, 35, 36, 231).

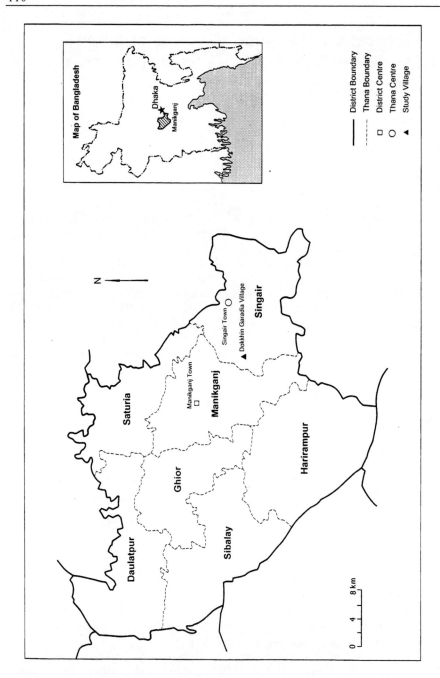

Map 6.1 Manikganj District: Location of the Study Area
Source: GIS Lab, International Centre for Diarrhoeal Disease Research, Bangladesh (ICDDR,B)

season and from 6 to 7.2 metres in the dry season. It is a fortunate region with a range of crops and agricultural products. Rice,[99] sugar cane, jute, pulses and vegetables predominate. Today, irrigation by tubewells is widely practised during the dry season, mainly for growing IRRI[100] rice. In the past, crop production was more dependent on the rivers. The Daleswari River forms the boundary to the west and partly to the north. To the south, the *thana* is bounded by the Kaliganga River. It is a recognised fact that the water table in Singair *thana* is declining at the rate of six inches per year. As a result, the Department of Public Health Engineering (DPHE) had to sink 128 tara pumps in the entire *thana* even though the area is more suitable for shallow tubewells. The recent problem of arsenic contamination also affects various parts of the *thana* (personal communication with ABDUS SAMAD, DPHE Singair).

Dokkhin Garadia is the southern part of Garadia village (see annex for map 6.2). The school represents the centre and separates the northern ward from the southern ward. Dokkhin Garadia is divided into five neighbourhoods, or *paras*. During the rainy season, occasional flooding occurs which forces the villagers to swim from house to house. Vegetation is abundant, especially bamboo, which is also cultivated.

6.1.2
Socio-economic aspects of the village

The household survey revealed that 1,615 people were living in Dokkhin Garadia in November 1996. This corresponds to 5.1 members per family. The age groups according to sex are presented in table 6.1. The population is very young: 48.3 percent of the inhabitants are under the age of 20. Although the level of education is increasing in the younger generation,[101] more than half of the population is illiterate. However, the literacy rate is considerably above the 1991 national average of 32.4 and the *thana* average of 21.1 (BBS 1997: 330 and 1996: 31).[102]

Map 6.3 (refer to annex) documents the socio-economic distribution of the households. The monthly income of the respondents and the housing material[103] were the determinants for stratification.[104] The income distribution according to *paras* confirmed what was observed in the field: the richest households are situated in Dokkhinpara and Moddhopara and the poorest households are in Noyapara.

---

[99] There are three major types of rice: *aus*, *amon* and IRRI (refer to the glossary of non-English words).

[100] IRRI is a high yielding variety of rice which was invented by the International Rice Research Institute (IRRI) in Manila in the course of the Green Revolution. IRRI paddy requires irrigation.

[101] Illiteracy in adolescents aged 10-14 is 12.3 percent, for adolescents aged 15-19 25 percent. In the age group 20-30, the percentage jumps to 56.5 percent.

[102] As expected, the male literacy rate is higher (49 percent) than the female (40 percent), due to socio-cultural constraints.

[103] See chapter 5.

[104] It is difficult to evaluate the socio-economic distribution of the households in the village. Ownership of land alone is not a sufficient factor for evaluation purposes. For example, a family might have no cultivated land, but belongs to the high middle class because one member is working abroad and others are involved in business.

Table 6.1 Dokkhin Garadia: Age Groups According to Sex (in Percentage)

age groups	% of total pop. n= 1615	male	female
1-4 years	10.8	47.7	52.3
5-9 years	13.4	49.5	50.5
10-14 years	12.6	48.3	51.7
15-19 years	11.5	49.7	50.3
20-30 years	21.7	46.0	54.0
31-40 years	11.7	52.9	47.1
41-50 years	7.9	49.2	50.8
> 50 years	10.5	54.4	45.6

Source: Household survey in Dokkhin Garadia (November 1996), own calculations

Dokkhin Garadia has remained a rural environment although it is very close to Dhaka. The main economic activity of the villagers is farming. 60 percent of those surveyed are farmers, half of them belong to the category of small scale farmers.[105] The main crops cultivated are: IRRI, wheat, *aus* and *amon*. IRRI dominates the cultivation cycle, which is primarily *amon* - IRRI. The majority of the farmers stated that they would like to extend IRRI cultivation because it is the most profitable crop for subsistence and sale.[106] Cash crop cultivation of lemon trees is increasing. The percentage of day labourers is high, followed by employment in business or as a wage labourer.

6.1.3
Institutional aspects of the village

Institutions have the function of taking decisions, settling disputes and representing the interests of the village to outsiders. The following institutions were looked at:

- matbor
- shomaj
- bichar
- shomiti

Matbor
Traditionally, the most powerful person in Bengali village society is the matbor. A village used to have only one *matbor* who had to mitigate between the parties in cases of conflict. The villagers of Dokkhin Garadia describe a *matbor* as a

---

[105] Three categories of farm households are distinguished: 1. small farm (0.05 to 2.49 acres), 2. medium farm (2.50 to 7.49 acres) and 3. large farm (7.5 acres and above) (BBS 1988a: 21). In Dokkhin Garadia, 11.4 percent were medium scale farmers and only 2.2 percent large scale farmers.

[106] Jute and sugarcane are grown for domestic sale but apparently there is no interest in increasing the cultivation of these crops.

powerful, intelligent and wealthy man who should know the national law and the socio-cultural rules of the Bengali-Islamic society. He should never be biased towards any party. His words represent the truth,[107] everyone follows his advice.[108]

When asked about the matbor's role today, the villagers gave a variety of replies. Some villagers stated that there is no longer a *matbor* in the village. Others say that everyone can be a *matbor*. Some villagers see the reason for this situation in the government act of 1975 which abolished the *matbor*-system. Others offer the explanation that Bangladeshi people in general have become more self-assertive and aware of their own decision making capacity during the last few years. Former loyalty towards a *matbor* has been replaced by a system of bribes.

About twelve villagers were identified as *matbors* in Dokkhin Garadia and they are still approached to mediate in conflict situations.

Shomaj

On a community level, the institutional matters are treated by the *shomaj*. In a social science context, the *shomaj* is a small community which organises *bichar* to mediate in cases of conflict within a group. *Shomaj* as a term means 'society, assembly, gathering, club'. A *shomaj* consists of people of the same neighbourhood (*para*) who support each other in difficult situations (JAHANGIR 1982: 38, 39).[109] In Dokkhin Garadia, a *shomaj* is not constituted geographically, according to *paras*, but is formed around a mosque and incorporates the central institution of protection and application of the ethical norms (*dhormo*). There are five mosques and therefore five *shomaj* in Dokkhin Garadia. The number of *shomaj* has increased in the village over the past few years because of the increasing rivalry among the villagers, which has led to the partition of large *shomajs*. Although every villager can become a member, the wealthy men dominate the *shomaj* because they are considered more influential. Obviously these people can reinforce and legalise their power through the *shomaj*. The head of the *shomaj* is the chairman and is always a respected *matbor*.

The *shomaj* represents the interests of the villagers. It discusses issues of village development such as the construction or maintenance of roads, bridges, mosques or Koran schools and also provides welfare services. The *shomaj* is also supposed to control the religious beliefs of the villagers.[110] As executive body, guided by the *matbor*, the *shomaj* is responsible for *bichar*.

Bichar

Bichar means judgement, decision, discussion and consideration, and *bichar kora* is justice. In this sense, *bichar* is a kind of a village court, organised by the *shomaj*. *Bichar* is called in cases of conflicts (KOTALOVA 1996: 79). The villagers

---

[107] *"Je ujid kotha bole, she matbor."*

[108] His power is manifested in the following expression of one villager: *"Ekjoner kothai uthe boshe, she matbor"* (When every one stands up and sits down according to his word, then this man is a *matbor*.)

[109] KOTALOVA (1996: 41) defines shomaj as: "the only institution through which 'community' beyond one's family and patriarchal line is created".

[110] The *dhormo*, the proper social and moral behaviour, is the measurement of control executed by the *shomaj* in the rural society (KOTALOVA 1996: 42).

of Dokkhin Garadia remember that in the past the major issues of *bichar* were about land issues. Jurisdiction was strictly followed by the Holy Koran. Any person who contravened the *bichar* was publicly punished. Today, problems in the relationships between men and women are the main issues of *bichar*. When asked about conflicts regarding water supply, villagers stated that they were not very common. No one could think of a *bichar* that was held due to disputes over the use of a hand tubewell or a pond, but sometimes quarrels arose if access to a water source is refused. As the number of shallow tubewells and ponds is increasing some people think that it may be possible that dissension over water issues will increase. In the case of tubewells for irrigation, for example, two cases have been brought to a *bichar* recently.

Shomiti
25 percent of the respondents in Dokkhin Garadia (n= 312) belong to a *shomiti*. A *shomiti* can be defined as an interest group or a club. There are three deep tubewell cooperative committees, two farmers' associations and a religious club. In addition, three of the major NGOs of the country are present in the village. Women are more represented in *shomitis* than men. 85 percent of the respondents are member of an NGO. 43 percent are affiliated with BRAC, 30 percent with the Grameen Bank and 12 percent with PROSHIKA.[111]

6.1.4
Religious aspects of the village

Dokkhin Garadia is a Muslim village. There are no specific religious institutions to guide village life. The three imams have no power. The religious code is quite liberally handled but there is a socio-economic stratification: the seclusion of women (*purdah*) is more often applied to wealthier women.[112] Furthermore, the people of Uttor Garadia disapprove of their neighbours who do not follow the Friday prayer as they are said to belong to a *polli elaca*, a rural area.[113]

6.1.5
Conclusions

When the researchers asked some villagers about the changes that they have seen in their village over the past few years, the following processes were mentioned:

---

[111] BRAC, Bangladesh Rural Advancement Committee, is the largest NGO of the country and specialises in rural development issues. The Grameen Bank has become famous internationally because of its credit system model which aims at supporting poor people's, especially women's, self-reliance. PROSHIKA is the third largest NGO in the country, mainly working in family planning and education.

[112] Although young brides always wear a *burkah* when they leave the village, women in general only cover their head with the end of the *saree* outside their house. The researcher found it surprising to see women returning home after their bath in the pond with their *saree* clinging to their body.

[113] According to the teaching of a former holy man, people in a rural area are excluded from the Friday prayer because their houses are too scattered for an assembly. This attitude has been especially attributed to the poor people in Noyapara.

- The high yielding IRRI rice is the most important crop today. It allows cultivation during the dry season because of tubewell irrigation. However, it is a fact that the water table is declining.
- The economic situation has ameliorated. Due to a better infrastructure, access to the markets has improved. The volume of sales and the demand for agricultural products, such as fertiliser, have increased. Furthermore, the export of labour to countries like Kuwait, Saudi Arabia or Malaysia has become an important source of income for the families. This has introduced a dollar prestige and also the understanding that education is important.
- Population has been increasing. The village is expanding to the south as many joint families are separating. This leads to segmentation of the land and water bodies and, as a consequence, to pressure on natural resources.
- The traditional institutions still exist in Dokkhin Garadia but their value has been transformed. The younger generation is more outwardly oriented. Minor disputes, such as conflicts between men and women, are discussed in *bichar*. Serious cases are often directly transmitted to the *union parishad*. *Shomitis*, in the form of NGOs, have gained importance in the villages, especially for women.
- Respect towards a single village leader (*matbor*) has faded. Individuals are much more conscious of their own decision-making capabilities. Institutions and religion are treated more pragmatically. Individualism is slowly undermining the protected family structure. [114] Relations based on the traditional values, such as land, property, aristocracy, patron-client relation, have been replaced by impersonal relations based on economic and technical activity and education.[115]

6.2
Village water supply in the past, processes of change and impact on ponds

This chapter describes the water supply of Dokkhin Garadia in the past and the processes of change which saw the introduction of new forms of pond management. In-depth interviews with eleven village elders, including both men and women aged between 55 and 92 years, and a focus group discussion with five village male elders provided the main data that is presented below.

In recent years, Dokkhin Garadia has developed a great deal. Due to an improved infrastructure a bus journey to Dhaka today takes approximately two

---

[114] According to ASFARUDDIN (1990: 63, 71, 91, 92) individualism is influencing the behaviour and the psychology of the people.

[115] There are ambiguous statements of older villagers about the past situation of law and order. One Hindu in Sahorail village (Singair *thana*) believed that life during the time of the *zamindars* was better because the British Rule was very strict and punished the criminals: "[...] that's why people were very good and honest." A Muslim neighbour had a different opinion: "If a Muslim went to a *zamindar's* place they gave them jute bags to sit on. They did not even allow Muslims to cultivate coconut trees. If they wanted to they said: Why do you want to cultivate coconut trees? Your parents did not, neither did your grandparents. You will die if you plant them."

hours. Two years ago Dokkhin Garadia was connected to electricity. Brick and iron-sheet houses in the village often indicate that some villagers have made money abroad. Local business is growing. Now there are five small shops in the village where items such as soap, locally made cigarettes, kerosene and biscuits are available. Every fourth household owns a hand tubewell.

6.2.1
Water supply in Dokkhin Garadia: past structure and processes of change

About 50 to 60 years ago, surface water was much more abundant and it remained for a longer period of time. The rains set in between mid-May to mid-June (*joystho*) and guaranteed water until mid-January to mid-February (*magh*). Fish was always available. The canal, which still crosses the village today, was much larger and deeper and, during three months in the rainy season, served as the main access point for commerce and communication. One villager remembers: *"Nowka chhara kono kothay ney".*[116] *Maowaris*, Indian merchants, passed by in big boats, loaded with goods, in particular jute from the factory in Baira. People could travel from the neighbouring location of Baira to other unions, to the District town Manikganj or even to Dhaka in four to five hours.

Today, flood waters are already dried up by mid-November to mid-December (*ogghran*). Surface water for bathing or washing cattle has become rare. Fish supply has been drastically reduced. Some older men believe that the recent large flood protection, drainage and irrigation projects, as well as the Indian Farakkha barrage (chapter 3.2), have contributed to the deviation of the river. The streams have silted up. One villager recalls:

> "In the past a greater amount of water arrived but it was not *bonna*. Now less water arrives but it looks like flood. During the rainy season, when the river is deep, more water is stored in the river but as the river is shallow now the water cannot remain."

Due to these processes the regular flood water (*borsha*) stays away, but the dangerous floods (*bonna*) now affect the land considerably after heavy rainfall.[117] Sometimes the present water shortage is also connected with the increasing number of tubewells in use today. The systematic introduction of tubewells started during the period when Pakistan was in control of the country. Government officials, a doctor and the union chairman visited the village to promote the use of hand tubewells and to warn people about the danger of consuming polluted surface water. However, some villagers were sceptical about the use of hand tubewells. An old woman remembered: "We thought, if we catch the tubewell then maybe something will happen." Another old woman assumed that hand tubewells brought gastric diseases: "Now we see that many people have diseases but in the past there were not so many diseases."

---

[116] There were no words without boats.

[117] SHAW (1992: 205) explains that *borsha* actually means monsoon season but is associated with regular inundation, whereas *bonna* is the extreme flood. She argues that the border between process and disaster is drawn differently in Bangladeshi society. SCHMUCK-WIDMANN (1996) who studied the Char-dwellers' livelihood, also looked closely at the local perception of floods.

The government programme determined the sinking of a certain number of hand tubewells per union. As the application procedure for a tubewell required political contacts with the union chairman for many years only rich villagers were able to have the privilege of obtaining a tubewell. Due to high subsidies tubewells were available at a cost of 300 Taka.[118] With the increasing demand for tubewells the private production of tubewells has become cheaper over the years. Today tubewells are an integrated part of the village water supply. During the household survey, the majority of respondents stated that they have recognised a significant impact on their personal well-being as a result of the introduction of the tubewells. In general, they appreciated that they have less diseases and that safe water is always readily available.[119] The older villagers are also convinced that cholera epidemics have disappeared since tubewells were introduced.

In the past, flood and canal water was used for all purposes whereas ponds were reserved for drinking water purposes. In Dokkhin Garadia, three ponds existed during the childhood era of the respondents. According to their reminiscences the oldest pond is probably the one of Yakub Ali. He moved to the southern end of the village about 60 years ago because his family was growing rapidly. When he constructed his house, he excavated a pond at the same time because there was no source of drinking water in the surrounding area. Noab Ali, one of his two sons, remembered:

" We built a *ghat* of bamboo and told the people to use the pond only from this side, don't spoil the water."

The women fetched water from the bathing site and carried it home for drinking, washing and cooking. Everybody frequented this pond especially during the dry season, when all the other water sources had dried up. A woman recalled:

"They didn't allow anybody to wash their feet, to wash cattle, they didn't allow washing of clothes. They took the water out. Now, there are more people, that's why they don't care anymore[...]."

One woman explained that a few years ago during the dry season several women descended knee-deep to fill their containers with water and later took their bath on the embankment. Noab Ali's brother got angry when he saw this and ordered the women to take the water home for bathing. However, some days later the women forgot about the order and continued as before. The environment of the pond has changed too. First there were no trees, today bush is growing around the pond. Noab Ali:

"We don't care for the pond as much as we did in the past. Now there are more people so who will care?"

---

[118] In 1997 DPHE increased the contribution fee for a public tubewell to 1,000 Taka (23.25 US$). For a public tubewell ten people have to hand in an application form which is examined at the union and *thana* level before the tubewell is granted. In the local market a tubewell costs between 2,000 and 5,000 Taka, transport and installment costs excluded (personal communication with ABDUS SAMAD, DPHE Singair).

[119] 50 percent (n=316) are aware that they have less diseases and 22 percent state that safe water is available without effort. But over 8 percent also complained about the presence of gastric diseases due to tubewell water consumption.

Another villager recognised that ponds were better maintained in the past. He explains:

> "Before, they [the pond owners, I.K.] were always conscious that cattle and people didn't defecate around the pond. They also forbade people to throw dead animals in the pond. Now, they take less care because everybody has tubewells."

Momtaz Fakhir's pond was the second pond in the village. Although some villagers explained that the pond was a gift of a rich man whom the Fakhir had healed, his wife tells a different story:

> "My husband was a healer. When his patients wanted to give him money for treatment he didn't take it. Afterwards all the patients decided not to give him money. Instead they bought some land and dug the pond for him [...]. We were using this *talab* water for every purpose, we did not go anywhere else. We did not allow anybody to bathe in the pond because we used it for drinking purposes. We took the water out [...]. Now, everybody has a tubewell, that's why the pond has no importance anymore. But in the past, the whole world came to our pond."

The third pond was the school pond, which Dhonu Mullah donated. He was a rich villager and also union chairman about forty-five years ago. He encouraged other influential villagers to contribute some land to build a school. Under his initiative the primary school, the Koran school, the pond and later the graveyard west of Dokkhinpara were constructed.

> "Basically, they needed soil for the school but afterwards they thought that they could make a pond, so the villagers could also use the pond water."

Dhonu Mullah's younger sister, remembered that he allowed everyone to use that pond and that nobody would be forbidden from doing so.

> "Several people gave this pond [...] they say it is a common pond (*shobar pukur*)[...] so everybody should take care because everybody uses it."

Although it was a common pond, the donors were expected to take more responsibility for its maintenance. They were also living close to the pond. As long as the pond was new they did not maintain it. Only when the pond started to silt up did the villagers requested permission from Dhonu Mullah to re-excavate

Photo 6.1 Hand tubewells provide safe drinking water. However, ecological problems and cultural prefernces limit their use.

Photo 6.2 Villagers enjoy bathing in ponds as one can swim and dive.

Photo 6.3 Pond water is often preferred for cooking purposes

it. But the re-excavation was not a joint action. Every user only re-excavated the part of the pond that he or she was using.

These three ponds normally did not dry up during the dry season. When the water table declined to a very low level the women still continued to fetch water with coconut shells and poured it through a piece of cloth that they stretched over the water container (*kolshi*), or they stored the water for one day before they drank it.

Some years later the graveyard pond was dug when the graveyard was placed on a mound. This pond was dedicated to ritual washings before a funeral, but later, when the water supply in the village became scarce, many villagers came to bathe in this pond during the dry season. Several villagers opposed this use of the pond because it was a form of desecration. When the graveyard was restored in 1996 a brick wall was built around the whole area, including the pond. Today this pond cannot be misused anymore.[120] One member of the committee justifies their action:

> "It is the graveyard pond, we should keep it clean. If people take their bath it will not be holy (*pobitro*) anymore because it is used for *janaja*.[121] In the past, the committee could not really forbid the villagers to take a bath there because there was no water elsewhere. Today, however, they have other sources - tubewells, ponds - so the committee will establish the rule that nobody can use this pond anymore."

6.2.2
The impact on the ponds in Dokkhin Garadia

The villagers pointed out several factors that invoked changes in the past structures of water supply, such as large-scale flood protection, drainage and irrigation projects, the introduction of tubewells and population growth. They are aware of the consequences on the general water supply in the village. These were:

- drastic reduction in fish supply
- decline of surface water (canal, river and flood water)
- more destructive flooding
- decline of groundwater

As a reaction to the new reality the role of ponds was also transformed. The household survey (n= 389) revealed that the respondents recognised the following changes in ponds: 46.8 percent stated that now there was more fish cultivation, 17.2 percent found that embankments had deteriorated, 15.4 percent explained that ditches became ponds, nearly 10 percent believe that water quality improved due to fish cultivation, 2.8 percent said that accessibility to ponds has been reduced and 2.3 percent indicated that there are more water plants. Taking all of the statements together the ponds have changed in various ways:

- The number of ponds has increased due to the decline of surface water and the growing demand for water. On the one hand, ditches are being improved. On

---

[120] This is pond 5 on the village map, which was excluded from further study due to the reasons mentioned.

[121] This is the prayer at the grave spoken after ablution.

the other hand holes, resulting from an increasing construction activity, are extended to ponds or at least to *maitals*. Finally a higher living standard makes the excavation of ponds affordable.

- Ponds are increasingly used for fish production. As hand tubewells provide safe drinking water ponds have become superfluous for this purpose and can be used instead to augment fish supply.
- Ponds have transformed from a common property resource (used for drinking purpose) to a private property resource (used for fish production).[122]
- Maintenance of the ponds has changed. Some believe that maintenance has improved because pond water is considered a scarce source of good water and fish production is a lucrative business.[123] Others however are convinced that maintenance has deteriorated. The embankments are destroyed, water plants cover the pond, vegetation is growing wild. The main reason is seen as the provision of tubewell water which has replaced the pond as the drinking water source.

"Jothno kom kore karon ekhon protteker ghore ghore tubewell ache."[124] "They are going to forget how to use pond water [...] for domestic purposes. Except for bathing, people don't use the pond."

- Another reason is that the number of users per pond has increased and consequently the pressure on the pond has risen. As the number of shareholders has also increased the allocation of the responsibility for maintenance has become difficult. There is not a single authoritative decision maker anymore.
- There are no strict regulations for pond use as in the past. Today, women walk into the water to fill their containers. Bathing and washing clothes and utensils in ponds, which are normally used for cooking, is no longer an exception. This lack of control has to do with a general degradation of respect towards village leaders (refer to chapter 6.1.3) but also with the perception that pond water is not used for drinking purposes anymore.
- In the past, ponds were often donated to a person or the village for goodwill. Therefore, the donor or the pond owner always had a high social prestige. Today pond owners have a high economic prestige, especially when they are successful in fish production.
- Accessibility to ponds has been reduced. In the past ponds for drinking water were open to all, whereas pond owners who produce fish, often prohibit others from using their pond. Nevertheless, these pond owners are respected because fish production is considered important.

This chapter has shown that exogenous factors, principally introduced by development programmes, caused major changes in the physical and social

---

[122] 35 percent of the respondents (n= 183) in the household survey believe that the change in ponds is due mainly to privatisation of ponds for fish production.

[123] One villager: "Now people take more care of the ponds because they think if they maintain the pond they can cultivate fish and solve the fish problem. When people realise that something is scarce then they consider it important. See, before there was no water shortage, we got water from canals, *beels* and rivers for cattle, for clothes. We had only some shortage of water for drinking and cooking."

[124] They take less care because every house has a tubewell.

122

environment of Dokkhin Garadia. The village has developed new social and institutional forms and the individual new strategies of tackling with the water supply situation. This has also led to a changed pond management. The next chapter will explore the decision-making patterns of the villagers that were responsible for their reactions to these changes. Firstly, the focus will be on the choice of water source for domestic purposes. It will be shown that the villagers' choice is rational, given the structures and is based on interactions with others. Later, it will be examined as to whether these assumptions are also true for pond management.

6.3
Village water supply and the choice for domestic purposes[125]

The Water Policy of the Government of Bangladesh focuses on water supply for agricultural production, especially on groundwater irrigation by tubewells. The sector of domestic water supply has been treated rudimentarily and was dominated by an intensive campaign for the overall use of tubewell water. Only recently the Policy seems to have changed in favour of ponds due to the arsenic problem.[126] Therefore, it is all the more important to emphasise the domestic water supply. The following points were examined:

- present sources of domestic water supply in the case of Dokkhin Garadia
- reasons why tubewell water is not preferred by many villagers for a majority of domestic purposes
- determinants of choice for a water source which are based on rational considerations of the users

The chapter utilises my own field data[127] which is compared with the relevant findings from existing literature.

6.3.1
Sources of domestic water supply

Generally, one has to distinguish between two forms of domestic purposes: water consumed for drinking and water consumed for other domestic purposes. In Bangladesh, the choice of a water source very much depends on this fact. Table 6.2 shows that, due to rigorous government promotion, tubewell water is the main

---

[125] Domestic purposes are defined as the use of water for drinking, cooking, ablution (ritual washing before prayer), washing clothes and washing kitchen utensils.
[126] See chapter 3.4.
[127] Besides data from the household survey this includes a survey with fifty poorer women of Dokkhin Garadia conducted during the dry season (April/May 1997). According to the findings of BRISCOE (1981) and SADEQUE & TURNQUIST (1995) it was assumed that poor people are usually deprived from access to private tubewells during the dry season and have to fall back on contaminated water sources.

source of drinking water in Bangladesh today. However, as far as other domestic purposes are concerned, other water sources are preferred. UNICEF (1997: 42, 43) for example demonstrates that rural households use 62.7 percent tubewell water, 43.4 percent pond water and 5.9 percent river or canal water for non-drinking purposes. In the study village a similar observation was made. Tubewell water was less consumed than the national average.[128]

Table 6.2 Sources of Water Supply for Drinking Purposes (in Percentage)

Source	National (% of total pop.)[a]	Singair *thana* (% of total pop.)[b]	Dokkhin Garadia village (n=312)[c]
tap/tubewell	97.2	94.3	89.7
well	---	5.03	10.0
pond	2.80	0.33	0.30
canal/river	0.60	0.34	

Sources: [a] UNICEF (1997: 42,43); [b] BBS (1996a: 36); [c] Household survey in Dokkhin Garadia (Nov. 1996), own calculations

Wells (*kua*) are still common as this water is considered safe. Figure 6.1 shows the percentage of hand tubewell use by the respondents for each domestic purpose. Tubewell water is principally consumed for drinking, ablution and washing kitchen utensils. But for cooking, bathing and washing clothes open water sources such as ponds and canals are preferred and depend on the choices of the users.

6.3.2
Determinants for choosing a water source

Several studies have been looking at the factors that determine the individual choice for a water source. Some studies investigated the topic from a regional point of view.[129] Other studies focused on women as the main actors responsible for obtaining domestic water.[130] WHITE, BRADLEY & WHITE (1972) are probably closest to reality when they state that the decision making model is more complex and cannot be reduced to only an economic optimum or to a technological or a traditional behavioural model.[131]

---

[128] The number of users per hand tubewell is almost equal for Singair *thana* and the study village. In the *thana*, 26.6 persons share a hand tubewell, in Dokkhin Garadia about 24 persons (HEALTH MINISTRY 1996).

[129] For example BRISCOE (1978 and 1981) for Bangladesh, and WHITE, BRADLEY & WHITE (1972) for East Africa.

[130] BWDB 1997; DPHE, & UNICEF 1995; ISHRAT & SALAHUDDIN 1994. These studies were mainly designed to integrate a software component in water development planning and range from economic models to gender based approaches.

[131] BRISCOE (1981) extends the economic model. He combines the preference model with a socio-economic stratification by comparing the marginal rate of substitution of a determinant

In Dokkhin Garadia, five factors were found to have a major influence on the decision making process of women when deciding upon a water source. These factors are: the seasonal availability of water, the quality of the water, the distance to the water source, ownership, security and family relationships relating to a particular water source and technical impediments. Furthermore, the source which is chosen is dependent on the purpose the water will be used for. Although the determinants are described separately it has to be noted that all the determinants are interlinked with each other and, as such, influence the decision making of the users for a specific water source.

6.3.2.1 The seasonal availability of water

In Bangladesh water supply underlies seasonal variations to a great extent. The monsoon rains which usually cover one third of the country's surface with water for several weeks also refill the groundwater storage. But during the dry season groundwater becomes scarce. Seasonal availability of water has therefore a major influence on the choice of water source.[132] The survey of fifty poorer women showed that tubewell water remained the only constant source of drinking water throughout the year, although a few women reported drinking water from wells. The reason for this conformity is the high tubewell coverage in the village and the acquired knowledge that tubewell water is the safest water for drinking. For cooking purposes, women use mostly surface water. During mid-July to mid-September (*srabon* and *bhaddro)* the women make use of the surplus water around their houses, such as the canal (*khal*) and the flooded fields (*chok*). This situation changes between mid-October and mid-December (*kartik* and *ogghran)* when ponds and *maitals* become the main source of water for cooking purposes. Only during mid-March to mid-May (*choyttro* and *boyshak)* when the surface water becomes drastically reduced, do more women draw water from tubewells. However, the majority of the fifty poorer women surveyed still collect water from ponds, mainly from those ponds traditionally set aside as sources of cooking water (see chapter 6.2).

The seasonal changes in location due to water availability is also noteworthy with regard to bathing. During the rainy season, over two thirds of the respondents bathe in the canal and almost one third bathe in the flooded fields. As soon as the open surface water withdraws, closed surface water bodies are frequented, these are mainly ponds and *dangas*. During the dry season women often move to the *dangas* in the field because the smaller ponds have dried up. But the use of tubewell water also increases and equals the use of pond water. The situation for washing clothes is similar to that of bathing. Open surface water

---

between poor and rich villagers. The System Rehabilitation-Project of the Bangladesh Water Development Board (BWDB 1997a) shows that the socio-economic situation of the main actors influences the coping strategies utilised in the choosing of a water source and the consumption of water. SADEQUE & TURNQUIST (1995) confirm that for Bangladesh the socio-economic status influences the use of tubewell water as poor women often face constraints in obtaining tubewell water.

[132] The household survey in Dokkhin Garadia revealed that 67 percent of the tubewell owners and 41 percent of those who do not own a tubewell admit that between mid-March and mid-April (*choyttro)* less tubewell water is available because of a general decline of the water table.

is preferred during the rainy season and is used as long as possible. Only between mid-December and mid-February (*posh* and *magh*) do closed surface water bodies replace open surface water bodies. Women also commence using tubewell water for washing. In the dry season, *dangas* are the washing site for one third of the women, about one quarter of the women use *maital* and tubewell water. For washing utensils and ablution the seasonal changes in the water source are not significant. Canal and fieldwater is used during the rainy season, but afterwards tubewell water becomes the most important source for the remainder of the year.

Seasonal availability of water is an important factor as it shows that the villagers use various water sources for different purposes at different times of the year. However, why they use a specific source implies other determinants.

6.3.2.2 Perceived water quality

According to WHITE, BRADLEY & WHITE (1972: 237) water quality is the most important factor for the selection of a water source. It is further related to the socio-economic status of the user and the domestic purpose that the water will be used for. BRISCOE (1981) found out that water quality is a more powerful determinant for the rich villagers than for the poor. This was confirmed in Dokkhin Garadia where the poorer women use tubewell water only for drinking because unlimited access to private tubewell water is not possible as will be explained in chapter 6.3.2.4. A report for DPHE & DANIDA (1998), states that the absence of iron, clarity versus turbidity and purity of water were perceived to be important indicators for water quality. BRISCOE (1981: 177) considers the following factors that influence water quality: colour, odour, taste, dirt, depth, *purdah* and the quality of the bathing site.

During field work in Dokkhin Garadia and the two additional study areas, an uniform concept of clean water emerged. Villagers prefer abundant and flowing water to small amounts and stagnant water. Open water is considered dirty, whereas closed water is considered to be clean. Dirty water is perceived as muddy, covered with leaves and polluted with human faeces or dead animals. Clear water is considered clean. Water sources that are protected by embankments, pipes or rings that keep away dirty run-off water are regarded as clean. However, there is also a commonly held belief about which specific water source is clean in a particular village. In Dokkhin Garadia, certain ponds were considered clean by everyone because they were formerly reserved for drinking water purposes. Such beliefs are difficult to change despite these ponds being highly contaminated. In Dokkhin Garadia, the presence of iron in the groundwater is a principal reason for refusing tubewell water for cooking, washing and bathing (see figure 6.2). Rice cooked with tubewell water turns red or black, it breaks up and loses its taste. Food needs to be boiled for a longer period and it spoils more quickly. Clothes washed with tubewell water have a tendency to become yellow or red. Some women claimed that they need more soap to wash clothes with and that their hair becomes sticky and their bodies turn red after bathing with tubewell water. Some women would not use tubewell water for bathing because they believed that they would get a fever or a cold.

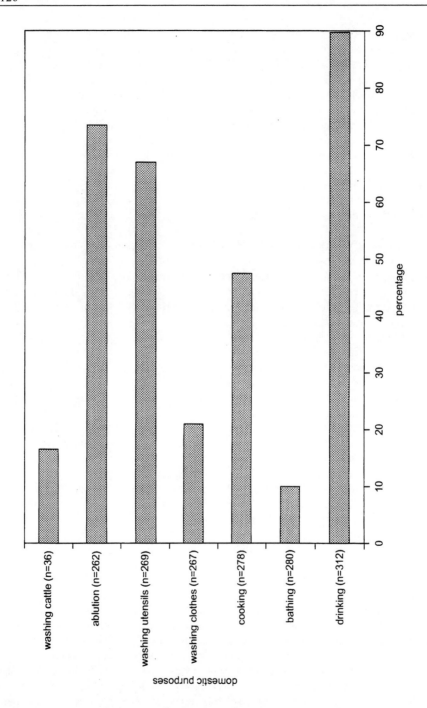

Figure 6.1 Tubewell Water Use According to Each Purpose
Source: Household survey in Dokkhin Garadia (Nov. 1996); own calculations

6.3.2.3 Distance to the water source

The availability of time and the energy a woman has to draw water determines the distance she will travel to the water source. According to WHITE, BRADLEY & WHITE (1972: 128) this will be a maximum of one mile. This appears to be the critical point with regard to the volume of water collected. Apparently, the distance factor is more important for certain domestic purposes than for others. Studies (DPHE & UNICEF 1995; BRISCOE 1981) indicate that women were more willing to cover a longer distance for obtaining drinking water than for other domestic purposes.

Map 6.4 illustrates poorer women's mobility in Dokkhin Garadia to obtain water. Normally, the closest water source is preferred if it corresponds with the other determinants such as the purpose that the water is used for. Tubewell water, for example is rarely used for bathing and washing as large volumes of water would have to be pumped and transported to the house. During the dry season, however, when water becomes scarce women move far away from their *baris* to *dangas* where water remain longest.

6.3.2.4 Ownership, security and family relationships

Do women choose a water source for social reasons; for example to meet other women, or not to be harassed by men or because of kinship relationships? WHITE, BRADLEY & WHITE (1972: 243) failed to prove that water sources in East Africa are social meeting points. They came to the conclusion that women avoid a water source where problems could arise or where they may feel insecure. The risk of being exposed to quarrels at a water source is a powerful determinant for poorer women during the dry season in Bangladesh because the pressure on the tubewell increases as there is less water available (BRISCOE 1981: 178, 179). It is in the dry season that tubewell owners sometimes ask for a remuneration or question the lack of monetary contribution, which may lead to disputes (DPHE & UNICEF 1995). Sometimes non-family members are only given limited access or are even prohibited from using tubewell water by private tubewell owners (SADEQUE & TURNQUIST 1995: 19, 20).

Therefore, to be the owner, to belong to his family or lineage, or to have a good relationship with the owner makes it much easier to draw water from a certain source, especially from a hand tubewell. In Dokkhin Garadia, the respondents who drink ring well water stated that they use this water because they own the ring well. Non-ownership of a tubewell was among the major reasons for not-using tubewell water (see figure 6.2). This could mean that villagers do not feel comfortable in using other people's tubewells for purposes other than drinking, because they would need to draw more water which the owner may disapprove. This could lead to disputes. Therefore, water sources are frequented where the possibility of conflict is less pronounced, for example public hand tubewells or open-access ponds.[133] This is particularly relevant for the poorer people. However, poor people in Dokkhin Garadia are rarely deprived from access to hand tubewells. Only six cases where negative incidences arose were reported. Four of these happened during the dry season when the tubewell owners drove people away because they feared that the well would break due to the increased pressure on the tubewell. In one case, a serious dispute was probably based on an personal argument.[134]

Other than the possibility of disputes, observing *purdah* may also restrict the choice for a particular water source in parts of Bangladesh. Some women are ashamed or feel that they lose dignity when they have to pass a male dominated public site, for example the market, to fetch water (DPHE & UNICEF 1995). Women in the more conservative coastal area of Patuakhali particularly expressed this fear.

6.3.2.5 Technical impediments

Defective public tubewells have been a major problem in rural Bangladesh for many years. The Department of Public Health Engineering (DPHE) who installed the hand pumps was not capable to provide the number of mechanics necessary for the repair tasks. DPHE tubewells therefore often became inoperable unless they were repaired by private initiatives. In Dokkhin Garadia, out of 68 hand tubewells seven are public, but only four of these are still working. With the general improvement of tubewell technology and the increasing availability of private tubewells, repair and replacement of spare parts is less of a problem. Nowadays, tubewells are more affordable as they have become cheaper and purchasing power has increased. However, pumping is a problem for many women, especially when they are expected to draw a larger volume of water, for example for bathing or washing clothes. The number 6 handpump is relatively easy to operate, whereas the tara pump requires greater extertion and may be difficult for many women.[135]

---

[133] Poorer women mainly refer to the public hand tubewell of Rajak Ali and of the village doctor (see map 6.4). Open access ponds are those which are reserved for cooking purposes (ponds 1, 6 and 13).

[134] A young woman was washing clothes at the public tubewell of Rajak Ali. When he saw this he got angry and ordered her to go somewhere else because she would need too much water. The woman countered that this was a public tubewell and open to all. But he chased her away, saying that he would have to repair the well in case of damage. The same evening the woman's father-in-law and his brother went to see Rajak Ali to discuss the matter. They started to quarrel and finally separated. From that time on they have not talked to each other.

[135] The number 6 pump is the standard hand tubewell in Bangladesh. It has a suction capacity of 7.5 metres whereas, the tara pump can lift water from up to 15 metres (KJELLERUP, JOURNEY & MINNATULLAH 1989: 9, 10). The operation of the tara pump requires physical strength as one villager in Madhabpur (Nachole *thana*) expresses: *"manush mara kol"* (a contraption to kill people).

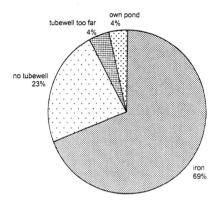

Reasons for not using tubewell water for bathing

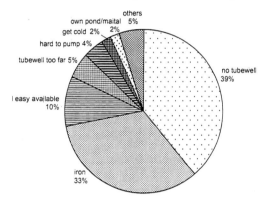

Reasons for not using tubewell water for washing clothes

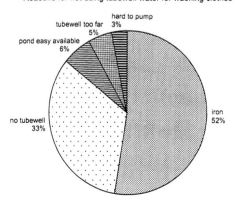

Figure 6.2 Reasons for Not-Using Tubewell Water for Various Domestic Purposes
Source: Household survey in Dokkhin Garadia (Nov. 1996); own calculations

6.3.3
Conclusions

Considering their workload and availability of time, the simplest choice for a woman would be to collect water from one source. But the reality is different. According to WHITE, BRADLEY & WHITE (1972: 233, 236) at least two sources are drawn upon, and a consultative report for DANIDA & THE MINISTRY OF FOREIGN AFFAIRS (1998) mentions two to three sources. Map 6.4 (refer to annex) illustrates the mobility of poorer women in Dokkhin Garadia for water sources. 42 percent of these women (n= 50) indicated that they frequented four different sources and 36 percent indicated five different water sources. In Dokkhin Garadia, it was observed that at first a choice was made between surface water and groundwater, then a choice between open and closed surface water. Finally, a distinction is made between different open surface water sources (canals, flooded fields) and different closed surface water sources (ponds, *maitals*, *dangas*). Among the latter, the pond is the most popular water source.

Today, a variety of water sources is required as surface water in the fields and canals dry up quickly and the demand for water is growing. Furthermore, tubewells cannot represent the unique water source because the groundwater quality is unacceptable in many parts of the country due to arsenic contamination, salinity and the high iron content, and because the water table is declining. Ponds have continued to be an important water source for rural dwellers. A pond is a convenient, traditional water source.[136]

Women carefully consider the multitude of water sources for a specific domestic purpose and various factors influence their decision making processes. Beside the above factors, habit and tradition as well as the behaviour of others and personal preferences are also important. Facing a changing water supply situation in the village the users have had to cope with the new conditions. The next chapter deals with pond management in Dokkhin Garadia and will document that the present pond management is a reaction to the changed system of the pond which was influenced by external circumstances such as water development projects, the integration into the market economy and population growth. It will explore why ponds are still important and that pond management also underlies a pragmatic and ecological decision making pattern, as in the case of the choice for a water source in general.

---

[136] HOQUE et al. (1990b) concluded in their study that the main reasons for not using tubewell
. water in rural areas were the inconvenience and the physical quality of the water.

7 Pond management in Dokkhin Garadia

The previous chapter has demonstrated the changes in water supply from the past to the present, the processes responsible for these changes and the adapting strategies of the villagers. This chapter shows that present pond management is a reaction to the changing social and ecological situations. The determinants the actors choose for the use and maintenance of ponds reflect their adaptation to a new reality. Even pond deterioration can be seen as one strategy among several to cope with the changes in the water supply situation. The five subchapters will treat:

- pond classification parametres for the operation period of the analysis
- the present pond water use and the determinants of pond water use
- the present maintenance practices and the determinants of maintenance
- the present state of the ponds in the village as per water quality analysis and an inventory of the pond environment
- processes of change exemplified through generations of pond owners
- problems and opportunities of ponds according to the findings of the case-study
- requirements for further studies and pond improvement projects

The chapter provides basic data on the structure and processes of the ponds and of pond management in Dokkhin Garadia that need to be taken into account for the future development of ponds for domestic purposes. The chapter concludes that pond management has to be considered as a viable alternative but it would involve some serious problems that would have to be tackled. First requirements will be offered.

7.1
Pond classification parameters

The first visit to Dokkhin Garadia took place in September 1996. In the company of the school headmaster's son, a college student, and with the help of passing villagers, the village was transected to identify ponds. The objective was to find a variety of ponds regarding age, size, use and ownership. As the village was still flooded not all the indicated ponds were accessible and their physical structure was hardly visible due to the fact that they were filled to the ridges with floodwaters. Finally fourteen ponds were selected, but in the course of the field work two had to be deleted.[137] A prepared checklist consisting of a set of parameters was used to interview each pond owner. This checklist offered a good basis for the formulation of a further list of pond parameters to analyse and compare the various ponds. The list included the following parameters:

- size of pond (surface in square metres)
- depth of pond (in metres)
- location of pond[138]
- age of pond
- reason behind pond excavation
- use of pond (purpose and frequency)
- drainage
- bathing site (*ghat*)
- pond maintenance practices
- cleanliness of pond (water quality)
- pond ownership patterns[139]

The operation of the parameters required the application of different methods such as physical measurement, narrative interviews, household survey, observation, various types of interviews and pond water analysis. Table 7.1 gives an overview of the parameters for all ponds.

To analyse the impact of the pond owners' socio-economic situation on pond management a list of socio-economic parameters was added[140], including the following:

- literacy status
- land ownership pattern
- family size and relations (inheritance pattern)
- occupation
- political position in the village

This information was drawn from the household survey and various semi-structured interviews. Table 7.2 presents the socio-economic parameters for all pond owners.

---

[137] Pond 12 turned out to be a *maital* and pond 5 had dried up because of work in the surrounding area.

[138] The parameter 'location of pond' proved not to be relevant for Dokkhin Garadia because the villagers had defined a pond as being located close to the house.

[139] ULLAH (1983) established a pond classification to investigate the potential development of ponds for fish cultivation. He included the following variables: pond size, age of pond, purpose of excavation, use of pond, flood vulnerability and depth. For the purpose of this study ULLAH's classification was extended because of the broader frame of the research.

[140] In this respect, ULLAH (1983) considered land ownership pattern, occupational profile, monthly cash earning, ownership of draught animals, duck raising, literacy status and fragmentation of pond ownership. For the study in Dokkhin Garadia several of these variables were not regarded relevant, for example the monthly cash income, the ownership of draught animals and duck raising.

Pond variable / Pond (number)	Size/Surface (square meters)	Depth inches/meters	Age (years)	Reason behind excavation	Drainage	Bathing site (ghat)	Ownership	Use
1	1280	171/4.3	45	drinking, cooking	no	no	public	cooking
2	245	148/3.75	8-18	bhithi	no	no	private (shared)	fish production, bathing, washing clothes
3	1478	108/2.7	10	fish production	no	no	private	fish production, bathing, washing clothes
4	250	----------	----	bhithi, multi-purpose	yes	no	private	bathing, washing clothes
6	811	203/5.1	55	drinking, cooking	yes	no	private (shared)	cooking, bathing, washing clothes
7	600	187/4.75	10	bhithi, multi-purpose	yes	no	private (shared)	cooking, fish production, bathing, washing clothes/utensils
8	724	164/4.1	10	bhithi, multi-purpose	yes	yes	private	cooking, fish production, bathing
9	316	----------	7	bhithi, fish	yes	no	private	cooking, bathing, washing clothes
10	458	198/5	3	bhithi, multi-purpose	no	yes	private	bathing, washing clothes
11	483	189/4.8	2	fish production	no	yes	private	fish production, bathing
13	899	162/4.1	50	drinking, cooking	yes	no	private	cooking
14	708	117/2.9	3	fish production	no	no	private	bathing, washing clothes

Table 7.1 The Ponds of Dokkhin Garadia: Comparison of Main Variables
Source: field study in Dokkhin Garadia (Sept. 1996 to August 1997)

Variable Pond owner	Occupation	Land ownership (decimel/acre)[a]	Number of possible heirs	Education (class/degree)	Political position
1	College teacher	-------	not relevant	M.A.	somaj member; matbor
2	School teacher	525/5.25	14	class 10	somaj member; matbor
3	Farmer	1575/15.75	4	class 10	-------
4	Business	30/0.3	4	class 10	somaj member; matbor
6	Farmer	-------	8 males	illiterate	former matbor
7	Farmer	175/1.75	2 males	class 5	-------
8	Farmer	70/0.7	1 male	illiterate [b]	-------
9	Farmer	175/1.75	3	class 5	somaj member; matbor
10	Farmer; Business	210/2.1	3 males	illiterate	somaj member; matbor
11	Farmer; Business	280/2.8	3	class 5	-------
13	Farmer	350/3.5	1	illiterate [c]	somaj member
14	Farmer; Business	525/5.25	6	class 3	somaj member; matbor

[a] 100 decimel = 1 acre
[b] Father. He is still the owner. The interview was conducted with the son whose educational degree is class 5. He is also a farmer.
[c] Father. He is still the owner. The interview was conducted with the son who has a M.A. and is a college teacher.

Table 7.2 Pond Owners in Dokkhin Garadia: Comparison of Main Variables
Source: village household survey, semi-structured interviews in Dokkhin Garadia

7.2
Pond water use and determinants of pond water use

Ponds are an integral part of the Bangladesh landscape and culture. Every Bangladeshi seems to have a relationship to a pond. Even city dwellers, who have grown up in the countryside, remember with fondness their daily bath in the village pond. In the following section it will be highlighted why villagers use ponds, why they prefer certain ponds to others and how they use ponds.

During the household survey (n= 312), 74 percent of the respondents stated that they use ponds and pond water for domestic purposes. The respondents were asked to give three reasons why they used ponds. The most frequent responses were:

- Bathing in a pond is very enjoyable because one can dive and swim and ones hair does not get sticky. This was the opinion of 15.1 percent, 10.3 percent and 3.5 percent respectively.
- The fact that pond water does not contain iron was mentioned as the second reason. The respondents prefer to wash clothes with pond water because they are cleaner than when washed with tubewell water and less soap is needed. Furthermore, food is tastier when cooked with pond water, it looks nicer and can be kept longer.
- Not owning a tubewell was considered the third most important reason for using ponds, and by 13.1 percent of the respondents as first reason.
- In the second and third response accessibility to the ponds was valued more. This means that it is easier to use ponds for certain domestic purposes, for example for washing clothes, but it could also imply that access to tubewells for other purposes than drinking is limited.
- Finally, 5.4 percent stated in their first response that they believe pond water to be clean and good for their health.

To cross-check the results of the survey on pond water use, pond observation was conducted at every pond for one day in three different seasons – post-monsoon (November), dry season (March), and monsoon season (August). Seven categories of pond use for domestic purposes were considered: bathing, ablution, water for cooking, washing kitchen utensils, washing clothes, cleaning cattle and refreshment[141]. As figure 7.1 indicates, the observations revealed that all the ponds serve a multipurpose function, and that no pond is used for drinking purposes anymore or to clean cattle. Although all ponds are used for several purposes some are used specifically for a main purpose.[142] This is the case with ponds 1 and 13, which are reserved for cooking purposes and used by over 80

---

[141] It was sometimes not possible to distinguish between pond water use for ablution and refreshment. During ablution (*oju*) a person washes the hands and arms, the ankles, the ears and nostrils. Some people only come to the pond to refresh themselves by washing their hands, arms and feet.

[142] Several authors ascribe to ponds a multipurpose function (KHAN 1990; ULLAH 1983). However, the importance that is attributed to a specific purpose should be differentiated.

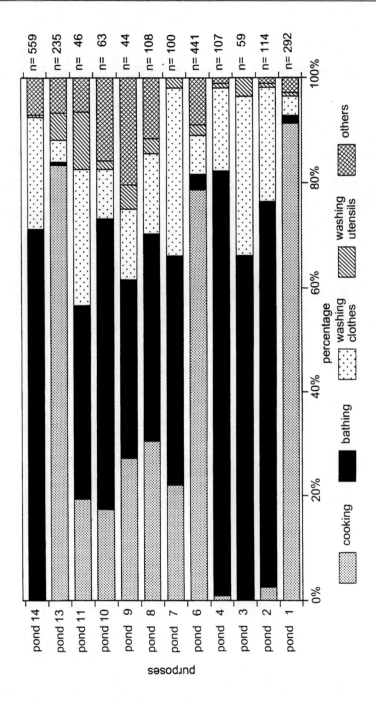

Figure 7.1 Pond Use According to Purposes (All Seasons)
Source: Observations in Dokkhin Garadia (1996/97)

percent of the respondents for this purpose (n= 292 resp. 235). Pond 6 is also used mainly for cooking purposes by 78 percent of the respondents (n= 441)[143]. Ponds 2, 4 and 14 are used for bathing by over 70 percent of the villagers (n= 114, 107 resp. 559). All other ponds are preferred for bathing purposes.[144]

The choice between different ponds is also, like water supply in general, determined by various factors. In the following chapter, it will be referred to by seasonal impact, perceived water quality, distance/time, ownership/accessibility, tradition/cultural habit and technical impediments.[145]

7.2.1
Seasonal impact

The monsoon rains replenish all surface water bodies. During the monsoon, water is everywhere and is used wherever it is most accessible.[146] But during the post-monsoon period (October to December), when evaporation exceeds precipitation, villagers take advantage of the replenished canals and *maitals*. In the dry season (January to May), surface water drastically recedes and people have to access ponds and *dangas* because they are larger and deeper and can retain water for a longer period.

The seasonal fluctuation of water availability is reflected in the villagers' frequency to use certain ponds. Two conclusions can be drawn from figure 7.2, based on observation:

1. The most frequented ponds are the most important ponds of the village. These are the three ponds dedicated to cooking purposes (ponds 1, 6, 13) and the most popular bathing pond (pond 14).
2. The most frequented ponds show the highest user fluctuation. The user peak of ponds 1, 6 and 13 is in March, because at that time water scarcity is acute in the village but these ponds still contain some water. Significant fluctuations also characterise pond 14. It is the most popular pond of the village but in March the pond dries up and cannot be used. The remaining ponds do not show relevant seasonal fluctuations because their user frequency is much lower.
3. The user peak of the ponds used for cooking water is in the dry season. This could mean that these ponds are deeper and better maintained although it is

---

[143] The researchers did not follow the women to verify whether the water was exclusively used for cooking purposes. But these ponds are generally said to be used for this specific purpose.

[144] Bathing is often combined with washing clothes: after bathing the men put on a fresh *lungi* and wash the wet *lungi*. Women wash the *saree* while bathing and change it later at home.

[145] These determinants almost coincide with the ones presented in chapter 6.3. During the comparative village studies (chapter 8), the determinants 'hydro-geomorphological conditions' and 'religion' were more important.

[146] The aspect of seasonal availability of water had its impact on the household survey when it was intended to find out which pond the villagers favoured. It turned out that the majority of the respondents did not refer to the twelve selected ponds but to other closed surface water bodies, such as *maitals*, *dangas* or *dobas*. At the time of post-monsoon, it is possible that people frequent these sources more than the ponds.

Photo 7.1 Pond in Dokkhin Garadia during post-monsoon season and...

Photo 7.2 ... during the dry season. It is mainly used for bathing and cooking purposes.

more probable that they are frequented due to their open-access character and to their perceived water quality.

7.2.2
Perceived water quality

Although the water table of those ponds used for cooking purposes, declines remarkably in the dry season, village women continue to fetch the muddy water. They justify this by saying that they use the water to cook rice and that everyone takes this water for cooking. Water quality is valued according to its effect on food, clothes and the body. The villagers, both men and women, in Dokkhin Garadia perceive good water as free of iron. Therefore, pond water is preferred to tubewell water in many cases (chapter 6.3). Nevertheless, the villagers know the health risks associated with pond water use. 66.5 percent (n= 312) reported having become sick after using this water. Despite this, the health impact of pond water consumption is less important. One reason could be that consuming pond water is not lethal anymore because the water is boiled or consumed only in small doses. In addition, the villagers may suffer chronic gastric diseases, which they consider as part of their normal existence. Consequently, they do not consider that there is an urgent need to improve their health situation.

Furthermore, pond water is considered clean. 80 percent of the poorer women (n=50) stated that pond water was clean because pond owners prohibit bathing, washing of clothes, the use of soap or washing cattle, and because the pond is protected by embankments there are no leaves or faeces in the water. The absence of water hyacinths (*kochuripana*) and algae in the water as well as a clean environment are also important factors in perceiving water as clean. Six out of the twelve pond owners consider that the water in their ponds is clean. Four of the owners use this water for cooking and three do not own a tubewell. This means that only one pond owner prefers pond water for cooking in comparison to tubewell water. Table 7.3 further indicates that tubewell owners consume less pond water for cooking purposes. It would seem that education is not an important factor when considering whether pond water is clean or dirty.

7.2.3
Distance/Time

For bathing and washing in particular, the closest water sources are always considered first because a large volume of water is needed. When washing clothes women like to swirl them in the water and when bathing everyone likes to dive. To save time and avoid a tiresome transport system, field and canal water is preferred during the rainy season, and ponds and *maitals* in the post-monsoon season. As *maitals* dry up in the course of the dry season, ponds are given priority as otherwise the women have to go further to the *dangas*. Certain *maitals*, whose water is perceived as good, are used for cooking purposes because they are located close to the house.

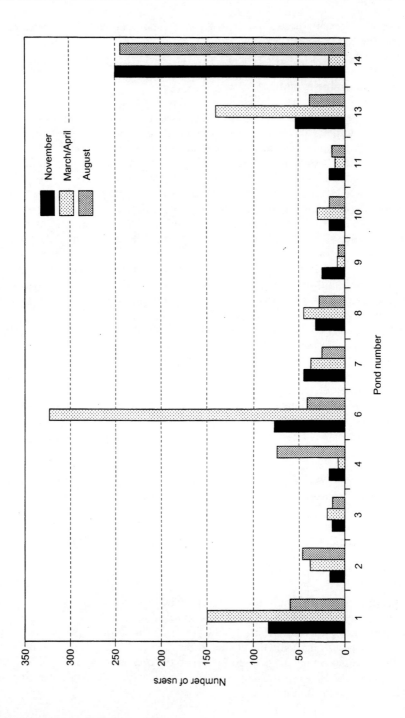

Figure 7.2 Number of Users According to Season
Source: Observations in Dokkhin Garadia (1996/97)

Table 7.3 The Impact of Pond Owners' Education on Perceived Water Quality and Pond Water Use for Cooking

Pond owner	Educational attainment	TW ownership	Use of pond for cooking	Pond water considered clean
1	M.A.	yes	no	no
2	class 10	yes	no	no
3	class 10	yes	no	no
4	class 10	yes	no	yes
6	illiterate	no	yes	yes
7	class 5	yes	yes	yes
8	illiterate	no	yes	yes
9	class 5	no	yes	yes
10	illiterate	yes	no	no
11	class 5	yes	no	yes
13	M.A.	no	no	no
14	class 3	yes	no	no

Source: Pond owner interviews, Dokkhin Garadia

7.2.4
Ownership and accessibility

The household survey revealed that for 13 percent of the respondents (n=248) being driven away from a pond is a recognised problem. Ponds which guarantee an easy and conflict-free access are preferred. The older ponds of the village (see chapter 6.2) are also the most frequented ones. Whether private or public these ponds have always been open to everyone as the provision of drinking water is considered a human right (refer to chapter 4.2.2.3). Although only pond 1, the school pond, is public, ponds 6 and 13 have never been restricted to any villager. However, access to three ponds is prohibited, namely pond 3, 5 and 11, and four ponds have limited access (ponds 2, 7, 8 and 10). These ponds are mainly recent ponds, which were not dug for drinking purposes. The owners are all wealthy villagers and they had a specific purpose in mind when they had the ponds constructed. The extent to which the villagers accept these decisions depends on different factors. Respect or fear attributed to a pond owner is a decisive factor. The owner of pond 3 is not popular in the neighbourhood because he has been refusing people the use of his pond.[147] Other owners are respected, but due to a weak control of the pond and external circumstances such as general scarcity of surface water, villagers are daring enough to use these ponds. During the dry season in particular the pond owners are more sensitive to access issues as pond water becomes scarce and fish production or provision of good cooking water is endangered. The owner of pond 2 is said to become angry because the added

---

[147] One woman said that ten to twelve years ago when the pond owner extended his *maital* to start fish cultivation he told her in a friendly manner not to come to the pond anymore for bathing. She did not protest ("It is their pond not mine") and has been using another pond since then.

pressure on the pond may harm his fish production. Other pond owners encounter less problems defending their ponds because they are situated away from frequented ways. Pond 9 for example is located at the end of the village and pond 11 is behind the house and surrounded by fields. In addition, the owner of pond 11, which is the newest pond in the village, made it very clear from the beginning that only his family members could use the pond because he wanted to produce fish. Nobody has opposed this decision so far. However, there are owners who even promote the use of their ponds. The owner of pond 4, for example, is very generous and allows everyone to bathe in his pond. But this may be because his pond is not useful for any other purposes, such as fish production or for cooking purposes. Pond 14 became the most popular pond of the village for bathing after the owner had given up his intention to produce fish.[148]

Disputes over access to ponds, which lead to *bichar*, were not reported. In the case where a *maital* caused a *bichar* the surrounding land was the reason.[149] One villager had observed that the relatives of Dhonu Mullah take the exclusive right to bathe and wash clothes in pond 1, which is public and used for cooking purposes. Generally, villagers do not care for the owner's order as demonstrated with pond 6 in chapter 6.2. However, if access to a pond is prohibited the villagers generally respect this decision. It seems that the acceptance is higher if a pond is new and dedicated to fish production, as in the case of pond 11, than in the case of a pond that was transformed from a common to a private user purpose (pond 3). However, pond owners who prohibit access to their ponds are unpopular.

7.2.5
Tradition/cultural habit

For generations, ponds 1, 6 and 13 have been used for cooking purposes. Although they are the most contaminated ponds of the village it would be difficult to convince women to stop fetching water from these ponds. The heir to the pond 13, a college teacher, believes that:

> "I can inform the users but they won't understand. They won't believe (me) because they need water, and they think that I lie because I want to start fish production."

---

[148] In the beginning, the situation was different. The pond owner had a big board fixed on the embankment saying: "Do not use soap!" When the villagers saw that the family members didn't respect this stipulation, they also started using soap. The fish production didn't begin well. In addition, as many people frequent the pond and the bottom is very sandy the embankments collapse from time to time and the remaining fish flush out of the pond. Finally, the owner decided to give up but he remained confident. As the villagers praise him for his generosity in giving free access to the pond he believes that Allah will reward him after his death.

[149] During the flood season, and also when the *maital* was frequently used, the adjacent land started to erode. As a result, the affected farmers called a *bichar* accusing the *maital* owners. They in turn requested the farmers to sell them some land in order to construct embankments for protection. The *bichar* did not bring any agreement. The decision was that both parties should take care when using the *maital*. Although the plaintiffs use this *maital* they are still .quarrelling with the owners.

The focus group discussion with five influential villagers at the end of the case-study disclosed that they were not aware of the extent of pond water contamination, particularly regarding of the ponds used for cooking purposes.

7.2.6
Technical impediments

The stability and longevity of a pond depends on the soil condition, the construction of the pond and its maintenance. The main technical problems that can occur are:

- part or an entire embankment collapses and fills up the pond
- drainage opens unintentionally and dirty outflow or predator fish enter the water, or fish are flushed out of the pond

18.5 percent of the respondents (n=248) considered the collapse of an embankment a serious problem. The water becomes muddy and consequently unfit for human use. In addition, repair costs are expensive as the reconstruction of the embankment has to be combined often with the excavation of the pond. Day labourers have to be hired for several weeks. The cost of reconstructing one embankment was reported to be between 1500-7000 Taka (35-160 US$). However, appropriate construction and maintenance are prerequisites for a good pond. But in Dokkhin Garadia pond owners do not seek any professional advice before constructing a pond but rely on friend's advice and their own ideas. This may have contributed to the two most recently built ponds already collapsing during the first monsoon season and then having to be rebuilt.

Normally pond owners do not recommend a drainage system for the ponds for the reasons stated above. But traditionally a drainage system was regarded as a natural sluice that regulated the amount of water between the pond and the open field and that permitted natural fish to flow into the pond during the rainy season. Six out of the twelve ponds had a drainage system in place.

7.2.7
Conclusions

Evaluating the different determinants of pond water use, the following conclusions can be drawn:

- Ponds are very important water sources, especially during the dry season
- Pond water is considered clean and good water for certain domestic purposes
- Perceived water quality is a more important factor than the impact of pond water consumption on health
- The ponds reserved for cooking purposes are the most frequented and therefore the most important ponds in the village
- Cultural habits significantly determine pond water usage. The image of old ponds is difficult to change

144

- Frequency of pond use depends on pond accessibility: the most frequented ponds are open-access ponds, the least frequented ponds have only limited access
- Drainage and collapsing embankments are recognised problems but measures are not taken to prevent these problems

It is obvious that the villagers' attitudes are markedly different from the attitude of a Western observer. Development projects have often disregarded these differences. It is essential to recognise local people's perceptions and needs, and to use local power structures and traditional concepts about purity and cleanliness at the initial phase in any development project. Having identified this knowledge the next step is to identify the problems and formulate activities with the people.

The next chapter turns to determinants of pond maintenance. Pond maintenance is also a consequence of villagers' decision making and is inevitably linked to pond use.

7.3
Present pond maintenance practices and the determinants of maintenance

The villagers[150] have a precise concept of a beautiful pond (*shundor pushkurni*).[151] It is deep, has four high and wide embankments and is planted with coconut trees, date palms and betel palm trees and it has a brick bathing site. A pond should be easily accessible and surrounded by a clean environment. There should not be any water hyacinths. If used for cooking purposes, the use of soap should be prohibited.

Obviously people have knowledge of how ponds should look and be maintained. But there is no pond in Dokkhin Garadia that corresponds to the villagers' ideal image. Only two ponds have a constructed bathing site[152] and no pond has four high embankments. Why do the ponds not correspond to the villagers' ideal concept of a pond? The answer is related to how the villagers consider pond maintenance. 95 percent of the respondents[153] admit that pond maintenance is essential, and 40.5 percent of them consider it important to keep the water clean. The pond owners mentioned the following principal maintenance practices:

- re-excavation of pond: to maintain the depth of a pond it is necessary to re-excavate the pond from time to time to avoid a gradual silting up
- reconstruction of embankment: the collapse of an embankment is a common problem, especially after heavy rains. A collapse may also occur when people walk on the embankment or when an embankment is too steep

---

[150] Data from the focus group discussion in Dokkhin Garadia (May 1997).
[151] This is the image of a *zamindar* pond, which was reserved for drinking purposes.
[152] They are made out of bamboo.
[153] Household survey Dokkhin Garadia (n= 312)

- cultivation of embankment: in the eyes of the people a beautiful pond should be surrounded by coconut, date palm and betel palm trees. Today cash crops of banana, lemon, papaya or mango are preferred and numerous types of leafy trees also grow exuberantly
- weeding the embankment: it is part of the care for a clean environment
- cleaning the pond surface: water hyacinths (*kochuripana*) are fast-growing water plants. If they are not regularly removed they quickly cover the entire surface and cause siltation (see chapter 4.2.4.1). But there is also a commonly held belief that water hyacinths are able to absorb dirty particles in the water.[154]

The maintenance practises of the pond owners differ from the suggested practices by the pond users. The users give priority to:

- removing the water plants and weeding the embankment
- collecting garbage
- informing the users about user rules, for example that bathing and washing with soap is prohibited

Pond owners are more aware of the technical side of pond maintenance than pond users who are more interested in a clean water source. Pond owners perceive a pond more as an investment, for the users it is a preferable water source for domestic purposes. This means that different opinions about maintenance practices reflect a different attitude about how a pond should be used. In general, three main determinants are decisive for owners and users when choosing a maintenance practice: purpose of pond use, capital and ownership. Maximising personal benefit and weighing the advantages and disadvantages, leads to the final decision on how to maintain a pond. Some of the considerations are as follows:

- Purpose of pond use: *Multipurpose function*: 20 percent of the respondents believe that maintenance is important in guaranteeing the multipurpose nature of a pond. Ponds are also often seen as an integrated production unit: the water is used for domestic purposes, natural fish provide a supplement to the diet as do vegetables and fruits grown on the embankment. Added to these, a pond represents a nice and pleasant site to sit and pass the time. *Ponds as an additional income source*: Nowadays fish production is a lucrative business for pond owners as fish supply has greatly decreased.[155] Plantation of profitable trees on the pond embankment is another income generating activity which is highly valued.
- Capital: Maintenance practises like pond re-excavation and reconstruction of embankments can be very expensive. Therefore, these repairs are only performed when ponds silt up or an embankment has collapsed. Ponds are frequently excavated in a step by step way according to money available.

[154] One pond owner was convinced by some villagers to leave the plants in the pond because it would clean the water. Another pond owner thinks that water hyacinths not only clean the water but also keep it cool.

[155] Although in Dokkhin Garadia only two pond owners have started professional fish production at least four pond owners intend to start in the near future.

However, regular re-excavation, over a sequence of three to five years, would be a positive maintenance method.

- Ownership: Shared ownership hampers the decision-making process for investment and maintenance ponds. For example, the two brothers of pond 2 have different opinions about the use of their pond and therefore cannot agree on the maintenance practise[156]

Current maintenance practices are a response to the changed environmental conditions. Today, tubewell water has replaced pond water for drinking purposes. Many villagers admit that ponds are maintained less now than previously. Almost 20 percent (n= 312) of the respondents believe that the main indicator of this is the fact that ponds dried up less in the past. The following reasons were given: 47.5 percent of the respondents made the increase in the number of tubewells responsible. This may be interpreted as that the careful maintenance of ponds became unnecessary because pond water was not used for drinking purposes anymore. 23 percent stated that the ponds were deeper in the past, 11 percent believe that there was more rain and 6.3 percent pointed out that ponds were better maintained and that less people used ponds. The replies show out that the villagers are aware of the poorer pond maintenance over the years. However, this awareness alone is not sufficient to initiate an improvement in the state of the ponds as people have their own reasons to maintain the status quo as described above.

Regarding the maintenance of the ponds the following conclusions can be drawn:

1. The interests of pond owners and users diverge: for pond owners a pond is mainly an additional income source. The younger generation wants to produce fish and cultivate cash crops on the embankment. For the users, ponds are pleasant sites for bathing and for the women to wash clothes.
2. Pond maintenance has adapted to the new water supply situation and corresponds to the new image of a pond. Ponds are not used for drinking anymore but to produce fish,[157] and for bathing and washing. Therefore, a certain level of contamination is acceptable.
3. Pond maintenance has deteriorated. Ponds are not very deep anymore, the embankments are flat, no bathing site is offered and drainage outlets are common. Bushes grows extensively around several ponds and the owners rarely give any instructions to the users on how to keep the water clean.

Figure 7.3 provides an overview of the influencing factors of pond management. Given the fact that ponds are an important water source for domestic purposes and that ponds are insufficiently maintained, the question remains as to whether pond water represents a health risk or not. If pond water is contaminated it will be essential to improve the ponds. The next chapter analyses the actual water quality and the environmental state of twelve ponds in Dokkhin Garadia.

---

[156] Shared ownership was observed to be an even more relevant determinant of pond maintenance in the study village of Sehakati (Patuakhali) (see chapter 8).

[157] Pond maintenance is sometimes even identified with fish production because additional care is needed, such as cleaning the pond with lime, releasing fingerlings, using fertiliser/chemicals and fish food.

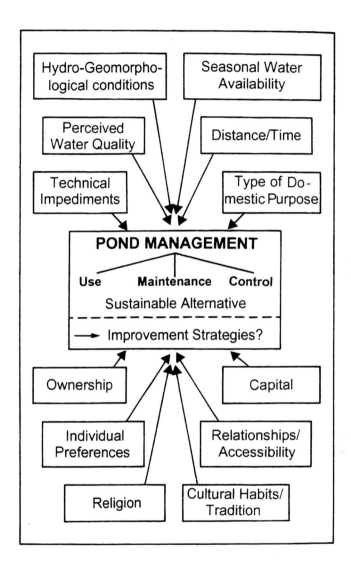

Figure 7.3 Physical and Social Factors Influencing Pond Management

7.4
State of ponds: water quality and environment

It is known that diarrhoeal attacks occur particularly during the post-monsoon season because faeces have been washed into open surface water bodies (HOQUE & HOQUE 1990: 182). As the ponds fill up and as they often lack high embankments they become highly contaminated. Furthermore, hanging latrines are considered another major cause for pond water contamination. Because of the awareness that contaminated pond water is a significant health risk, hand tubewells were introduced and their use was promoted in Bangladesh since the 1950s. One intention of this study was to identify the extent of pond water contamination in the study village and to explore possible causes of this contamination. Consequently, both the water and the pond environment were analysed.

7.4.1
Pond water quality according to seasons

The taking and analysing of water samples was conducted by the Environmental Health Programme (ICDDR,B). The methodology and its related problems were described in chapter 5.3.3. Surface water analysis in general has a limited validity. Since the condition of surface water depends on numerous factors the water quality is highly variable. Therefore, the results should be seen as being arbitrary. Water samples were taken during October (post-monsoon), March (dry season) and July/August (monsoon season). The arithmetic and log mean of faecal coliform counts for each pond and month is listed in table 7.4. The results, represented in figure 7.4, can be summarised as follows:

- The total antilog of all ponds in each month shows that coliform counts increase significantly from October over March to July/August.
- The coliform counts of all ponds, except pond 10, increase over the period of measurement. Pond water quality is best in October (post-monsoon) and worst in July/August (monsoon). This does not coincide with the findings of HOQUE & HOQUE (1990) who expect high contamination ratios for the post-monsoon period.
- A possible explanation would be that the ponds were fully recharged during the post-monsoon season in 1996 which may have diluted the faecal inputs to a certain extent. Moreover, the validity of the October measurements has to be questioned as discussed in chapter 5.3.3. Finally the monsoon season of 1997 provided very little rainfall. Therefore, the ponds were not properly refilled, and as the number of users increased due to the heat this may have caused a concentration of feacal contamination.
- Two ponds (2, 13) had very high coliform counts throughout the measurement period. In comparison to the other ponds, these two are surrounded by bamboo bush and dense vegetation. It might be that these sites are preferred by villagers, especially children, for defecation. The faeces is washed off into the pond during precipitation.

Table 7.4 Pond Water Quality: Counts of Faecal Coliform Units (cfu) of 12 Ponds in Dokkhin Garadia

cfu/100ml mean Pond	October 96		March 97		July/August 97	
	arithmetic	log	arithmetic	log	arithmetic	log
1	1250	3.09	2400	3.38	3425	3.53
2	10.000	4	13.750	4.13	3150	3.49
3	30	1.47	225	2.35	4850	3.68
4	80	1.9	6150	3.78	7400	3.86
6	820	2.9	1600	3.2	5322	3.72
7	140	2.14	700	2.84	2047	3.31
8	1050	3.02	1000	3	2510	3.39
9	120	2.07	7250	3.86	3955	3.59
10	3000	3.47	2250	3.35	285	2.45
11	30	3.47	1110	3.04	2600	3.41
13	10.500	4.02	1900	3.27	10.102	4
14	370	2.56	850	2.92	1000	3
mean	2282.5	**2.67**	3265.4	**3.26**	3887.25	**3.45**
antilog		**467.7**		**1819.7**		**2818.3**

Source: Analysis by the laboratory of the Environmental Health Programme (EHP), ICDDR,B; own calculations.

- All the cooking ponds (1, 6, 13) have a log that is higher than 3, and are therefore highly contaminated. It may be that children defecate on the embankment or in the bush. In the case of pond 6, the family members also bathe in the pond and wash clothes which could be contaminated with faeces. The water in these ponds represent a health risk throughout the year.
- Only one pond (10) saw a reduction in the coliform counts over the measurement period. A reason for this could not be found.
- The colifom counts of the two least frequented ponds (3, 11) amazingly rose in the course of the year. The pond owners were not able to give an explanation. In fact, this data is difficult to interpret as contamination cannot occur from the latrine run-off caused by the lack of embankments. It may be that the plastic pipes leading into the ponds contained dirty run-off and contaminated the ponds.
- Pond 14, which is among the most frequented ponds, had a rather low faecal contamination rate. Therefore, it would seem that the number of users is not a decisive factor for the extent of pond water contamination.

Although it is not possible to draw firm conclusions from the water analysis of the ponds in Dokkhin Garadia, the tests have shown that pond water poses a health

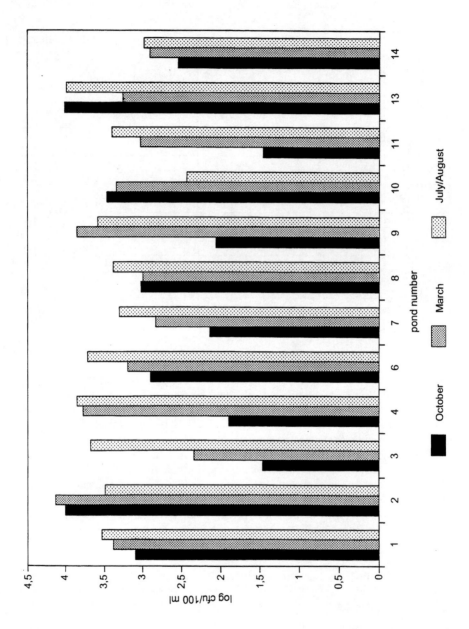

Figure 7.4 Seasonal Variations of Faecal Coliform Counts of 12 Ponds in Dokkhin Garadia
Source: Analysis by the laboratory of the Environmental Health Programme (EHP), ICDDR,B;
own calculations.

risk and that the contamination peaks are in both the dry season and the monsoon season. Pond water consumption during these periods therefore should be reduced or replaced. During the rainy season water is abundantly available, however, it is difficult for the villagers to find other water sources in the dry months for bathing and washing.

It is obvious that all ponds greatly exceed the International Standards for Drinking Water which is 0 faecal coliform units per 100 ml and 2 total coliform units per 100 ml.[158] Five ponds fulfil the standards for recreational water (200 total cfu/100ml) in October but no pond achieved this standard during the other measurement periods. However, all ponds would be suitable for fishing for which the standard total coliform count is 5000 cfu/100ml (JAPANESE ENVIRONMENT CORPORATION 1996).

7.4.2
Pond environment

The pond environment was assumed to have a considerable influence on pond water quality. The main question was how faecal coliform contamination of ponds could occur. In general, there are different possibilities:

- There might be hanging latrines along the embankment
- Women often wash dirty children's clothes in ponds
- Villagers, especially children, often defecate on the embankment, and particularly in the bushes
- The pond consists of a drainage outlet that may cause dirty run-off to enter the pond

Some of these assumptions were tested by observation around the ponds in Dokkhin Garadia. The following parameters were checked:

- latrine proximity
- waste around the pond
- animals in or around the pond
- drainage
- plantation (cultivated and uncultivated)
- water plants

The proximity of open latrines, waste or faeces around the pond, the presence of animals (and therefore faeces) as well as the existence of a drainage outlet would allow conclusions to be drawn on the faecal coliform contamination of pond water. The variety and growth of the plantation around the pond, both on the embankment and behind it, was chosen as an indicator of a preferred defecation site. The variety and growth of water plants is primarily an indicator of pond maintenance but also of the ecological condition of the pond.

Pond environment observation revealed the following:

---

[158] See chapter 4.2.4.3.

- No pond had a hanging latrine adjacent. In close proximity to two ponds (4, 8) home-made latrines were discovered, and behind one embankment of pond 8 an open latrine was detected. During the flood season it is possible that contaminated run-off flows into these ponds. But in normal conditions, contamination does not occur because of the proximity of latrines to the ponds.
- In general, the pond environment looked clean. Waste in the form of paper or plastic was only noticed once during observation of ponds 1, 4, 13 and 14.
- Ducks and chickens are common in and around the ponds. Goats were observed at pond 1. However, no pond was used to wash cattle, for this purpose farmers prefer the canal or *dangas*.
- Six of the twelve ponds observed have a drainage outlet which leads to the open field.
- All the ponds have planted embankments, although the embankments of ponds 7, 9 and 14 are sparsely planted. It is possible to distinguish between cultivated and wild plantations. Ponds 1, 3, 7, 8, 9, 10, 11 and 14 belong to the first category.[159] Ponds 2, 4, 6 and 13 are surrounded by wild vegetation.[160]
- The presence of water plants indicates seasonal variations. Some ponds hardly ever had water plants (1, 6, 9, 11, 14) others had many throughout the year (2, 8, 10, 13). The most frequent and profuse water plant is the water hyacinth (*kochuripana*. Other water plants observed were duckweed *(kutipana)*, water lily (*shapla*), *kolmilota* and *araly*.

The state of the ponds can be summarised as follows:

- All ponds are highly contaminated with faecal coliform bacteria, ponds reserved for cooking purpose are among the most contaminated.
- The source of contamination remains vague. Hanging latrines are placed over *dobas*, never over ponds and the villagers are aware of this. Animal faeces was not directly observed. However, there is a high probability that people, mostly children defecate on embankments especially in the bushes, as this is a preferred defecation site. This could explain the high coliform counts at the ponds 1, 2 and 13. Further drainage may also lead to water contamination, especially during the monsoon season when accumulated sewage flows into the pond. This may explain the high bacteria counts during July and August in the ponds 4, 6, 8, 9 and 13. Finally, the impact of washing children's dirty clothes on the pond water contamination remains unclear.
- Pond environment is generally clean.
- Leafy trees are supposed to harm water quality. An increasing amount of biomass in the pond can affect pond ecology because the amount of oxygen declines and favours eutrophication of the pond. This, however, cannot explain the faecal contamination of pond water. Water hyacinths (*kochuripana*) have

---

[159] The most common cultures are banana- and papaya trees. Date palm and betel palm trees are also very popular. Even lemon trees, jackfruit trees, coconut trees and mahogany trees are sporadically cultivated on embankments. One side of the embankment is sometimes reserved for vegetable cultivation. Eggplants, beans, pulse and pumpkin are the most favoured vegetables grown.

[160] There are some fruit trees and there is a dense vegetation of bamboo and other leafy trees such as *Neemtree, Mandartree, Boroitree, Koroytree, Gabtree, Jiggatree,* and *Shishutree*.

an ambiguous reputation. On the one hand they are considered harmful and on the other hand they are said to clean the water (refer to chapter 4.2.4.1).

Pond environment observation has weakened the general assumption that hanging latrines are a major cause of pond water contamination. The villagers in Dokkhin Garadia even define a pond as a place with a clean environment (see chapter 3.1.2.2). But in other parts of the country, animal faeces and garbage around a pond was often observed, especially in urban sites where many ponds resemble ditches. Some assumptions were reconfirmed, for example the influence of the drainage on pond water contamination. This fact has been neglected so far because drainage is regarded important to regulate the water for irrigation and to allow the flow of natural fish, which again proves that hardly any attention has been given as yet to the use of ponds for domestic purposes. Furthermore, it would appear that an abundant vegetation of leafy trees around the pond does lead to contamination of the water. This has less to do with an increased eutrophication of the pond but with the local concept that the bush offers a protected environment for defecation. Local concepts of cleanliness also determine whether a pond is considered clean or not. Some people do not believe animal or baby's faeces to be harmful and some villagers believe in the purifying effect of water plants, such as the water hyacinths. Therefore, washing children's dirty clothes in pond water and taking water for cooking from underneath the water hyacinths are still common.

The investigation of 12 ponds in Dokkhin Garadia revealed that the concept of the pond, determined by pond water use, pond maintenance practises and pond water quality has changed from the past to the present. Therefore, the older ponds should be compared with the recent and the new ponds in the village to confirm this assumption.

7.5
Processes of change: comparing pond-generations

The ponds studied were grouped according to their age (see table 7.5). Three pond generations resulted. For comparison the following five parameters were chosen: age, size and depth of the pond, reason behind digging, actual pond use and access to the pond, and the extent of faecal contamination (cfu/100ml).

Older ponds
- The oldest ponds are between 45 and 55 years old. These are ponds 1, 6 and 13.
- They have an average size of 996.6 square metres and an average depth of 4.5 metres.
- These ponds were mainly excavated for drinking and cooking purposes by influential villagers for the welfare of the people.
- Today they are still used for cooking purpose and are open to the public.
- The log records of cfu/100 ml for these three ponds in all seasons is on average 3.44, which means that they are highly contaminated.

Recent ponds
- Ponds 2, 3, 7 and 8 belong to this category. They are between 10-18 years old.
- They have an average size of 761. 7 square metres and an average depth of 3.8 metres.
- The were initially excavated to provide mud to construct the homestead mound (*bhithi*). Some have been excavated over many years by their owners, who are wealthy farmers.
- They serve a multipurpose function but access is mostly limited.
- The log record for cfu/100 ml of all ponds on average over all seasons is 3.06, this is slightly lower than in the older ponds.

New ponds
- Ponds 10, 11 and 14 were excavated two to three years ago.
- Their average size is 549.6 square metres and the average depth 4.23 metres.
- They were excavated for fish production and bathing by wealthy villagers.
- Two are principally used for fish cultivation and bathing and one exclusively for bathing. Access to the fish ponds is prohibited.
- The average log record of cfu/100 ml is the lowest with 2.85 for all seasons.

The comparison reconfirms what has been described before: The older ponds were designed as drinking water reservoirs. Therefore, they are the largest on average and still remarkably deep. The new ponds are also deep, but smaller in size because they were constructed to meet the needs of one family. According to the findings of the water tests, the older ponds are more contaminated because they are no longer maintained properly: two of the three ponds are surrounded by wild vegetation and have drainage outlets. The reasons for excavating a pond and the purposes of pond use have changed. While older ponds were sources of drinking water, more recently constructed ponds result from the need to obtain mud to build the homestead mound and are used for various domestic purposes. The new ponds are dug with the intention of fish production. It is no longer a matter of social prestige to own a pond, although a pond has become an economic asset for wealthy villagers. Finally, fish ponds are strictly private and access prohibited while former drinking water ponds are still open to the public.

Before the chapter is concluded, a list of the problems and opportunities of pond management, resulting from the above analysis is presented. This also poses the question as to the limits of this case-study and what the requirements would be to tackle the problems and to promote ponds for domestic purposes.

Pond Variables:	Older Ponds			Recent Ponds					New Ponds	
	1	6	13	2	3	7	8	10	11	14
size (square meter)	1280	811	899	245	1478[d]	600	724	458	483	708
depth (meter)	4.3	5.1	4.1	3.75	2.7[e]	4.75	4.1	5	4.8	2.9
cfu/100ml[a]	2358	2580	7500	8966	1701	962	1520	1845	1246	740
reason behind digging	cooking	drinking, cooking	cooking	*bhiti*	*bhithi* bathing	*bhithi*, cooking bathing clothes/ utensils	*bhithi*, cooking, bathing, washing	*bhithi*, domestic purposes	fish production	fish production
domestic use	cooking	cooking, bathing, washing clothes	cooking	bathing washing clothes	bathing, washing clothes	cooking, bathing washing clothes/ utensils	cooking, bathing washing clothes/ utensils	bathing, washing clothes	bathing	bathing, washing clothes
ownership	public	private	private	shared	private	shared	private	private	private	private
fish production	no	no	no	some	yes	no	no	no	yes	no
user frequency[b]	292	441	235	114	59	100	108	63	46	559
maintenance[c]	little	little	little	little	some	some	some	much	much	some
pond owner status	initiator was famous personality	former *matbor*	father was healer	*matbor*	-	*shomaj* member	-	-	-	-
pond owner education	irrelevant	irrelevant	irrelevant	class 10	class 10	class 5	illiterate	illiterate	class 5	class 3

Source: pond owner interviews, pond observation, water sample analysis and measurements in Dokkhin Garadia
[a] Arithmetic mean over all measurement periods
[b] Total users observed during the days of observation
[c] Regular maintenance tasks: re-excavation, repairing of embankments, cleaning of the environment and of the pond surface); controlling the users.
[d] This corresponds to the demarcation of the future pond. The actual pond is only about one third of the total surface.
[e] Indication of the pond owner, as measurement could not be taken.

Table 7.5 Pond Generations According to Variables
Source: pond owner interviews, pond observation, water sample analysis and measurements in Dokkhin Garadia

7.6
Conclusions

7.6.1
Problems and opportunities of present pond management

Figure 7.5 summarises the chapters 6 and 7 (refer to annex). Several processes have led to a change in pond management. Current pond management represents the reactive response of pond owners and users to the new situation. Facing external problems, such as an increasing demand for water and contaminated or bad quality groundwater, requires alternative water sources. Ponds incorporate a viable alternative but at the same time the current pond management strategies face serious problems. These problems must be addressed in order to guarantee a sustainable water source.

- User conflicts: Fish production in ponds is not really compatible with the multipurpose use of ponds for domestic purposes. When ponds are treated with chemicals or fertilisers the pond owners use tubewell water for bathing during this period.[161]
- Health risk: Despite the fact that ponds are not used for drinking purposes anymore the water analysis revealed that ponds represent a considerable health risk when bathing, during ablution or when pond water is used for cooking.
- Privatisation: Fish production is a lucrative business and, as a result, pond owners guard their ponds. Less ponds will be available to the public as more ponds will be used for fish cultivation.
- Shared ownership: The increasing number of owners of one pond impede an effective and safe maintenance of the pond. The pond becomes useless and a health risk. Table 7.2 indicates that, due to the inheritance law in Bangladesh, the future pond owners will be numerous. Normally the present pond owners do not bother about the future distribution of their pond. How their heirs, whether there will be six or fourteen people, manage the pond will be their decision.
- Knowledge: Although pond owners and users have a certain traditional knowledge about pond construction and maintenance it may no longer be adequate. Individual pond construction techniques and opinions about the effect of water purifying methods are questionable.

On the other hand ponds offer several opportunities. Ponds:

---

[161] For the same reason, the owner of pond 8 plans to buy a tubewell because he does not intend to use pond water for cooking purposes any longer. A shareholder of pond 7 however, does not exclude the use of pond water for cooking despite fish production. He would reserve a place in his pond for cooking purposes where he grow water hyacinth. Another pond owner does not want to start fish production because it would mean that bathing in the pond would no longer be possible.

- are a popular and culturally accepted water source as they are a central part of the culture and the ecology of Bangladesh.
- represent an appropriate technology as local material is used and the costs are relatively low if no labour has to be hired.
- are a profitable income source through fish production and tree plantation.

Pond management has to be seen as a reaction to changes of the system. The factors that determine pond management have shifted because people's *life world* and their concept of the pond has changed. Priorities are set differently. However, it is necessary to improve the ponds in order to provide a sustainable water source for the future. For any project that intends to improve ponds the initiative has to arise from the people. The actors' experiences, needs and knowledge has to be considered first, their strength strengthened, their weaknesses weakened. External assistance could help to facilitate this process and provide outsider's knowledge where necessary.

7.6.2
Requirements for further research and for pond improvement projects

From the findings and conclusions of the case-study in Dokkhin Garadia arose the question whether this situation may be transferable to other regions of Bangladesh. It was assumed that under different hydro-geomorphological conditions management strategies may vary and that a under different economic situation other determinants are more relevant for people making decisions with regard to pond management. In particular, two regions would be interesting to test these assumptions, the coastal area and the High Barind in Northern Bengal. Both areas face problems with groundwater supply and consequently tubewell coverage is lower than on the national average. The following hypothesis arose:

- If tubewell coverage is low do people rely more on ponds, even for drinking water?
- If people rely more on ponds how do their management strategies differ from Dokkhin Garadia? Do they have local knowledge about effective pond management which could be utilised to improve the general situation of ponds in order to obtain a sustainable water source?

The investigation of these questions is subject of chapter 8.

Two requirements emerge to be most relevant for future considerations about pond improvement projects: control over the pond and information about pond water quality. Based on the experience that local people's decision-making patterns are rational and that local resources should be regarded, it will be necessary to explore the possibilities of local institutions for pond control.

In chapter 6.1.3 the institutions of Dokkhin Garadia village were presented. In the context of pond management, two questions are important: firstly, has any institution influenced pond management or contributed to its deterioration?

Secondly, which institution may be appropriate to address for pond improvement in the village?

Before the independence of Bangladesh in 1971 the system of the *matbors* regulated village affairs. In Dokkhin Garadia all the older pond owners were politically active and respected people, either *matbors* or union chairmen. When the government started to distribute and sink hand tubewells village leaders allocated them. They were the mediators between the government, development agencies and the villagers and all development programmes were implemented through them. Therefore, to possess a hand tubewell became an indication of power like pond ownership was before. Of course, the distribution of water sources was unequal. Did these powerful men exercise their influence in a negative way over the common people? It would seem, supported by the findings from Dokkhin Garadia, that access to ponds and hand tubewells has always been open to everyone as long as the water was used for drinking. The provision of drinking water was, and still is, a religious and moral obligation. However, many pond and tubewell owners limit the access to these water sources as soon as an economic benefit is involved or the villagers begin to extract large volumes of water. So far conflicts about access to ponds and hand tubewells have not required any trial (*bichar*). Conflicts may occur, though, in the future as the demand for water increases.

Are the powerful men in the village responsible for the deterioration of the ponds? These people were the first to have safe tubewell water and therefore might have lost interest in maintaining pond water quality for drinking purposes. This may be partly true, but some pond owners continue to use their ponds for drinking purposes because they are used to pond water and dislike the taste of tubewell water. This was observed in Dokkhin Gardadia. In general, the deterioration of the ponds has to be seen as part of a process of change. The continuous acceptance of tubewell water for drinking has changed people's opinion about the function of the pond.

Ponds that have deteriorated should be improved to reduce health risks. In the case of the three ponds used for cooking in Dokkhin Garadia the owners and former *matbors* are no longer able to exercise control over their ponds. Their former prestige is gone. But also part of the problem is that people are not conscious of pond water contamination. Information and education about the risks of water-related diseases is necessary. As these ponds were always open to the public, many people fear that the future owners may transform their ponds into fish ponds which would impede their use for domestic purposes. Therefore, it seems reasonable to transmit the responsibility for a public pond to a public institution, such as the *shomaj* where the final responsibility for the pond is with the villagers. However, in the case of private ponds with open access a solution for the mutual benefit of both parties has to be found. It is obvious from the observations made during the field work that clearly defined allocations of duties were missing. This has contributed to the deterioration of the ponds due to insufficient maintenance. Therefore, ensuring the allocation of responsibilities is one of the most important issues for pond maintenance. This subject will be taken up in the last chapter of this study.

8 Pond management in two additional field areas

Two additional field sites were selected to test and compare the findings of the village case-study in Dokkhin Garadia focusing on the questions:

- Are ponds utilised more for domestic purposes in areas with low tubewell coverage?
- Do local people in those areas also manage their ponds pragmatically according to the given environment? What determinants are decisive for pond management?
- Do they have local knowledge about how to maintain ponds, for example about water treatment methods or about construction?

To attempt to answer these questions this chapter was structured in order to parallel the former chapter. However, due to the specific objective of the study, the different environmental conditions and the time constraint, slight changes to the former case-study had to be taken into account. Five subchapters are distinguished:

1. Presentation of the survey parameters.
2. Introduction to both field areas.[162]
3. Comparison between the two village studies, analysing present pond water use and its determinants, the state of the ponds as well as maintenance practices and their determinants.
4. Description of the past pond management situation in both sites, focusing on endogenous maintenance practices and the processes of change.
5. Conclusions with implications for pond improvement projects.

8.1
Survey parameters

Methodologically the former survey of Dokkhin Garadia was modified, meaning it was compressed and shortened, but the main variables were retained to guarantee the comparability with Dokkhin Garadia. Whereas in Dokkhin Garadia a multiple method approach was undertaken, the additional studies were based on a single method approach, namely a short survey with pond owners. Due to the different regional context some parameters were added, which were not very relevant for Dokkhin Garadia. These parameters were the location of the pond,

---

[162] In both villages the same survey was conducted for reasons of comparability.

the number of ponds privately owned, inheritance patterns and traditional water purification methods. In addition to the survey, pond observation and narrative interviews were also conducted. The survey was based on the following parameters:

- number of ponds owned
- number of shareholders
- size and depth of pond
- age of pond and reason for excavating the pond
- pond ownership and inheritance
- pond use according to the location of the pond
- traditional water purification methods
- individual preferences: pond or surface water, pond or tubewell water
- individual perception of water quality: cleanliness of ponds
- maintenance techniques
- number of embankments
- drainage
- bathing site *(ghat)*
- plantation
- waste
- water plants

In addition, the socio-economic condition of the pond owners was collected by asking their occupation, literacy status and family size. Information about tubewell ownership, use and problems was also collected.

8.2
Introduction to the two field areas

Due to their hydro-geomorphological conditions the coastal area and the High Barind are two areas of Bangladesh with an inadequate groundwater supply. As special wells are required to draw water, hand tubewell coverage is markedly below the national average. Along the coast the water table is very high but it has a high saline content down to 300 metres (WHO, DPHE & UNICEF 1990: 1). As a result, deep tubewells are the only possible way to draw suitable groundwater. The High Barind Tract is a geologically uplifted area, characterised by a low water table. Due to seasonal fluctuations the water table can vary between 11 and 25 metres. As well as deep tubewells, tara pumps are needed. One village in Patuakhali *thana* on the coast and in Nachole *thana* in the High Barind were chosen for comparison (see map 5.1).

A short introduction of the physical and social conditions of the two selected field sites follows. The information ranges from *thana*- to union- to village level.[163]

---

[163] Data was mainly taken from the Bangladesh Population Census 1991 for the correspondent *zillas* (districts). Village specific statistical data was hardly accessible.

8.2.1
Sehakati village (Patuakhali union, Patuakhali *thana*)

Geomorphologically, Pathuakhali *thana* belongs to the Ganges tidal floodplain which consists mostly of non-calcareous clays deposited by various tidal rivers (BRAMMER 1996: 65). Of the 2,543 square kilometres almost 20 percent of the *thana* surface is covered by rivers (RASHID 1990: 164). Although the rivers are freshwater, salt water penetrates in particular into the southern unions of the *thana*. In the dry season, soils become saline which limits agricultural production and hampers water supply. In addition, the heavy clay soils are difficult to cultivate during the wet as well as during the dry season (BRAMMER 1996: 154). The water table fluctuates seasonally between two metres in the rainy season and five metres in the dry season (personal communication BODUR RAHMAN). The *thana* is further characterised by an unstable climate and a proneness to cyclones. The communication system is poor (BRAMMER 1996: 154).

Patuakhali *thana* consists of 17 unions with a total population of about 315,000 people. The average household size is 5.58 persons. Almost 10 percent of the population live in urban areas, mostly in Patuakhali Sadar (town). The main source of income is agriculture. Cereal, *aman* and *aus* rice are the most frequently cultivated crops (BBS 1988b). The sanitary conditions are unsatisfactory. There is a high percentage of unsanitary (87.9 percent) and open latrines (9.5 percent). Drinking water is mainly taken from tubewells (72 percent) and from ponds (17.64 percent) (BBS 1992). To date 150 persons on average share a DTW in Patuakhali *thana*, The target of DPHE for the year 2000 is the provision of one DTW for 75 persons (personal communication BODUR RAHMAN).

The study village Sehakati belongs to Jainkati union, which is situated southeast of Patuakhali town. In 1991 Jainkati union had 14,714 inhabitants living in twelve villages. According to a survey of EHP/ICDDR,B in 1997 DPHE has installed 125 DTWs in Jainkati. This corresponds to about 120 persons per DTW.

Sehakati village is situated along a canal that flows south into the Lohalia River. The village consists of 505 households of which two thirds subsist on agriculture (BBS 1988b). There are two markets, one in the northern and one in the southern end of the village, adjacent to the canal and the river. The settlements are spread out and form clusters. A cluster normally consists of several households (*baris*) inhabited by families of the same lineage. In almost every cluster there is at least one pond or ditch. For the survey, only the southern part of the village (Dokkhin Sehakati) was considered.

8.2.2
Madhabpur village (Nachole union, Nachole *thana*)

Nachole thana is part of the Barind Tract. Geographically the Barind Tract includes Greater Rajshahi, Rangpur and Bogra Districts of Bangladesh and a part of Maldah District of West Bengal (India). Geologically the Barind Tract is an area of uplifted blocks or terraces of Pleistocene age that underlay the Mahadpur clay (RASHID 1991: 13, 14; BMDA 1998:1). The region is characterised by an elevated terrace-like relief, frequently dissected by valleys, heavy red-mottled clay and poor vegetation. The instability of the silty topsoil places constraints on agriculture because the soil not only becomes wet quickly but also dries out quickly and is not very fertile. In the absence of irrigation only transplanted *aman* rice can be cultivated. Otherwise HYV *boro* rice is widely planted (BRAMMER 1996: 25, 166). Large seasonal variations in temperature, from 3°C in winter to 44 °C in summer, and a comparatively low annual rainfall are other limiting factors for agricultural in this region (BMDA 1998: 1). The water table also fluctuates markedly. During the dry season in 1995 the water table was at 25.46 metres and increased in October to a minimum of 11 metres. In 1997, the corresponding values were 22.1 metres and 10.77 metres (BMDA 1997).

Nachole *thana* belongs to Nawabganj district, which once was strategically and commercially important due to its location at the junction of the Ganges and Mahananda Rivers. In 1991, there were 16,880 households in Nachole *thana* with an average of 5.75 persons per household. The main source of income is agriculture. The sanitary conditions are comparable to Patuakhali, although the number of open latrines is much higher: over 71 percent of the households use open spaces for defecation. In comparison to Patuakhali, drinking water is predominantly taken from tubewells (75 percent) and wells (18 percent) (BBS 1996b). As the water table tends to decline and fluctuates greatly, shallow tubewells (STWs) with an extraction capacity of 6 metres become inoperable. As a result, STWs have to be replaced by other pumps, such as deepset tubewells or tara pumps whose sucking capacity is between 18.2 metres and 30 metres. At the present time approximately 150 people share a tubewell in the *thana* (personal communication MD. SOMSER ALI, DPHE).

Madhabpur village is located north-east of Nachole Town. Madhabpur is also the name of the *mauza* that consists of seven villages. The total population of the *mauza* is about 2,500 people, the population of Madhabpur village however is only about 800 people. In the *mauza* there are 360 ponds, in the village between 25 and 30 ponds and about 25 hand tubewells (personal communication MOGIDUL HAQUE, ex-union chairman).

When comparing both areas the following picture becomes apparent:

- In both areas groundwater supply is insufficient, in Sehakati due to the high saline content and in Madhabpur because the water table significantly fluctuates seasonally.
- Expensive hand tubewells are required to draw water from underground sources. In Sehakati deep tubewells are adequate, in Madhabpur deepset tubewells and tara pumps are required.
- The hand tubewell coverage is similar in both areas and below the national average. About 150 people share a hand tubewell in both areas.
- Drinking water is taken principally from hand tubewells, but in Patuakhali *thana* ponds also play an important role in drinking water supply, and in Nachole *thana* ring wells are used.
- Sanitary conditions are poor in both areas. In Nachole, the majority of people still use the open space for defecation. In Patuakhali, non-sanitary latrines are predominantly used.

8.3
Comparison of pond management in the two field areas

8.3.1
Socio-economic conditions

In Sehakati, 28 pond owners were visited and in Madhabpur 20 owners.[164] More farmers were among the respondents in Madhabpur than in Sehakati and more pond owners are involved in business in Sehakati than in Madhabpur. The average size of the respondents' households was similar in both villages: 7.3 members in Sehakati, 7.9 members in Madhabpur. Pond owners in Madhabpur are better educated than in Sehakati. 40 percent have a higher education in Madhabpur, 10.6 percent in Sehakati. But the percentage of illiterate pond owners was almost identical in the two villages.

The pond sample size in Sehakati was 29. One pond was public, the others private. In Madhabpur 21 ponds were surveyed, 1 public and 20 private. The 28 private pond owners of Sehakati village reported having a total of 55 ponds. This corresponds to 1.89 ponds per owner on average. In Madhabpur, the 20 pond owners possess 75 ponds in total, which corresponds to a mean of 3.75 ponds per owner. Comparing the average size and depth of the ponds in Sehakati and Madhabpur, the results were as follows: On average, the ponds in Madhabpur are larger and deeper than the ponds in Sehakati. The average size of a pond in Madhabpur was 111.5 *decimel* (1.1 acre), in Sehakati 68.5 *decimel* (0.68 acre). The average depth of a pond in Madhabpur came to 98.9 inch (2.5 m) and in Sehakati to 78.2 inch (1.98 m). It must be noted that all the indications are estimates of the pond owners and are not based on the researcher's own measurements. In general, all ponds are of a relatively large size but not very deep in comparison to the Pond Survey stratification criteria.[165]

The ponds in Madhabpur are on average older. Although in Madhabpur only 42 percent of the ponds are older than 50 years (in Sehakati 43 percent) 85.5 percent are older than 31 years, in Sehakati only 63 percent are this old. This corresponds with the inheritance pattern in both villages. In Sehakati, 62 percent of all ponds are inherited and in Madhabpur 50 percent are inherited. As the inhabitants of Madhabpur came from West Bengal after the partition of India they either bought ponds from the former *zamindar* or leased them from the government (see chapter 8.4.1). In both villages, the pond owners who had their ponds excavated themselves, stated that they dug a pond mainly for domestic purposes but also for fish cultivation.

After the introductory comparison of the two villages, the following three major themes will be described and discussed:

---

[164] In Sehakati three times the wives of the pond owners were interviewed because their husbands were not available.

[165] Size and depth of the ponds were stratified according to the suggestions of the Pond Survey (BBS 1994: 2, 13). There, three categories of pond size are distinguished: 1. 0.01-0.1 acre; 2. 0.11-0.3 acre; 3. > 0.31 acre. For pond depth five categories are set up: 1. < 5 ft; 2. 5-9 ft; 3. 10-14 ft; 4. 15-19 ft; 5. > 20 ft.

1. Pond water use and determinants of pond water use
2. Observed pond environment and determinants of maintenance and control
3. Changes from the past to the present pond management

8.3.2
Pond water use and determinants of pond water use

Figure 8.1 shows pond water use for Sehakati and Madhabpur compared with Dokkhin Garadia. In both villages ponds are never used for drinking purposes and rarely used to clean cattle. Some differences become apparent though: in Sehakati, pond water is generally used more for domestic purposes such as cooking, bathing, washing and ablution than is the case in Madhabpur where tubewell water is preferred for many purposes, for example ablution and cooking. Furthermore, in Sehakati pond water is not used for irrigation but in the high Barind village of Madhabpur pond irrigation is vital. Combined with irrigation fish production is more popular in Madhabpur, and it is also undertaken more professionally in this northern region than on the coast.[166] Hence, the attitude about ponds varies between the two villages: in Sehakati, a pond is considered a source of subsistence whereas in Madhabpur it is a commercial investment. The relevant factors that determine pond water use are: location of pond, ownership of tubewell, seasonal availability of water and perceived water quality. The importance of each factor for the pond management in both villages is explained as follows.

8.3.2.1
Location of the pond

Table 8.1 points out a remarkable difference regarding the location of the ponds between the villages. The separation of ponds in "behind the house" and "in front of the house" is clearer and stricter on the coast than in the Barind. In Sehakati, ponds are more an object of prestige and evidence when situated in front of the house. They are used by the men for bathing, but they also serve to produce fish and to embellish the site. When located behind the house, ponds are dedicated to women for their exclusive use in order to maintain seclusion *(purdah)*, as the coastal area is more conservative. Women in Sehakati do not like to draw water from tubewells that are located in public places, like the market. They either send a male member of the family to fetch water or they use the pond behind the house. Although these ponds are mostly smaller and in a worse condition than the ponds in front of the house, women use them for bathing and ablution. The high number of ponds in the fields in Madhabpur refers to the importance of ponds for irrigation in this area. But generally they are used for all kinds of purposes

---

[166] The Pond Survey (BBS 1994: 50, 146) compared the frequency of fish release in different regions of Bangladesh. In Patuakhali District yearly fish release is 13.9 percent whereas it is 67.5 percent in Rajshahi District.

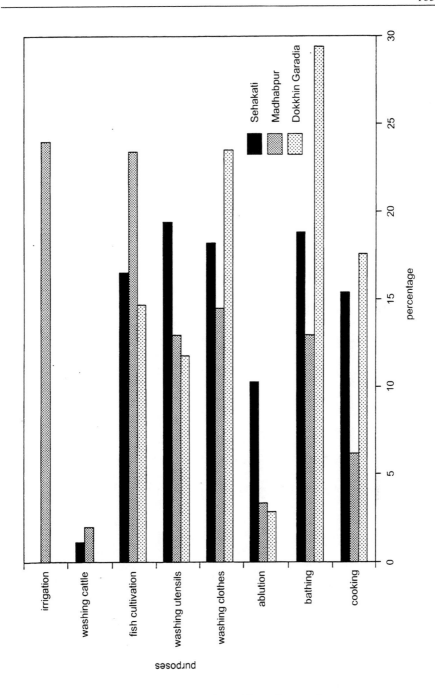

Figure 8.1 Pond Use According to Purposes: Three Villages Compared
Source: Pond owner interviews in Sehakati, Madhabpur and Dokkhin Garadia (1996/97)

including bathing and fish production. However, for cooking purposes water from ponds in the front of the house is collected.

Table 8.1 Location of Ponds in Sehakati and Madhabpur (in Percentage):

Location Village	in front of house	behind the house	in the field
Sehakati (n= 49)[a]	53	37	10
Madhabpur (n=61)	20	20	60

Source: Village surveys in Sehakati and Madhabpur, October/November 1997: [a] total number of ponds owned by the respondents.

8.3.2.2 Ownership of a tubewell

Slightly more than half of the pond owners in both villages own a tubewell. In Madhabpur 70 percent of the pond owners take tubewell water for both drinking and cooking purposes, and 10 percent use it for all domestic purposes. In Sehakati however, 96 percent of the respondents only use tubewell water for drinking. Neither in Madhabpur nor in Sehakati is tubewell water use significantly related to socio-economic status or the level of education of the pond owner. But it can be said that pond water is still used more in Sehakati than in Madhabpur. A cross-check confirmed this. Ten out of twelve tubewell owners of Sehakati use pond water for cooking, six consume the water from the pond behind the house. In Madhabpur however, only two of the nine respondents, who own a tubewell, use pond water for cooking.

8.3.2.3 The seasonal availability of water

In Sehakati, fewer ponds dry up than in Madhabpur. In Madhabpur, ponds are important for irrigation as groundwater irrigation by DTWs is not possible for geological reasons. Irrigation coincides with the dry season when evaporation is high and an increasing amount of water is also needed for domestic purposes. Although the ponds are bigger and deeper than in Sehakati, they dry up before they can be replenished by the monsoon rains. In addition, Madhabpur doesn't have alternative water sources in the surrounding area. Sehakati on the other hand, is intersected by canals some of which are perennial. But during the monsoon season when the coastal area is flooded for several weeks, ponds are regularly exposed to damage such as the collapse of embankments.

8.3.2.4 Perceived water quality[167]

60 percent of the respondents in Madhabpur and 71.4 percent of the respondents in Sehakati believe that pond water is clean, particularly when the pond contains a

---

[167] For technical reasons it was not possible to take pond water samples for analysis of coliform .bacteria counts in the additional study villages.

great deal of water. But in Madhabpur, good water in general is associated with the flowing water of the Padma, which is not in the vicinity of the village. The villagers of Sehakati prefer pond water because of the pond's proximity to the house and because the water is considered clean and good/sweet. Nevertheless, the majority of all respondents prefer tubewell water for drinking to pond water because it is considered sterile, safe and clean as it is covered and originates from underground. In both villages, the perceived water quality is related to pond maintenance. Clean ponds in Sehakati are identified as having good embankments, no drainage and no leaves on the surface. The same applied to Madhabpur. The question arises: Are the ponds maintained according to these criteria?

8.3.3
Conditions of the ponds[168]

After the interviews with the pond owners, observation of the pond environment was undertaken to verify the respondents' ideas about the condition of the ponds. The observation revealed that 27 of 29 ponds in Sehakati had some kind of embankment but only four ponds had the necessary four embankments. In Madhabpur, no pond was found with four embankments, and twelve did not have any embankment. 60 percent of the ponds in Madhabpur have a drainage outlet but in Sehakati less than 30 percent had one. A nice bathing site (*ghat*) with steps or a bamboo construction was rarely observed. Basic *ghats* however, which are made out of a tree trunk or a stone, are common. In Sehakati, 22 ponds are equipped with a basic *ghat*, one pond had a constructed *ghat*. There were more ponds without any type of *ghat* in Madhabpur (eight out of 20) but also more ponds with a constructed *ghat* (four out of 20).

Pond environments were rarely clean. Only five ponds in Sehakati (n= 29) and 1 in Madhabpur (n =21) were free of waste. There was animal faeces everywhere. In Madhabpur there were two latrines close to the pond and human faeces was observed around a pond in Sehakati. Water plants were scarce in both villages. One pond in particular stood out from the others in Sehakati. The surface of the water was covered with green algae and the water is used for cooking purposes. In both villages most of the trees on the pond embankments were palm trees (date, betel and coconut palm trees) followed by fruit-trees and leafy trees. Vegetables were rarely cultivated.

Pond environment observations revealed that:

- Pond owners of Sehakati and Madhabpur villages do not maintain their ponds as they should in order to obtain an ideal pond.
- Although the ponds in Sehakati generally have embankments, a *ghat,* but no drainage, the embankments are insufficient to protect pond water. Furthermore, they are quite shallow which indicates a tendency to silt up.

---

[168] For observation and check list of the pond condition and environment only one pond per owner was visited.

- In Madhabpur, most ponds have an inlet or outlet which leads into an adjacent field for irrigation purposes. The protection of the pond from in-flowing water is not guaranteed as there are no good embankments.

How can this disparity between the ideal image that pond owners have of clean ponds and the existing conditions be explained? Pond owners in both villages agreed that pond maintenance is essential and it is assumed that pond owners measure maintenance from their own perspective. Therefore, the present maintenance practices and the determinants of maintenance have to be examined.

8.3.4
Maintenance practices and determinants

Figure 8.2 shows the various types of pond maintenance practices as stated by the pond owners in both villages. The most important maintenance activities in Madhabpur are:

- re-excavation of ponds
- weeding
- different cautions or warnings[169]
- repairing embankments
- adding fertiliser

It seems that the pond owners in Madhabpur consider it important to uphold the storage capacity of a pond because they give priority to re-excavation. Furthermore, they are interested in fish production as adding fertiliser is considered a maintenance task.

In Sehakati, the main maintenance practices were:

- weeding
- removing dirty things
- re-excavation
- adding lime to the water
- caution or warnings for pond users

Pond owners in Sehakati care more for a clean water surface and for water quality. Control of the ponds is considered less important than in Madhabpur because a pond is not valued as a profitable asset but serves the domestic needs of the family. If a pond project intends to change the condition of a pond it is important to first clarify with the owner the purpose of the pond and whether he is interested in any measures that would change the function of the pond.

For pond owners in Madhabpur, ponds have priority:

1. for fish production
2. for domestic purposes
3. for irrigation

The pond owners in Sehakati set other priorities. The purpose of a pond is:

---

[169] Washing cattle and children's dirty clothes and also defecation at the pond and throwing dirty things into the water are all prohibited.

1. to meet the demand of water for domestic purposes
2. to save a supply of clean water
3. to produce fish
4. for recreation
5. to maintain *purdah*

Comparing this list of priorities with the maintenance practises indicated above, it is obvious that the purposes for which a pond is used determine the maintenance practices. In Madhabpur, ponds are important for fish production and irrigation, and therefore re-excavation is the most essential practice in order to retain water in the pond as long as possible. In Sehakati, ponds are used more for domestic purposes. Therefore, clean ponds are considered important and weeding, removing dirt and adding lime are regarded appropriate maintenance practices. But ponds also have a considerable recreational value and are preferred by women to maintain *purdah*.

Nevertheless, the ponds are in a poor condition as they are not properly maintained. One pond owner in Madhabpur and four in Sehakati do not maintain their ponds. Financial considerations are a main reason as pond re-excavation and repairing embankments is expensive, but generally improperly maintained ponds can be attributed to the number of shareholders in a particular pond. In Madhabpur, the average number of shareholders for one pond is 3.75, but in Sehakati it is 10.48 persons. This is the result of the hereditary laws in Bangladesh according to which the entire possessions of the head of a household are divided amongst his offspring after his death. The large segmentation of land in Bangladesh is a well-known and often described phenomena[170]. Ponds, like land, are also divided according to the number of offspring. A plot of land can be allocated individually but it is not possible to divide a pond. The profit from a pond, either as source of fish supply or as a common water source for domestic purposes, is easily divided amongst the shareholders. However, obligations with regard to investment and pond maintenance are not likely to be proportionally shared amongst the shareholders and this becomes more difficult when there is a large number of shareholders. In situations where there are many shareholders, a pond becomes a common commodity for which no one wants to take responsibility. Additionally, the older the pond is there is less interest and effort on the part of the shareholders to improve the pond. Finally, the more dilapidated a pond becomes the more expensive the maintenance costs will be.

Furthermore, the decision to do important maintenance work, such as re-excavation or repairing of embankments, is often less a financial problem as some shareholders are always willing to contribute more than others for the benefit of all. The main problems are conflict of interest and absenteeism. Some shareholders do not want to invest their money to start fish production because they fear they will be cheated. In other cases, some shareholders agree to produce fish but then they are mostly absent from the village and therefore do not take any

---

[170] JANSEN (1990) discusses this issue in the context of scarcity of land in rural Bangladesh.

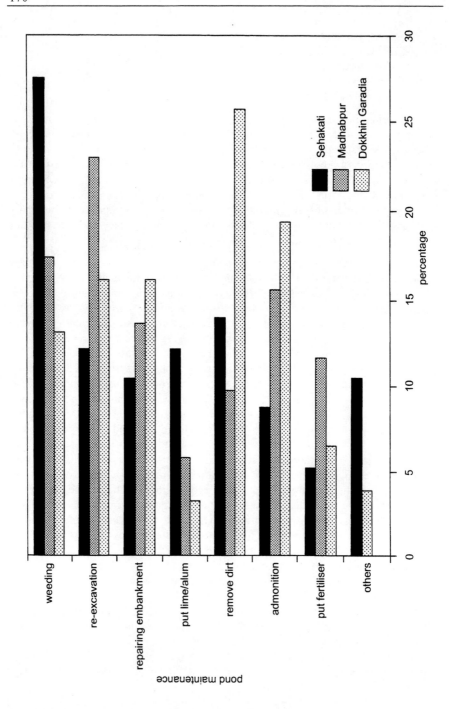

Figure 8.2 Pond Maintenance Activities Compared in Three Villages
Source: Pond owner interviews in Sehakati, Madhabpur and Dokkhin Garadia (1996/97)

responsibility for pond maintenance. But at the time of harvest, they demand their equal share. This often leads to disputes among the shareholders.

Hazards due to local climatic conditions also influence pond maintenance to a certain extent. On the coast, the land is largely flooded during the monsoon season and the pressure of the flood waters affects the ponds as drainage outlets become broken and embankments collapse. As these are regular occurrences, pond owners often do not have the money for the necessary repairs.

8.3.5
Conclusions

In summarising the results of present pond use and maintenance practices in the two additional village studies there are some conclusions to be made:

- In Sehakati and Madhabpur it was found that additional determinants can influence pond use, such as hydro-geomorphology, location of the pond and religion (*purdah*).
- However, some determinants are as important in selecting a particular pond for a certain purpose as they were in Dokkhin Garadia. These determinants are: perceived water quality and seasonal availability of water.
- Villagers have a precise picture of an ideal pond, but this type of pond could not be found. The reason is that an ideal pond corresponds to a drinking water pond, but these ponds are no longer required due to the availability of water from hand tubewells.
- Today, villagers consider other purposes important, especially fish production, and therefore other maintenance practises are given priority.

Nevertheless, observations confirmed that present maintenance practices are not adequate to uphold the determined purpose of a pond. Due to poor water quality, which was clearly visible, ponds represent a health risk. Eroding embankments, drainage and silty water affect fish production and irrigation. Therefore, ponds should be improved to guarantee people a sustainable source of water and a possible income. In the past, pond water was a source for drinking water. Older villagers who were interviewed praised the earlier quality of the water. It can be assumed that pond maintenance was better during earlier times. The older women in Sehakati used to treat water with *fitkiri* in the past. The question can be asked as whether there were other water treatment methods known then. Maybe endogenous knowledge can contribute to measures for future pond improvement. With the help of narrative interviews the past pond management in Sehakati and Madhabpur will be described in order to investigate the given assumptions.

8.4
Previous pond management in the two field areas

A brief historical description of pond use in former Bengal was given in chapter 4.2.1. To understand the following narratives of villagers from the coastal belt and the Barind Tract, some central historical facts are repeated. Under the British Rule, land cultivation and taxation were delegated to the *zamindars* - landlords of mostly Hindu origin. The *zamindars* land cultivation management procedures were based on an extensive hierarchical system throughout Bengal. The right to excavate ponds and the property derived from ponds always remained a privilege of the *zamindars* who often offered ponds to their tenants for domestic purposes, including for drinking purposes. Due to the emigration of Hindus to West Bengal after the partition of India in 1947, many ponds became derelict. The ponds, which the former landlords had not sold, became government property and were called *khas* ponds. Before the statistical inventory of ponds in 1961, many ponds were taken over by Muslim farmers to extend their cultivable land. Other farmers bought land adjacent to ponds and then leased the ponds. However, many *khas* ponds became silted and were useless for the villagers.

In East Bengal, public health efforts only started to gain ground in the late 1920s. *Kacha* and *paka* wells (*kua*) were sporadically sunk for common people and some hospitals were built. In the houses of the *zamindars* wells were already common, and the first tubewells were introduced in the early 1930s (see chapter 3.3.2).

Recalling the past water supply situation and pond management this chapter intends to discover changes in pond management and endogenous techniques of pond maintenance. In addition to the two study villages, one village in each Patuakhali *thana* (Taktakhali) and Nachole *thana* (Ghion) were also visited. The villagers of Taktakhali were using surface water exclusively until two years ago. It was assumed that they may have a greater knowledge about pond management strategies. Ghion was chosen because it is one of the few villages in this area where eye-witnesses from the British period could be found.[171]

8.4.1
Past pond management in Patuakhali

According to the reports from Patuakhali, every household used to have a pond, or at least a ditch. Although they were mostly used for all domestic purposes a certain distinction was made. Good ponds, characterised by clear (*forsha*) water and no insects, were only used for drinking and cooking. During the rainy season flood water was preferred and during the dry season river water if it was available. Except for the good ponds, which didn't need any treatment, women used to put *fitkiri*[172] in the water which was then stored for a while before consumption. As *purdah* had to be maintained, women could not bathe in the river but had to use the ponds behind the house, which were mainly ditches where dirty clothes and kitchen utensils were washed. The ponds with the best water quality were always controlled by an authority. In Taktakhali village, the owner of the mosque pond would not allow anybody to bathe in the pond, especially women during menstruation and animals were driven away. The owner also had

---

[171] These are mainly people from tribal minorities, such as the Saotal. Some of them remained in the country after the Independence of India.

[172] Potash alum (see chapter 4.1.1).

the pond re-excavated several times and removed leaves from the surface. The pond had high embankments and a *ghat* made out of a date palm trunk.

In Sehakati, the *zamindar* of the area provided two ponds for the villagers. The *zamindar* commissioned his manager, the *nayeb*, for the excavation of one of these ponds and some land was bought from farmers to construct the embankments. These farmers in turn were allowed to lease the embankments for their own purposes, for example for grazing their cows. After the completion of the pond, the responsibility for the pond was transferred to the villagers. Nothing changed in the use and maintenance of this pond over all these years until it became derelict. Intervention over a short time by the chairman, who constituted a *shomiti* to cultivate fish, failed twelve years ago. Today, the pond is totally covered with water hyacinths. Recently the chairman leased the pond to a man who lives in Dhaka.

At the southern end of Sehakati, there was a second *zamindar* pond, the Kacharibari pond. This pond was only used for drinking purpose, and it was strictly controlled by the *zamindar's* employees. Abdul Mojid, who had the title *Mirda* at that time because he was a tax collector, remembers:

> "In Kacharibari there were many big rooms. They [the *zamindar's* employees, IK] were living there for two to three months to collect taxes, afterwards they left.[...]. I stayed during the day, at night only the guards stayed. [...]. There were some guards, two, three guards for the office. There was another man, especially for the pond. He was called 'Haldar'. He was responsible for keeping the pond and the embankments clean, and he kept cattle away from the pond. The *zamindars* kept the water very clean, they didn't allow anybody to misuse this pond [...]. They didn't even allow people to take water out of the pond to bathe on the embankment. But the employees did bathe in the pond. [...]. This water was very good, we didn't get any disease."

The villagers could fetch water only for drinking and cooking purposes. They respected the rules ("*manush pani opobitro kore na*")[173]. However, another villager recalls the following incident:

> "Once a man came to this village and went to the *zamindar* pond for bathing. He was an educated person. Then the guard caught him and brought him to the Kacharibari. There they asked him: "You look like an educated person. Don't you know, that people here take this water for drinking? So why do you bathe in this pond?" The man replied that he didn't know that people would care that much for this pond."

After the departure of the *zamindars* the Land Revenue Department sent employees who were living there to supervise the ponds. These employees had helpers who took care of the pond but the rules were no longer as strict. The villagers still used the pond in the same way although some took their bath secretly in the pond. When the tubewells were introduced people started to use the pond for everything. During the liberation war, the office buildings were destroyed. Bushes started to grow and animals grazed in the woods near the pond. Nobody dared to approach the pond anymore. In 1986, a teacher convinced the villagers to clear the bush, to construct a school and to repair the pond.

The older villagers agree that the quality of pond water has deteriorated.

---

[173] People did not pollute the water.

"This kind of water, where do we get it? We always misuse our own pond water. We take our bath, we do this and that, we cultivate many trees on the embankments, throw dirty things in the pond [...]. So, it is not suitable for drinking anymore",

declared one respondent. An old woman of Taktakhali village affirmed:

"[..] Before they forbade the misuse of the pond because we had to drink this water. At that time people respected their word but now nobody respects anybody anymore."

Another woman in Taktakhali stated that no one cares for the mosque pond anymore because now there are too many owners (*"amra ekhon bhag bhag hoyeche"*)[174].

Comparing the past water supply situation with that of today, the older villagers confirm that they do not care sufficiently for their ponds anymore. One reason is that natural resources are split amongst the heirs of an owner, which impedes a clear allocation of responsibilities. Since people today only use pond water for cooking, the deterioration of the water is considered harmless. The historical accounts also show that the drinking water ponds were never the property of the farmers. Either these ponds belonged to a local landlord or to the community. The communal ponds were not controlled because they were common property for which no one took responsibility. Therefore, they deteriorated quicker than the controlled ponds of the ruling authority.

8.4.2
Past pond management in Nachole

The demographic shift, induced by the partition of India, is far more obvious in the north of Bangladesh. The inhabitants of Madhabpur village are exclusively Muslim immigrants from West Bengal. The Hindus all moved to India as did the tribal minorities with few exceptions. Some Saotal still live in Ghion, about 15 km from Nachol town. They remain the only people who remember the situation before 1947. An 80 year old Saotal person recalled that during the time of the *zamindars* ponds were used for all domestic purposes. But one pond, with a constructed *ghat*, was reserved for drinking purpose:

"We used this water only for drinking. We didn't allow anybody to go into this pond and prohibited the washing of cattle."

The villagers received the right to use this pond for drinking purposes from the *zamindar* because he was not living in the village and the pond therefore became a common pond. The village superior, the *Morol*, assumed the control over the pond. The school master remembers:

"[...] the *Morol* told that we should not bathe and wash cattle there, that we should only use it for drinking and cooking."

As everyone was afraid of the *Morol* everybody acceded to the verbal rules. This pond was deep and had high embankments and maintenance was not necessary. But when the Hindus left and the Muslims immigrated from neighbouring West Bengal things started to change. The old Saotal explains:

---

[174] Now the families have split.

" The immigrants from India cut the trees, they sold them and also used them for fuel and to construct houses [...]. When people took land from the *zamindar* they used all of it for cultivation. They also destroyed the embankments to get soil and started to cultivate them. When the old residents told them not to use the ponds they answered: 'These are our ponds, don't tell us what to do!'"

Consequently, deforestation began to devastate the landscape and the ponds silted up. The former drinking water pond had lost its brick *ghat* in the early 1960s. It was sold to another village and the owner leased out the land surrounding it. Although cattle were still prohibited in the pond, bathing became common. But as there was no other water supply in Ghion, people still had to use this water for drinking and water was taken from the opposite side of the *ghat*. The pond slowly transformed from a single purpose to a multipurpose resource because the controlling authority left and a general scarcity of water in the area forced the people to use pond water.

The Muslim immigrants stated that they already knew wells and tubewells from India but they did not find any in Madhabpur. Ponds were the only source of water supply and they were in a bad condition. An old Muslim who immigrated from West Bengal to Madhabpur in the 1950s remembers the water situation in his new homeland:

"There was no water. We had to use pond water because there were no tubewells, no wells [...]. Some ponds we kept clean, only for drinking purposes. We didn't allow anybody to go there and wash cattle [...]. When someone saw cows at the pond he drove them away. Sometimes we had meetings when we felt that we should clean the pond."

In Madhabpur, two ponds were reserved for drinking purposes but probably they were also used for other purposes. Disease was a problem: "When we drank this water [pond water, IK] our belly grew, and we got fever."

Until the first wells and tubewells were installed by the government in the 1960s, the new settlers also sporadically collected rainwater. With the introduction of HYV crops irrigation with pond water began. Ponds were not vital anymore for drinking water purposes. At that time farmers started to lease *khas* ponds and re-excavated them. Ponds became private and could not be commonly used anymore. Due to irrigation, ponds began to dry up in the course of the dry season. Disputes over pond water often resulted in fatalities: "They cut heads, killed people", said one villager. Nobody wanted to share water anymore. The increasing demand for land for cultivation made the farmers fill up derelict ponds. One woman complained that in the past they were living peacefully but now there were too many people (*"ekhon manushta beshi"*). The tendency towards a profit-oriented agriculture and demographic pressure contributed to a deterioration of many ponds. The Barind area slowly became an exploited area for natural resources.

8.4.3
Conclusions

The narrative interviews from both field sites can be summarised as follows:

- On the coast, ponds have always been important for women to keep *purdah* but in general other surface water, such as flood and river water, was preferred.
- In the High Barind ponds were always the most important water source.
- In the past, ponds were used for all domestic purposes but only the good ponds, characterised by deep and clear water, high embankments and a brick *ghat,* were used for drinking and cooking purposes.
- Drinking water ponds always belonged to an authority, mainly to a *zamindar.*
- Ponds handed over to the community were not maintained as no tasks were assigned. In the case of Sehakati, each farmer cared for his plot on the embankment but the farmers did not maintain their common pond together.
- The most effective maintenance practice was control. The authority, but not necessarily the owner, made sure that no villager entered the pond or cattle were washed in the pond.
- Ponds for drinking water became derelict in both areas because the former authority had left and because of unclear property rights.
- Water purification methods were known in Patuakhali. Women used to put *fitkiri* in the water container before consumption. In Nachole, this method was not common.[175] This has probably to do with the fact that the majority of the people interviewed there were descendants of immigrant Muslims from India whose fathers were already familiar with tubewells when they settled in the former East Pakistan. But it cannot be completely supported that water purification methods were really unknown in North Bengal.

The conclusions reveal a gap between the two kinds of ponds that existed: the good, large ponds of the *zamindars* used for drinking water and the inferior, smaller ponds of the local farmers. The previous chapters indicated that villagers still refer to the *zamindar* ponds when they are asked to define a pond. An assumption is made that this may be the reason why communal ponds were not managed and why *zamindar* ponds have upheld the image of good ponds. The assumption is that there are two concepts of ponds, one is situated on a spiritual level and one on a pragmatic level. On the spiritual level, there is the concept of the *zamidar* pond. As most *zamindars* were Hindus the pond was Hindu property. Chapter 4.2.2 described ponds as having a remarkable importance in Hindu mythology. Stories about ponds that are still known in Bangladesh today often go back to these roots. Though it may be that a *zamindar* pond was a symbol for the spiritual collective orientation of a community. Every one was attached spiritually to a pond and through it to the entire community. Although in the present Muslim society of Bangladesh, the spiritual relationship to a pond is being lost, some remnants have survived. On the pragmatic level, there is the pond of the common

---

[175] The survey in the two villages confirmed this: 62 percent of the respondents in Sehakati remembered their wife or mother having used *fitkiri* or sporadically *korpur* to clean water for drinking and cooking purposes. In Madhabpur this practise was not applied at all.

farmer which represents a physical asset of a family that contributes to its livelihood.

This assumption could explain why villagers, exemplified in Shehakati, did not maintain the common pond that was transferred to them. That pond was the entire responsibility of the *zamindar* because the pond was excavated on his land, he was the constructor and the owner. The transfer to the villagers was neither physically nor spiritually legitimised, and therefore involved no effort on the part of the community. *Zamindars* were feared but also respected by the common people. Their status may be compared with the status of a *raj* (king) who were often conferred with supernatural powers. The power of the *zamindars* has remained uppermost in people's mind up to today. These considerations are decisive when a concept of pond improvement should be established, as will be the intention of chapter 9.

8.4.4
Processes of change from past to present pond management

64.3 percent of the pond owners in Sehakati and 71.4 percent of the owners in Madhabpur recognised a change in pond use over the years. In Sehakati, the major change is evident: 77 percent do not use pond water anymore for drinking. In Madhabpur, the answers were less homogeneous: 22 percent of the respondents stated that they don't use pond water anymore for drinking or for cooking purposes. 33 percent stressed that ponds nowadays were used for professional fish production and also for irrigation, whereas this was not the case in the past. Furthermore, the narrative interviews revealed that pond water quality has deteriorated. Some of the processes which have led to these changes are listed below:

- With the introduction of wells and tubewells less pond water was consumed for drinking. Thus, the necessity to keep pond water clean became futile. Maintenance was considered less and ponds were used in multipurpose ways. "Our pond is not very clean anymore because we don't drink the water anymore" or "Our pond is clean but not for drinking purposes", and "Now, pond water is bad/condensed[176]", were common statements of the respondents in both villages.
- Control over pond use greatly diminished. Two reasons are mainly responsible for this: control was considered less important because pond water was not used for drinking anymore and the role of the authority weakened. The feared *zamindars* and their employees had left the country, the *zamindar* system was abolished and those now responsible were either absent or had lost their prestige due to an increasing self-consciousness of the people as Bangladesh has developed into an individualistic society over the past decades.
- Another factor is population growth. According to one respondent about fifty years ago, 150 to 200 people were living in Taktakhali village. Today, there are about 400 to 500 people. In one cluster there are 20 families of the same

---

[176] *"Ekhon pukurer pani mota lage."* *Mota* means heavy and is used in contrast to tubewell water which is considered *patla*, or light.

lineage, with 150 members. The consequences are evident. More water is needed but the proportional supply of ponds is not guaranteed. Therefore, ponds are overused, spoiled and consequently create a health risk. In addition, there are too many shareholders to decide on the maintenance tasks. Therefore maintenance becomes obsolete.

- With the introduction of HYV crops in the course of the Green Revolution, farmers in the Barind started to irrigate their crops with pond water. The shift was accompanied by a transfer in the pond ownership pattern. In North Bengal, ponds always were the property of the *zamindars*. Ponds were considered separate from land, whereas the pond embankments have always counted as land. For this reason all ponds, which were not sold by the *zamindars* before their departure, became government property (*khas*) and were transferred to the Land Revenue Department in 1957. Farmers were now able to lease these *khas* ponds. Either they used them for irrigation or they started to cultivate crops as soon as the pond had silted up. Some farmers tricked the government by showing fake documents which they had obtained before 1957. Many ponds though have been converted from public to private holdings and consequently turned from a common into a private good, from a source of public profit (drinking) into a source of private profit (crop production, fish production). Conflicts arising from unclear allocation of pond property are still common.

As for the case-study in Dokkhin Garadia this chapter also confirms the assumptions of chapter 4 that present pond management reflects the changes in the concept of the pond along the spiritual – secular, domestic – productive and communal – individual dualities. The question is what remains of the former concept of the pond and the knowledge about pond maintenance.

8.5
Evaluation: pond concept and local knowledge

The comparison study revealed that ponds were not used conspicuously more in villages where less tubewells were available due to groundwater problems. The observation indicated that maintenance of these ponds is not better and sometimes even worse than in Dokkhin Garadia. Knowledge about a local water treatment methods could only be discovered in Sehakati on the coast. Although all pond owners confirmed the importance of maintenance, their ponds rarely corresponded to these concepts. Summarised, the following conclusions can be drawn from all three study villages:

- The present concept of a pond nowhere corresponds with the ideal concept of a pond. Suggested pond maintenance practises are not realised but adapted pragmatically to the given situation. As a consequence, insufficient pond maintenance influences the water quality of the ponds.

Concepts about water quality were found to be quite homogeneous. Good water is flowing and clear, bad water is stagnant and muddy. Pond water is considered good water, which is mainly linked to the concept of a *zamindar* pond.

Individual ponds are often perceived as clean, although water quality tests indicated high levels of contamination.

An obvious consequence of these findings would be to take measures to improve the maintenance of the ponds. These would be:

- regular re-excavation
- ensure high and strong embankments
- closing the outlets
- clearing the embankments and the environment of bush

According to the narrative interviews there is no evidence that any ponds were maintained more regularly in the past. A pond was usually only re-excavated, or the embankment repaired, when it was in danger of silting up. But the large *zamindar* ponds were probably less vulnerable to defects because they were well constructed. The individual farmers were too poor to maintain their ponds and were also able to use pond water from *zamindar* ponds for drinking.

The most effective maintenance practice was control. People did respect the words of the authority concerning the use of ponds for drinking water. Today, the best controlled ponds are fish ponds as they are worth greater investment. Owners therefore guard them and watch out for thieves. Villagers respect these pond owners because today fish is scarce, as was good drinking water in the past. Ponds, which are only used for domestic purposes, and therefore do not produce any economic profit, are not considered worthwhile investments. Control is not regarded important and regular maintenance is not necessary. Therefore, conflicts only occur today at ponds used for commercial purposes, either for fish production or irrigation. However, it is possible that the concept of the pond is changing again because safe drinking water is becoming scarce due to the arsenic contamination. Whether this would be incentive enough to increase investment in ponds and pond maintenance by the owners is unsure. But it is worthwhile to re-consider ponds as a valuable water source for domestic purposes, maybe even for drinking purposes.

The narrative interviews illustrated that despite rigorous control, water related diseases were very common in the past. All the older villagers reported that epidemics regularly swept their region, especially during the months of the dry season (*coyttro*) and during post monsoon (*kartik/ogghran*). Mojid Mirda of Sehakati remembers: "In my house many people died. I saw 14 to 15 people die at a time."

It is evident that people did not know of the relationship between contaminated water and diseases. In the 1950s, the Pakistan Government launched a campaign to eradicate cholera. The systematic sinking of tubewells started and health education was provided on a union level. These public health measures initiated the effective reduction of serious epidemics like cholera.

Moreover, the water treatment method with *fitkiri* was the only one mentioned. At the household level, women were turning a piece of *fitkiri* in the water container for a while and storing the water before consumption.[177] Sometimes *fitkiri* was also put in larger doses into the pond. However, one has to keep in

---

[177] This method is sometimes still applied today when pond water is used for cooking.

Photo 8.1 Protected *ghats* to maintain *purdah* are common in the coastal districts

Photo 8.2 Inviting *ghat* of a pond in Madhabpur (Nachole *thana*)

mind that *fitkiri* does not disinfect the water but only coagulates it. Although one respondent reported that they sometimes boiled the water for drinking purposes this method was rarely considered as fuel was scarce and expensive. Rainwater collection was rarely practised. Although the older respondents commended the water quality of the *zamindar* ponds it remains unclear to what extent this water was really safe as no water quality tests can show what the situation was in the past. On the other hand the physical resistance of the rural dwellers was probably rather high.

The empirical study provided information for suggestions as to which aspects would have to be considered for any project based around ponds:

- Identification of local concepts of cleanliness in order to evaluate whether these concepts are detrimental or conducive to the project and to the overall benefit of the people.
- Include women in the process of identification because their knowledge may be more significant in the domestic field of water management since they are the main actors.
- Identification of the importance a pond has for the livelihood of an individual owner or the community. This implies the view of a pond as an integrated system, including economical, ecological, cultural and spiritual aspects. The role of the pond for domestic purposes should be discussed and investments and alternatives weighed.
- Testing the effectiveness of traditional water purifying methods, for example *fitkiri*.
- Discussion about possible solutions concerning the multiple ownership problem of ponds with the people concerned. This is particularly relevant for Bangladesh where population pressure increasingly affects the natural resources system.

The next chapter introduces an institutional framework to include all the suggestions which the empirical findings have provided. Having learnt from previous development failures the community management approach was chosen because it was considered the most appropriate approach for a sustainable and self-reliant development.

9 Community management for pond improvement

Due to external influences, for example the introduction of hand tubewells for drinking purposes, the *life world* of people in rural Bangladesh has changed and with it their attitude towards the ponds. Ponds have become a secularised, individualised object, dissociated from the supernatural and the communal benefit. As a consequence pond management is valued differently today. The productive aspect of ponds is of increasing interest but rural dwellers still consider ponds important for non-productive, domestic purposes. However, despite available local knowledge and the resources to manage ponds, there is insufficient pond management due to such problems as conflicting interests, ownership patterns and missing information. The neglect of pond maintenance poses a health risk to the pond users. Considering the fact that ponds represent a vital water source in Bangladesh it is necessary to improve them. Moreover, the arsenic threat requires feasible alternatives to groundwater supply and ponds are one important option.

Chapter 4 introduced some sustainable pond water treatment methods. Knowing about the technical options the question is now: which *institutional* approach would be appropriate for pond improvement taking into account the problems and opportunities of present pond management? The review of economic development theories in chapter 2 demonstrated that supply driven, large-scale development approaches have not produced sustainable results in many cases. The main reason for the failure has been attributed to the alienation of development aid from local people. Finally, it was argued that the community management approach entails all the elements that are regarded important to render a project self-reliant and sustainable (see chapter 2.4.4): it should be actor-oriented, conducted on a small-scale and with an integrative perspective. With this background chapter 9 intends to evaluate the community management approach for the purpose of pond improvement. The rationale for this attempt is the following:

1. Since the 1980s donor agencies started to recognise that development projects are more sustainable when directed by participatory approaches. It was re-discovered that the people always had their own management strategies (MCCOMMON, WARNER & YOHALEM 1990: 1, 3). However, external agencies did not to take them into account and hence contributed to an inactivation of traditional structures.
2. Communal management strategies have a long standing tradition in Bangladesh. Village communities are used to establish educational, cultural

and religious institutions (BHUIYA & RIBAUX 1997: 8).[178] In past years community management projects have become more significant. In 1990 the government launched the Social Mobilisation (SOC-MOB) programme (see chapter 3.3.2). On the union level Water Supply and Sanitation (WATSAN) committees were formed chaired by the respective union chairman. Later the committee was extended to the village level in order to improve dissemination to the people (HOQUE et al 1995: 1-3; 14, 16).[179] In 1994 ICDDR,B and the Swiss Red Cross launched the Chakaria Community Health Project which can be considered a realistic self-help approach.[180] Since then this approach has stimulated other development projects: the WATSAN Partnership Project (WPP) financed by Swiss Development Cooperation (SDC), which was initiated in early 1998, follows up certain aspects for implementation in the water sector (RIBAUX, ISLAM & MOTALEB 1999).[181]

3. The community management approach helps to establish democratic structures at the grassroots level. This is the more important because neither the efforts of the government nor of the various NGOs will be sufficient to tackle the numerous problems that Bangladesh faces in the future (BHUIYA & RIBAUX 1997: 7).

The chapter starts with general aspects of a community management approach. Then, the conditions for the application of approach to improve ponds is discussed. The chapter concludes with a scenario for Bangladesh.

9.1
Characteristics of a community management approach

Originally the UNDP/World Bank policy in the water sector was based on the assumption that local communities were not capable of managing and maintaining their basic water supply. Therefore, it was considered the role of the public sector to provide these services (BRISCOE & DEFERRANTI 1988: 12, 17-19). The paradigm change in the water sector management from the mid-1980s onwards has induced a shift in the role of the government and donors from providers/implementors to facilitators of development activities (MCCOMMON, WARNER & YOHALEM 1990: 28). But despite the general concession of

---

[178] Most of the primary and secondary schools in Bangladesh go back to community initiatives, and were only later registered and supported by the government.

[179] A research project conducted by the Environmental Health Programme of ICDDR,B revealed that strengthening the cooperation between different partner organisations and the active participation of the local people can bring successful results. For example, the rate of using tubewell water for cooking purpose rose from 24 to 72 percent, the rate of washing both hands before eating from 6 to 71 percent, and the rate of sanitary latrine use from 23 to 64 percent (HOQUE et al. 1997: 7).

[180] See BHUYIA & RIBAUX (1997) and EPPLER, BHUYIA & HOSSAIN (1997).

[181] The objective of the WPP project is "to improve users' sustainable access and use (i.e. hygiene behaviour practices) of affordable water and sanitation facilities[...]" (RIBAUX, ISLAM & MOTALEB 1999: 1-2). It is a community based project whose implementation is facilitated by three international NGOs each having its specialised knowledge and experience in a particular sector (community management, technical development and hygiene education).

international development agencies and donors that community management approaches are most appropriate for sustaining the water supply sector (BRISCOE & DEFERRANTI 1988), until recently hardly any attempts have been undertaken to implement this approach for water management projects in Bangladesh. Regarding pond projects the situation is somehow different. Various projects have involved the community and invited people to participate.[182] However, these projects have excluded the domestic aspect of ponds. In addition the community management component consequently was not often implemented.[183]

In contrast to the past supply driven approaches the community management approach is demand-driven, which means that:

- the community takes the initiative and the decisions about the services
- the community contributes to the arising costs and is involved in fund controlling
- the community is the owner of the services and responsible for their maintenance
- the project activities are managed and coordinated by a democratically elected village committee
- the government acts as facilitator and provides the necessary legal and political framework (RIBAUX, ISLAM & MOTALEB 1999: 3-2)

Community management, thus, is decentralised management leading to self-reliance. Due to heavy external support over the past 25 years the relief mentality is still strongly rooted in rural Bangladesh. Therefore, the implementation of the community management approach can be problematic when people repeatedly demand financial or material inputs. The experiences with the Chakaria Project confirmed that it is essential to strictly refuse these demands and to emphasis continuously the community's "respect for self-help" (BHUIYA & RIBAUX 1997: 23). Hence, external assistance in community management projects should be based on the following:

- The role of the project staff is one of a facilitator. The project assists in community meetings and offers, on the community's request, advise and skill development but it does not provide any material or financial help. Furthermore the programme has to be built up on existing local resources.
- The external project staff has to emphasis continuously its role and strengthen the consciousness of the community to make them feel like real participants of the programme and owner of their project.
- The external providers facilitate the coordination between the community and external partners, such as government agencies and NGOs that are active in the area and in the particular sector (EPPLER, BHUIYA & HOSSAIN 1997: 15-17).

---

[182] The European Commission in cooperation with the Department of Fisheries, for example, is active in participatory rural pond acquaculture (FELTS, AKTHER & MAHAL 1997).

[183] This is the result of an evaluation of three pond improvement projects: the PSF project of DPHE/UNICEF (see chapter 4.1.2); the PRISM duckweed cum fish production project (see chapter 4.1.4); and the pond re-excavation project of the Bangladesh Multipurpose Development Authority (BMDA) in which ponds are leased for fish production through an auction system.

After having presented the general characteristics of a community management approach the perspective has to focus next the specific conditions of the ponds for such an approach. Two questions are relevant in this context:

- Are there experiences from the past with traditional community pond management which could be used?
- What are the obstacles of and requirements for community pond management?

9.2
Implications of community management for pond improvement

9.2.1
Initial situation

Two considerations are important for planning the improvement of ponds based on the community management approach: the reasons for pond mismanagement and a failing traditional community pond management. These will briefly be discussed below.

The pond ownership patterns and the low priority people attribute to pond water quality can lead to mismanagement. It became apparent in the case-study of Dokkhin Garadia that privately owned ponds with private access are better maintained than shared ponds or private ponds with open access. Multiple ownership leads to dissension and indecision about which pond management strategies to apply. Furthermore, pond owners are not respected anymore when advising the villagers how to use their open access pond. Finally, family members who affirm that their pond water has deteriorated are still satisfied with its quality. They justify their minimal pond maintenance with the statement that they do not use the water for drinking anymore. When pond water quality does not correspond anymore to their needs those who do not own ponds simply use a different source of water. The numerous health education campaigns resulted in people drinking tubewell water but consciousness about water-related diseases and disease transmission is still low.

In contrast to many traditional community management projects – even in surface water management (see DUYNE 1998) – ponds have not been traditionally managed by the community. This was the result of the historical accounts during the case studies (see chapter 8.4.3). Former drinking water ponds were mainly provided by local *zamindars* or influential villagers for the use of the community and were surveyed and maintained by the owners themselves. Sometimes a *zamindar* transferred the responsibility for a pond to the community. But the witnesses stated that the community did not maintain the pond, yet, they used it for drinking purposes. This unwillingness of the community to maintain the pond could have the following reasons:

- The *zamindar* transferred the responsibility but not the *ownership* of the pond to the community. The community always remained in the status of tenancy, it

Photo 9.1 Demonstration of a pond sand filter in Patharghata

Photo 9.2 Community management is the most appropriate way for sustainable pond management.

possessed the pond but it never had the opportunity of becoming its owner. As a consequence the community did not feel responsible for pond maintenance.

- The main source of production was (and still is) land. In one documented case the farmers divided the embankments around the pond for agricultural use. One can conclude that ponds were, above all, viewed as a derivative of land. This may be one reason why fish production was neglected although it could have been very profitable. But surely, unclear property rights among the community members and the fear that the pond owner would reclaim their output played the major role.
- People distinguished between good and bad ponds. Many *zamindar* drinking water ponds were highly appreciated for their cleanliness. Therefore, the question occurs why a community did not make any effort to maintain a drinking water pond when it was deteriorating. As described in chapter 6.3 the behaviour of the villagers' water drawing pattern is determined by various factors. Pond water can often be substituted by other, similarly acceptable sources. When a pond silted up people shifted to another pond or another available water source. If there were no other source available, as in the case of the High Barind area, people chose the best place in the pond to fetch drinking water from either opposite the washing site or underneath the water plants. It cannot be denied that at that time people were ignorant about water borne diseases and disease transmission.

These considerations have the following implications for pond improvement:

- Pond owners and users have to be made aware of the disadvantages of pond mismanagement and the advantages of an improved pond with respect to their health, their personal preferences, their time and cost budget and their prestige.
- If ponds are to improve as a drinking water supply a communal open access pond is more appropriate. The access to and availability of pond water for domestic purposes must be guaranteed to all members of a village society. The arsenic problem may additionally disfavour the poor as they may be deprived from the access to safe (i.e. arsenic free) tubewell water. Therefore, the community needs to be the owner of the pond and must allocate the responsibilities effectively. The next subchapter illustrates how such a community management approach for ponds may be designed.

9.2.2
A scenario: pond improvement by community management

The central conditions for a demand-driven, decentralised community management approach are to build up existing resources (institutional, material, financial etc.) and to emphasise the community's ownership of the project. It is of utmost importance for self-help projects that the allocation of the ownership, and hence responsibility, is clear. There are four possibilities for a community to become owner of a pond:

- there is already a communal pond in the village, for example the mosque or school pond

- there is a private pond with open access. If the owner is willing he may transfer the ownership to the community, either by sale or donation of his pond
- there is a *khas* pond in the village. In this case the community can lease the pond but in the long run the government should guarantee that it transfers ownership of the pond to the community. Otherwise the chances for sustainable management will be low
- there is no appropriate pond in the village. The community may consider excavating a pond for which it may have to purchase a plot of land

In any case, the initiative to improve (or even construct) a pond has to emerge from the community which must be convinced of the advantages of a communally managed pond. Decision-making is preceded by a situation analysis during which the community should:

- lay down the problems regarding ponds and pond management
- discover existing maintenance techniques and knowledge of pond water treatment methods
- initiate a discussion about the importance of ponds for domestic purposes and, in arsenic contaminated areas, for drinking purposes, and to stress the relation between water-related diseases and good health
- elaborate possible ways to overcome the existing problems

Community ponds are often the property of religious or educational institutions like the mosque committee or the school. In those cases these existing institutions could take on the responsibility for their particular pond, if they fulfil the criteria of a self-help organisation.[184] Consequently pond improvement measures can be added directly to the respective committee agenda.

The committee represents the community which will approve its achievements in regular elections. To be able to participate in the decision-making process the community needs to be informed about pond water quality and the activities of the committee. This requires the overall consciousness of the community that safe water is a scarce good and that polluted water has serious health impacts.

A possible strategy to offer for a self-administrative pond management would be as follows: part of the committee's financial resources will be used to meet the fixed costs (tools for re-excavation or pond construction, eventually costs of pond purchase). Normally the major financial burden is the current costs of pond maintenance. These maintenance costs (re-excavation, reconstruction of embankment, water treatment, water quality control, weeding etc.) would be borne by the community. Every member would have to pay a yearly fee calculated according to the pond budget. Any household which is unable to contribute any money would commit itself to an equal amount of work at the pond. It would be the task of the committee to fix and adapt the budget costs and calculate the cost of maintenance in working hours according to changing conditions.

In case a community requests support from an external organisation, an NGO for instance, this organisation should limit their help by giving training, such as:

---

[184] A self-help organisation is an organisation "initiated by the villagers without any external input" (BHUYIA & RIBAUX 1997: 14, 18). It should consist of a committee having ongoing activities and sufficient financial resources.

hygiene education with special reference to water-related diseases, managerial courses to the committee members and orientation courses about water treatment techniques and pond construction. Private pond owners could be invited to participate in those courses. To sustain the efforts of the committee and the quality of the project it would be important to conduct regular water quality monitoring. Every community is in charge of water treatment according to its selected technique. As water quality control requires know-how and is cost-intensive respective research institutions, such as ICDDR,B or EAWAG should make efforts to find appropriate technologies for communities.

9.3
Conclusions

For many years development projects were largely supply-driven and enhanced the dependency of the beneficiaries from external providers, donors, international organisations and national governments. Technology, know-how, managerial personnel and finances were imported to build up economic structures comparable with the Western countries which were supposed to bring economic growth and general welfare. This development made people in developing countries think that they were unskilled, poor and dependent on external help. In Bangladesh people sometimes said during interviews that they did not know anything because they were too poor. In the meantime it is widely recognised that local knowledge is an important element for the integration of development programmes and that a project will only endure when a self-reliant community is in charge of it.

The community management approach is considered the appropriate development approach for Bangladesh because it helps to awake people from passivity and relief mentality. People are encouraged to respect themselves and to rely on their own capacities. In this way people regain self-confidence and self-determination.

Pond improvement for domestic purposes is desirable because Bangladesh needs alternatives to the contaminated groundwater and also because improved ponds sustain people's health and social well-being. Technical aspects of pond improvement, such as re-excavation, stabilising the embankment and making them higher, cleaning the pond environment of bush and closing existing in- and outlets, are obvious. Effective pond water treatment methods are also feasible, either applicable at the source or at the consumption level (chapter 4.1). For a sustainable implementation of these technical aspects community management is considered the best approach for open access ponds that are reserved for drinking purposes.

The most important factor for successful community pond management is that the community is the owner of the pond and fully responsible for it. This will be the case when the initiative for pond improvement emerges from the community. It will be the community to decide on the use of the pond, to elect a responsible committee and to provide the necessary money or labour for pond maintenance.

Given the fact that rural people have stopped drinking pond water it might be difficult to make them understand that ponds could be an alternative to tubewell water. It will be the task of governmental bodies, for example DPHE and the Health Ministry, to encourage people to reconsider ponds for drinking purposes. In such an undertaking, it is absolutely essential that the people's awareness regarding the importance of pond water quality is raised. Health education remains very important and should include information about water-related diseases, disease transmission, waste disposal, the effectiveness of water plants, pond protection and water treatment methods.

Summarised, pond improvement consists of a package comprising three aspects:

- technical aspect: water treatment methods, pond construction and maintenance techniques
- institutional aspect: sustainable management, i.e. sustainable maintenance and control according to the defined purpose of the pond
- information aspect: training and education regarding water/environment and health, exchange of information regarding water quality control and effectiveness of different water treatment methods.

10 Synthesis: relevance for theory and policy

This final chapter offers a synthesis of the main results of this study. The first part reviews the theory and the hypotheses with respect to the empirical findings. The second part discusses the implications of the study for theory and policy and provides suggestions for the three parties that the study had to account for:

- the discipline of geography
- the sector of public health as represented by the ICDDR,B and the Basel Cantonal Hospital/Switzerland
- the development agencies through the Swiss Development Cooperation (SDC)

10.1
Theory and hypotheses

10.1.1
The empirical relevance of the theory

This thesis has argued that many economic development theories had adversely affected development. Therefore, the focus is on alternative approaches that lead away from economic standardisation and toward people-centred development. Two arguments were expounded:

1. Development interventions influence and change the traditional system, which may have positive as well as negative effects on the target area and the target groups
2. Development projects have contributed to an alienation and separation of the individual from its natural habitat and the community

Both assumptions were confirmed with examples from Bangladesh. Development interventions in the form of large-scale technocratic projects like the Flood Action Plan and standardised, centralised projects like the tubewell programme demonstrated the negative effects on the environment and the society. The traditional pond system also attested to that. It was found that the concepts of pond and pond management have changed due to direct and indirect external interventions: the introduction of the tubewell technology directly induced a deterioration of pond maintenance. Indirect factors of development, such as population pressure through improved public health, reduced water supply resulting from large-scale flood control, drainage and irrigation projects, and increased purchasing power facilitating investment in fish production, have influenced the decision making of the actors regarding pond management.

Development interventions were principally designed to raise the GNP and the individual purchasing power. The emphasis on economic and technical aspects implied external support that increased the dependency of the local beneficiaries on national and international agencies. Moreover, the FAP and the tubewell programme indicated that local beneficiaries, influential villagers excluded, were not involved in the decision-making process of these projects. The external interventions also affected the traditional water source pond. Ponds shifted from being largely a socio-cultural to being a predominantly economic object. It was shown that present pond management is a reaction to the changing of people's *life world* which is reflected in rational and pragmatic adjustment strategies of pond owners and users. Priorities are established differently regarding a new living situation. However, it was also demonstrated that the present conditions of ponds is problematic, particularly for the health of the users since pond owners and users do not consider the contamination of pond water a problem.

Responding to the reductionist approaches of development theories a broader methodological approach was established that enables us to deal with more complex issues, such as development issues. The integrative system approach, as applied in geography, was considered appropriate to investigate and explain processes of change. This is regarded necessary to provide solutions for development practice. Contrary to conventional development approaches the integrative system approach is based on interdisciplinary, small-scale and locality oriented research and stresses the cooperation with local actors and the integration of their knowledge and their resources. The community management approach was selected as the most convenient approach to apply in the context of Bangladesh and the improvement of ponds for domestic purposes.

10.1.2
Affirmation of the hypotheses

Two general hypotheses were established.

1. Pond management has changed, principally due to external development intervention with the introduction of tubewells. This change is visible both in the deterioration of pond maintenance and in a shift of the function of the pond.

The empirical study confirmed that the traditional system of the pond, the concept of the pond, and accordingly pond management, have changed. Compared with the "ideal" concept of a pond, the physical structure of the pond has deteriorated: four high and firm embankments could rarely be detected. Many ponds are too shallow and risk drying up during the dry season. Ponds are often surrounded by dense vegetation and bushes which provide preferred defecation places for villagers. Bathing sites in the form of a simple or a constructed *ghat* were hardly found. Ponds which are still reserved for cooking purposes are not specially protected any longer. Women descend into these ponds to fetch water ignoring the owner's warnings, whereas in the past everyone obeyed the rule of not to put one foot into the pond. Outlets into these ponds, which increases the risk of contaminated inflow, were common. Water quality analysis confirmed that pond water was highly contaminated with faecal coliform bacteria. Paradoxically, ponds that were considered safest because they were traditionally set aside for cooking purposes, proved the worst in terms of contamination. Around various ponds animal faeces and, sporadically, human faeces were discovered. According to the majority of the respondents, the main reason for their careless behaviour is that they do not rely anymore on pond water for drinking since they use hand tubewell water for this purpose. The introduction of hand tubewells was confirmed to be a direct cause for the deterioration of pond maintenance.

The function of the pond has also changed due to a shift in the concept of the pond. A pond is no longer an important source of drinking water but people now acknowledge its importance for fish production. Indirect causes, such as the rapid decline in fish supply and a growing demand for water and fish due to population pressure also promote the productive function of the pond. Moreover, the improved economic living standards in rural Bangladesh facilitate fish production. The pond as a beautiful, romantic place has lost its *genius loci* to a great extent, as it has been transformed into an economic object. The secularisation of the pond is followed by privatisation when pond owners restrict or even prohibit the access to their pond. Although conflicts regarding the access to or the use of ponds (and also hand pumps) could not yet be observed, the competition for water, whether for domestic purposes or irrigation, may increase in the future considering the acute water crisis in Bangladesh.

2. Ponds may be a viable alternative for future water management in Bangladesh if the inherent problems are dealt with. Any pond project should emphasis the domestic function of the pond and consider local people's knowledge, particularly regarding water treatment methods, and pond construction and maintenance techniques.

The empirical findings confirmed that ponds are a viable water source because ponds were highly valued, particularly for domestic purposes. It can be said that even today ponds form a part of Bangladeshi culture. However, the conditions of the majority of the ponds impede the proper functioning and even pose a health risk, particularly when used for domestic purposes. Some of the problems that hamper effective pond maintenance are failing awareness of water related diseases and their impact on human health, multiple ownership, population pressure and the lack of financial resources. To provide a viable alternative water source ponds need to be improved. It was intended to explore local knowledge concerning water treatment methods and pond construction and maintenance techniques in order to include it in pond improvement projects. Pond owners and village women traditionally used *fitkiri* to purify pond water but it remains scientifically unclear to what extent potash alum is an effective water treatment method. Although (small) ponds were traditionally common in many homesteads of rural Bangladesh the large drinking water ponds, that villagers referred to, were mostly provided by *zamindars* or mosques. These ponds were privately maintained. Once such a pond was offered to the community it was not regularly maintained. It can be argued that the deprivation of any ownership rights to these ponds was mainly responsible for this.

10.2
Implication for theory and suggestions for policy

This study was conducted in partial fulfilment of the requirements of a PhD degree in Geography. This was made possible by an interlinkage programme between the University of Basel, the Basel Cantonal Hospital and ICDDR,B. Finances were partly provided by the University of Basel/Basel Cantonal Hospital and Swiss Development Cooperation (SDC). Accordingly, the study had to account to three different fields: the field of geography, the field of public health and the field of development cooperation. Therefore, the conclusions of this study will be discussed on two levels: the implication for theory will refer to the field of geography, and the suggestions for policy to the fields of public health and development cooperation.

10.2.1
Implications for theory: integrative system approach and water management projects

Conventional water policy has been accused of following a unilateral, technologically driven sector policy. This simplistic perspective has contributed to a dissociation of water resource from other resources and the environment in general. Therefore, a new water policy should drawn up on a complex, holistic perspective as FALKENMARK & LUNDQVIST (1996: 189-91) propose:

> "[..] we have to start thinking not of water resources in general, but of water in relation to the landscape through which it is continuously moving. This makes the landscape a useful starting point, since it is the scene for human activities. We need an easily understandable mental image of the water moving though that landscape, above and below the ground from the water divide down to the mouth" (FALKENMARK & LUNDQVIST 1990: 190).

This view corresponds with the integrative system approach described in chapter 2.4. Water management issues, like development issues, are complex and, therefore, need to be handled in an holistic approach. Hydrological processes are expressed in space. Water management requires the investigation of physical and human interactions in the hydrological system in order to detect the potential resources volume for the users in a particular place without compromising others or affecting the system as a whole. The cooperation of various disciplines will be needed to propose solutions. Although it is a prerequisite to understand the global (hydrological) system and to establish global and national water management guidelines, solutions have to be found and measures taken according to the local water supply and demand situations. Such an approach has to take into account the local actors and their needs. The integrative system approach, therefore, provides a methodological framework for complex problems. The methodology has to follow a small-scale, people-centred approach, considering the specific locality of action.

10.2.2
Suggestions for policy: water policy and pond projects for Bangladesh

The study revealed that ponds are a viable alternative water source for Bangladesh but have to be improved for sustainability. The implications are based on this statement. Before they are discussed the importance of sustainable water management for the future shall be briefly pointed out.

10.2.2.1 The need for sustainable water management in Bangladesh

Many policy makers agree that water will be one of the most controversial issues of the 21st century. Declining water tables and conflicts about water in many parts of the world already indicate an increasing global water crisis. On the one hand, the demand for water will steadily rise due to population growth and better living standards; on the other hand the increasing contamination of water sources and the competing interests will exacerbate the pressure on water as a resource. In this context, a new water policy is urgently needed, which should reflect the concept of water as a vulnerable and scarce resource (BISWAS 1991).

Development agencies have acknowledged that generally water resources management in the future should aim at:

- creating a water policy for the entire sector
- improving the efficiency of water management projects
- decentralising water management programmes
- involving the community
- strengthening the coordination and cooperation of the different agencies involved in the water sector, from the grassroots to the government level (REPETTO 1986: 27: THE WORLD BANK 1993: 10, 13)

Chapter 3.2 described the multiple aspects of a water crisis that will continuously affect Bangladesh in the future. In Bangladesh the estimated population by the year 2050 is 253 million (BISWAS 1991: 220). This would correspond to 1,714 people per square kilometre (1999: 755 according to BBS 1997: 3). Being aware of the proneness to flooding and the increasing groundwater crisis, Bangladesh is been seriously challenged. In particular, the alarming fact of arsenic groundwater pollution will force the government to provide solutions as quickly as possible. Among the coping strategies, the government will consider alternative water sources, such as ponds or rainwater. At the end of 1998 the National Safe Drinking Water Supply and Sanitation Policy, which still has to be ratified, included the following statement:

> " One pond will be excavated/re-excavated in every village and reserved for supplying water for drinking. Measures will be taken to keep this pond free from pollution."

Thus, the government has seriously reconsidered the use of pond water even for drinking purposes after it had vehemently opposed its use during the past 25 years. This study concludes by making theoretical and practical contributions to the water crisis in general and for pond improvement in particular.

To draw any conclusions for Bangladesh in this respect it is necessary to introduce the administrative structure of the national water policy. In Bangladesh three ministries are involved in water policy:

- The Ministry of Local Government, Rural Development and Co-operatives (MLG, RD&C). This ministry is divided into two divisions: The Division of Local Government (LGD) and the Division of Rural Development and Co-operatives (RD&CD). Two implementing bodies are placed in the LGD: the Department of Public Health Engineering (DPHE) which is responsible for the rural water supply and sanitation (RWSS) programme. The second implementing agency, the LGED, is not relevant for the water sector as it is concerned with rural infrastructure programmes.
- The Ministry of Water Resources. Under its respective Water Resources Division the Bangladesh Water Development Board (BWDB) is the principal implementing agency for Flood Control, Drainage and Irrigation projects.
- The Ministry of Agriculture. Most irrigation projects fall into the Agricultural Division whose implementing agency is the Bangladesh Agricultural Development Corporation (BADC) that is responsible for minor irrigation programmes (personal communication with PETER TSCHUMI, SDC Bern).

In this context Bangladesh's water policy should discuss the following issues:

- Merging the different fields of the water sector in one ministry: Despite the fact that the Ministry of Water Resources and the Ministry of Agriculture cooperate in certain cases the water sector policy is rather disorganised. Placing the different fields, rural and urban domestic water supply, flood control and drainage and irrigation, under one common umbrella would facilitate planning and increase the efficiency of water management programmes. The present structure may also explain the lack of a clear policy for improving ponds. Ponds as a water source cover the productive (fish production, irrigation) and the non-productive (domestic water supply) field of water management. However, none of the three ministries deals with pond issues. The first statistics on ponds for example, was conducted by the Land Revenue Department and most pond projects have been undertaken by the Ministry of Fisheries and Livestock through the *thana* fishery offices.
- Stressing the domestic aspect of water management projects: Water management projects have largely focused on the use of water for productive purposes on large-scale. However, the provision of water at the household level is vital for any productivity and has, therefore, to be emphasised. This implies the involvement of women in water management projects because they are the water managers at the domestic level.
- Decentralising decision-making in water management projects: The Second Report on Human Development in Bangladesh (UNDP 1993) underlines the need for decentralisation to assure efficient resource allocation. A demand-driven approach is necessary, which requires the involvement of the people concerned, who in turn are able to offer their own strategies and institutional arrangements to deal with water management issues. Decentralisation also means transferring responsibility to the decision-makers.

- Cooperation and coordination between micro- and macro level institutions: Although project responsibility should be decentralised, a national policy has to provide the framework for action. It will become increasingly important for government agencies to act as facilitators and for the NGOs to coordinate the transfer of information between the communities and the government agencies.

10.2.2.2 Suggestions for pond improvement projects

When making suggestions for pond improvement one point needs to be stressed at the end of this study: open water source are always badly polluted. Groundwater would be the safest drinking water source but because of the arsenic contamination alternatives are required. Alternative removal techniques, though, will probably not be applicable to all the different regional hydrogeological zones. Pond water should be boiled before it can be considered for drinking purposes, but unfortunately firewood is often scarce in rural Bangladesh. Therefore, afforestation programmes should be promoted. They would also contribute to balance the water table which is declining. However, any negative side-effects have to be carefully prevented.[185] If boiling the water is impossible the pond sand filter method or solar water disinfection may be applied under a strict and regular control of the water quality. Moreover, any initiative to improve a pond has to come from the people themselves. Without the people's interest and willingness to take responsibility for ponds, a pond improvement project will not be sustainable, as the pond sand filter project demonstrated. Villagers know what a drinking water pond should look like, according to the ideal image of a *zamindar* pond. This technical knowledge is assumed as common knowledge. However, technical assistance, particularly regarding water quality monitoring, would be essential to guarantee the success of a project. Moreover, the role of external facilitators should be to raise villagers' awareness of the ecological interrelations and of water as a precious and vulnerable resource. Areas where external development agencies and public health experts may provide valuable contributions are considered to be the following:

- Providing advisory services regarding pond construction: The suggestions concerning the physical structure of a pond for domestic water supply are as follows: such a pond should have four high embankments, which are not too steep, covered with grass and planted with non-leafy trees in order to let wind and sunlight pass. It should have a size of about 1500 square metres and be about 5 metres deep. There should not be any outlet but a constructed ghat. Villagers have a traditional knowledge concerning pond construction, and guidelines for construction were also established by different institutions, for example IFADEP and BMDA. But as soil conditions and distance to the water table influence the construction of a pond villagers should be given the opportunity to seek advice for pond (re-)excavation. An institution on the thana or union level may be appropriate to offer this advisory service.

---

[185] BMDA successfully transformed the formerly deserted Barind Tract into a green area. The method applied, however, has been criticised because the afforestation was accompanied by large-scale deep tubewell irrigation! In the Southeast of the county the Government is in charge of another afforestation programme but corruption is hampering its success.

- Institutionalising water quality monitoring: If ponds are to serve drinking purposes, their water quality needs to be regularly monitored. Water quality standards for Bangladesh do exist. Although a monitoring system would have to be established at the national level by the respective ministry, its implementation should be decentralised as far as possible. This would require the development of an intermediate technology for water quality monitoring and a training programme for pond owners.
- Ecological education: Villagers do not consider it as important as in the past to maintain their ponds because now they use tubewell water for domestic consumption. The groundwater problem in Bangladesh forces a behavioural change in this respect. In the future, water must be valued as a limited and vulnerable resource. Interviews revealed that villagers care more for scarce resources when they are aware of the scarcity. Respect for water as a scarce resource is needed, this was a common thread in the mythological tales of the Hindu period. Nowadays, respect needs to be built on an understanding of the ecological processes, of the water cycle and the human interventions that affect it.
- Public health education: Not only respect for the water resource is required but also an understanding of the impact of water quality on human health. It was shown that the concept of cleanliness is often determined by cultural factors and habits which can be very harmful to health. Although today health education is an integrated part of water supply and sanitation projects, their limited success may be due to the fact that villagers do not fully understand the messages. Linking health messages with ecological messages and their direct impact on daily life will improve their effectiveness.
- Strengthening self-reliance: The transmission of ecological and health messages has to be undertaken in a participatory process with the people. Only with the participation of the people, will there be a complete understanding of the connection between water, health and human productivity, and only then will it raise people's interest in respecting the use of water and in sustainable pond maintenance in order to obtain safe water. People will then feel responsible for their ponds and they will also understand their obligations with regards to water control when using these ponds.

Geographisches Institut
der Universität Kiel

Glossary of Non-English words

aman:	variety of rice, harvested in October/November
aus:	variety of rice, harvested in June
bari:	house, household
baor:	dried up river course
beel:	natural surface water body
bhithi/bhitha:	homestead mound
bichar:	(in)formal trial
bigha:	measure of area. 3 bigha = 1 acre = 4,046.8 square meters
boro:	dry season crop; non-irrigated crop
burkah:	long dress with veil, worn by orthodox Muslim women
chula:	earthen fireplace, here also household unit
chok:	open field
danga:	here: a pond in the open field
decimel:	square measure: 33 decimel = 1 bigha, 100 decimel = 1 acre
dhormo:	religious belief
dighi:	big pond
doba:	here: ditch
fitkiri:	potash alum
ghat:	here: bathing site
haor:	large-scale natural water body
imam:	Muslim priest
IRRI:	variety of rice, requires irrigation; harvested in April/May
kacha kua:	well, dug in the soil
khal:	canal
khas:	government (pond)
kutipana:	duckweed
kochuripana:	water hyacinth
kolshi:	earthen or metal water container
lakh:	100.000
lungi:	long piece of cloth, local men's dress
madrasa:	muslim religious school
maital:	locally for small pond
matbor:	influential villager, arbiter in a bichar
mauza:	demarcated area for land taxation purpose (almost equal to a village)
oju:	ablution, ritual washings done before prayer
paka kua:	brick lined ring well
par:	pond embankment
para:	neighbourhood

pir:	local Muslim saint
pobitro:	holy, sacred, pure
pukur:	pond
purdah:	seclusion of women according to islamic tradition
pushkurni:	pond
rajbari:	house of the former Hindu landlords
saree:	typical women's dress
shalish:	informal village court
shomaj:	community institution
shomiti:	club, union, interest group
Taka:	currency of Bangladesh (average 1996/97: 43 Tk = 1 US$)
talab:	pond
thana:	administrative unit between district and union
union:	lowest administrative unit
union parishad:	political body of the union, represented by the union chairman
ward:	kind of political unit
zamindar:	landlord
zilla:	district

Bengali months

boyshakh :	Mid April - Mid May
joystho:	Mid May - Mid June
ashar:	Mid June - Mid July
srabon:	Mid July - Mid August
bhaddro:	Mid August - Mid September
ashin:	Mid September - Mid October
kartik:	Mid October - Mid November
ogghran:	Mid November - Mid December
powsh:	Mid December - Mid January
magh:	Mid January - Mid February
phalgun:	Mid February - Mid March
choyttro:	Mid March - Mid April

List of Personal Communications

1. Dewan Md. Ali, chairman of Baira union, Baira (15.3.97)
2. Mr. Fedas, Thana Fishery Officer, Singair (24.3.97)
3. Prof. Dr. Suzanne Hanchett, consultant, Dhaka/Portland (12.8.97; 13.2.98)
4. Bodur Rahman, District executive engineer DPHE, Patuakhali (8.9.97)
5. Abdus Samad, sub-assistant engineer DPHE, Singair (23.9.97)
6. Md. Ikramullah, Chairman PRISM Bangladesh, Dhaka (1.10.97)
7. Azizur Rahman: Secretary BMDA, Rajshahi (19.10.97)
8. Kairul Anam: Pond Project Officer, BMDA, Rajshahi (20.10.97)
9. S.M.A. Mannan: Monitoring Officer, BMDA, Rajshahi (20.10.97)
10. Amjad Hossein, executive engineer, BMDA, Rajshahi (2.11.97)
11. Somser Ali, sub-assistant engineer DPHE, Nachole (3.11.97)
12. M. Chowdhury, engineer, BMDA, Nachole (3.11.97)
13. Mogidul Haque, ex-union chairman, Madhabpur, Nachole (4.11.97)
14. Prof. Dr. Md. Mahbubar Rahman, Department of History, Rajshahi University (9.11.97)
15. Monoar Hossein, executive engineer DPHE, Barguna (19.11.97)
16. Mr. Azad, formerly of UNICEF, Dhaka (2.12.97)
17. Abdul Rahman, former assistant engineer DPHE village sanitation, Dhaka (11.2.98)
18. Babar N. Kabir, Head Water and Sanitation Programme, the World Bank, Dhaka (18.2.98)
19. Saidur Rahman, retired, formerly of Bangla Academy, Dhaka (9.3.98)
20. Shafiul Ahmed, engineer, formerly of EHP, ICDDR,B, Dhaka (12.3.98)
21. Bilqis Amin Hoque, Head EHP, ICDDR,B, Dhaka (15.10.98)
22. Prof. Dr. Rudolf Baumgartner, NADEL, ETH Zürich (27.11.98)
23. Claude André Ribaux, consultant, St. Gallen (26.1.99)
24. Peter Tschumi, SDC sector Asia 1, Bern (13.4.99)

Bibliography

ACHARYYA, S.K. et al. (1999): Arsenic poisoning in the Ganges delta. - = In: Nature 401/7 October: 545.

ACRA, A. et al. (1980): Disinfection of Oral Rehydration Solutions by Sunlight. - In: The Lancet 6: 1257-1258.

ADDO, H. et al (1985): Development as Social Transformation. Reflections on the Global Problematique, Colorado: Westview Press.

AFSARUDDIN, M. (1990): Society and Culture in Bangladesh, Dhaka: Book House.

AHMED, K., JAHAN K. & I. HUQ (1984): Decontamination of Drinking Water by Alum for the Preparation of Oral Rehydration Solution. - In: The United Nations University Food and Nutrition Bulletin 6/2: 54-57.

AHMED, M. F. (1998): Water Supply Strategy in the Arsenic-Affected Rural Areas. - = In: HOQUE, B. A. et al. (eds.): Measurements and Litigation Strategies for Arsenic in Drinking Water at the Field Level. Outcome of a Workshop, 30-31 March 1998, Dhaka: The World Bank: 11-15.

ALAERTS, G.J., RAHMAN M. MD. & P. KELDERMAN (1996): Performance Analysis of a Full-Scale Duckweed-Covered Sewage Lagoon. - In: Water Resources 30/4: 843-852.

AL-SAFADI, M. C. (1992): Customary Water Rights and Associated Practice in Yemen, Sana`a, Sana'a: High Water Council of the Republic of Yemen.

APPADURAI, A. (1990): Technology and the Reproduction of Values in Rural Western India. - In: APFFEL, M. F. & S. A. MARGLIN (eds.): Dominating Knowledge. Development, Culture and Resistance, Oxford: Clarendon Press: 185-216.

ARIYARATNE, A. T. (1988): The Power Pyramid and The Dharmic Cycle, Ratmalana: Sarvodaya Vishna Lekha.

ATKINSON, A. (1991): Principles of Political Ecology, London: Belhaven Press.

AZIZ, K.M.A. et al. (1990): Water Supply, Sanitation and Hygiene Education. Report of a Health Impact Study in Mirzapur, Bangladesh, Washington: UNDP/World Bank Water Supply and Sanitation Program.

BANGLADESH BUREAU OF STATISTICS (BBS) (1987): The Bangladesh Census of Agriculture and Livestock 1983-84. Zila: Nawabganj, Dhaka: BBS.

BBS (1988a): The Bangladesh Census of Agriculture and Livestock 1983-84. Zila: Manikganj, Dhaka: BBS.

BBS (1988b): The Bangladesh Census of Agriculture and Livestock 1983-84. Zila: Patuakhali, Dhaka: BBS.

BBS (1992): Bangladesh Population Census 1991. Zila Patuakhali, Dhaka: BBS.

BBS (1994): Report on the Survey of Ponds 1989, Dhaka: BBS.

BBS (1995): Statistical Yearbook of Bangladesh, Dhaka: BBS.

BBS (1996a): Bangladesh Population Census 1991. Zila Manikganj, Dhaka: BBS.

BBS (1996b): Bangladesh Population Census 1991. Zila Nawabganj, Dhaka: BBS.

BBS (1997a): Agricultural Census 1996: Preliminary Report, Dhaka: BBS.

BBS (1997b): Bangladesh Data Sheet, Dhaka: BBS.

BANGLADESH ENVIRONMENTAL NEWSLETTER (1995): Salinity Increased Alarmingly in Southwest Bangladesh 6/4 Oct.-Dec.: 3.

BANGLADESH ENVIRONMENTAL NEWSLETTER (1997): Understanding Arsenic Chemistry and Toxicity 8/1 Jan.-March: 1;7.

BANGLADESH WATER DEVELOPMENT BOARD (BWDB) et al. (1997a): Water Management in Flood Control and Drainage Systems in Bangladesh. - = Systems Rehabilitation Project. Technical Report 1/50, Dhaka: BWDB.

BWDB et al. (1997b): Investigating Women and Water Management. A Rapid Water Management Appraisal Focused on Women in Dardaria Khal. - = Systems Rehabilitation Project. RWMA Technical Note 35, Dhaka: BWDB.

BARG, U. et al. (1996): Inland Fisheries. - In: BISWAS, A. K.: Water Resources. Environmental Planning, Management, and Development, New York: McGraw-Hill: 439-476.

BARIND MULTIPURPOSE DEVELOPMENT AUTHORITY (BMDA) 1998: Barind Tract: Its development activities, Rajshahi: BMDA mimeo.

BARRETT, P.R.F (1996): Aquatic Weeds. - In: BISWAS, A. K.: Water Resources. Environmental Planning, Management, and Development, New York: McGraw-Hill: 477-528.

BARROWS, H. H. (1923): Geography as Human Ecology. - In: Annals of the Association of American Geographers, XIII/1: 1-14.

BATEMAN, M. O. et al. (1995): Prevention of Diarrhea Through Improving Hygiene Behaviors. The Sanitation and Family Education (SAFE) Pilot Project Experience, Dhaka: CARE/ICDDR,B.

BERKES, F. (ed.) (1992): Common Property Resources. Ecology and Community-Based Sustainable Development, London: Belhaven Press.

BERNARD, R. H. (1994): Research Methods in Anthropology. Qualitative and Quantitative Approaches, London, New Dehli: Altamira.

BETZ, M. J., MC GOWAN, P. & R. T. WIGAND (eds.) (1984): Appropriate Technology: Choice and Development, Durham, North Carolina: Duke Press Policy Studies.

BHUIYA, A. & C. A. RIBAUX (1997): Rethinking Community Participation. Prospects of health initiatives by indigenous self-help organizations in rural Bangladesh, Dhaka: ICDDR,B.

BHUIYAN, MD. K. (1994): Economics of pond culture in Bangladesh, Dhaka: BIDS.

BISWAS, A. K. (1991): Water for sustainable development in the 21st century. - In: Water Resources Development 7/4: 219-224.

BODIAN, S. (1995): Simple in Means, Rich in Ends. An Interview with Arne Naess. - In: SESSIONS, G. (ed.): Deep Ecology for the 21st century. Readings on the Philosophy and Practice of the New Environmentalism, Boston, London: Shambhala: 26-36.

BOOT, M. T. & S. CAIRNCROSS (1993): Actions speak. The study of hygiene behaviour in water and sanitation projects, The Hague, London: IRC Int. Water and Sanitation Centre, London School of Hygiene and Tropical Medicine.

BRAMMER, H. (1996): The Geography of the Soils of Bangladesh, Dhaka: University Press Limited.

BRISCOE, J., AHMED S. & M. CHAKRABORTY (1978): Domestic Water Use in a Village in Bangladesh I: A Methodology and a Preliminary Analysis of Use Patterns During the "Cholera Season." - In: Prog. Wat. Techn. 11/1, 2: 131-141.

BRISCOE, J., CHAKRABORTY M. & S. AHMED (1981): How Bengali Villagers Choose Sources of Domestic Water. - In: Supply and Management 5: 165-181.

BRISCOE, J. & D. DE FERRANTI (1988): Water for Rural Communities: Helping People help themselves, Washington: The World Bank.

BROWN, L. A. (1988): Reflections on third world development: Ground level reality, exogenous forces, and conventional paradigms. - In: Economic Geography 64/3: 255-278.

BURKEY, S. (1993): People First. A Guide to Self-Reliant Participatory Rural Development, London, New York: Zed Books Ltd.

CAIRNCROSS, S. (1988): Health Aspects of Water and Sanitation. - In: Waterlines 7/1: 2-5.

CAIRNCROSS, S. & R. G. FEACHEM (1983): Environmental Health Engineering in the Tropics. An Introductory Text, Chichster: John Wiley & Sons.

CAPONERA, D. A. (1973): Water laws in moslem countries. Irrigation and drainage paper 20/1, Rome: FAO, Water Resources and Development Service, Land and Water Development Division.

CARR, M. (1985): The AT Reader. Theory and Practice in Appropriate Technology, London: Intermediate Technology Publications.

CHAKRABORTY, R. L. & H. NOMA (1989): Agricultural and rural development in Bangladesh, Dhaka: Japan International Cooperation Agency (JICA).

CHAMBERS, R. (1985): Rural Development. Putting the Last First, London, Lagos: Longman.

CHATTERJI, M. (ed.) (1990): Technology Transfer in the Developing Countries. - In: SAEED, K.: Prevention of Dysfunctional Environmental and Social Conditions in Technology Transfer, Houndsmill, Bansingstoke: Macmillan: 129-139.

CHAUKAN, S. (1983): Who puts water in the taps? Community participation in third world drinking water, sanitation and health, London: Earthscan, International Institute for Environment and Development.

CHOWDHURY, A. M., HAKIM A.M. & S. A. RASHID (1989): Changes in Land Ownership and Use in Rural Bangladesh. A Study of Seven Mouzas of Bogra District 1920-1987, Bogra: Rural Development Academy.

CHOWDHURY, A. M. R. & Z. N. KABIR (1991): Folk Terminology for Diarrhea in Rural Bangladesh. - In: Reviews of Infectious Diseases 13/4: 252-254.

CLEAVER, H. M. Jr. (1972): The Contradictions of the Green Revolution. - In: The American Economic Review LXII/2: 177-186.

COX, K. R. (1988): Locality and Community: Some Conceptual Issues. - In: European Planning Studies 6/1: 18-30.

DAG HAMMERSKJÖLD FOUNDATION (1975): What now - another development. Dag Hammarskjöld Report on Development and International Cooperation, Uppsala: Dag Hammarskjöld Foundation.

DANISH INTERNATIONAL DEVELOPMENT AGENCY (DANIDA) (1979): Drinking Water to Rural Areas in Bangladesh. An Evaluation of the Rural Tubewell Water Supply Project, Dhaka: mimeo.

DANIDA (1989): Country Strategy for Strengthening Environmental Considerations in Danish Development Assistance to Bangladesh, Dhaka: Danida, Department of International Development Cooperation.

DANIDA & MINISTRY OF FOREIGN AFFAIRS (1998): Five Districts Water Supply and Sanitation Group. Consultancy Services for DPHE-DANIDA Urban Water and Sanitation Project Bangladesh. Baseline Survey 1 Summary and Recommendations, Dhaka: mimeo.

DAVID, S. (1997): Amphibian Blessings. - In: India Today July 21: 10.

DEPARTMENT OF PUBLIC HEALTH ENGINEERING (DPHE) & UNICEF (1989): A Report on the Development of a Pond Sand Filter, Dhaka: mimeo.

DPHE & UNICEF (1994): Study to forecast declining groundwater level in Bangladesh. Final Report. Executive Summary, Dhaka: mimeo.

DPHE & UNICEF (1995): Women in the Context of Sanitation, Water Supply and Hygiene: A Village based study. Voluntary Health Services Society (VHSS), Dhaka: mimeo.

DESOUZA, A.R. & J. BRADY-FOUST (1976): World Space Economy, Columbus, Toronto: Merrill.

DE VRIES, P. (1992): A research journey. On actors, concepts and the text. - In: LONG, N. & A. LONG (eds.): Battlefields of Knowledge. The Interlocking of Theory and Practice in Social Research and Development, London, New York: Routledge: 47-84.

DOS SANTOS, T. (1981): The Crisis of Development Theory and the Problem of Dependence in Latin America. - In: BERNSTEIN, H. (ed.): Underdevelopment & Development. The Third World Today, Middlesex: Penguin Books: 57-80.

DUYNE, J. E. (1998): Local Initiatives: People's Water Management Practices in Rural Bangladesh. - In: Development Policy Review 16/3: 265-280.

EAWAG (1998): Project Proposal. Solar oxidation and removal of arsenic from drinking water (SORAS), Dübendorf: EAWAG.

EISEL, U. (1992): Individualität als Einheit der konkreten Natur: Das Kulturkonzept der Geographie. - In: GLAESER, B. & P. TEHERANI-KRÖNNER (eds.): Humanökologie und Kulturökologie. Grundlagen, Ansätze, Praxis, Opladen: Westdeutscher Verlag: 107-151.

ENVIRONMENTAL SANITATION INFORMATION CENTER (ENSIC) (1982): Surface Water Filtration for Rural Areas - Guidelines for Design, Construction, Operation and Maintenance, Bangkok: ENSIC.

EPPLER, P., BHUIYA A. & M. HOSSAIN (1997): A Process-oriented Approach to the Establishment of Community-based Village Health Posts, Dhaka: ICDDR,B.

EHLERS, E. (1996): Traditionelles Umweltwissen und Umweltbewusstsein und das Problem nachhaltiger landwirtschaftlicher Entwicklung - unter besonderer Berücksichtigung asiatischer Hochgebirge. - In: Heidelberger Geographische Gesellschaft 10: 37-51.

ERLER, B. (1994): Tödliche Hilfe, Köln: Dreisam Verlag.

EVANS, D. D. & L. N. ADLER (eds.) (1979): Appropriate Technology for Development: A Discussion and Case Histories, Boulder, Colorado: Westview Press.

FALKENMARK, M. & J. LUNDQVIST (1996): Looming Water Crisis: New Approaches are Inevitable. - In: OHLSSON, L. (ed.): Hydropolitics. Conflicts over Water as a Development Constraint, Dhaka: University Press Limited: 178-212.

FELTS, A. R., AKHTER, K. R. & K. C. MAHAL (1997): Integrated Food Assisted Development Project IFADEP-SP2. Case Studies. Success and Failure in Rural Aquaculture for Ponds developed with Food for Work. Consultant report for the European Commission and the Government of Bangladesh, Dhaka: IFADEP.

FLICK, U. (1995): Qualitative Forschung. Theorie, Methoden, Anwendungen in Psychologie und Sozialwissenschaften, Hamburg: Rowohlt.

FREEDMAN, B. (1995): Environmental Ecology. The Ecological Effects of Pollution, Disturbance, and Other Stresses, San Diego: Academic Press.

FURTADO, C. (1981): Elements of a Theory of Underdevelopment - the Underdeveloped structures. - In: BERNSTEIN, H. (ed.): Underdevelopment & Development. The Third World Today, Middlesex: Penguin Books: 33-42.

GADGIL, M. & R. GUHA (1995): Ecology and Equity. The use and abuse of nature in contemporary India, New Dehli: Penguin Books.

GAIN, P. (1998): Bangladesh Environment: Facing the 21st century, Dhaka: Society for Environment and Human Development (SEHD).

GALTUNG, J. (1986): Development Theory - Notes for an Alternative Approach. - In: SIMONIS, U. E. (ed.): Entwicklungstheorie - Entwicklungspraxis. Eine kritische Bilanzierung, Berlin: Duncker & Humblot: 75-89.

GALTUNG, J. (1988): Self-Reliance. Beiträge zu einer alternativen Entwicklungsstrategie, München: Minerva Publikation.

GARDNER, K. (1991): Songs at the River's Edge. Stories from a Bangladeshi Village, Calcutta: Rupa & Co.

GEISER, U. (1993): Ökologische Probleme als Folge von Konflikten zwischen endogenen und exogen geprägten Konzepten der Landressourcen-Benutzung, Zürich: Sri Lankan Studies 5.

GHAI, D. P. et al. (1978): The basic-needs approach to development. Some issues regarding concepts and methodology, Geneva: International Labour Office.

GLAESER, B. (ed.)(1987): The Green Revolution revisited. Critique and alternatives, Boston, Sydney: Allen & Unwin.

GOVERNMENT OF BANGLADESH & MINISTRY OF WATER RESOURCES (1995): Guidelines for People's Participation in Water Development Project, Dhaka: GoB/MoWR.

GOVERNMENT OF BANGLADESH & MINISTRY OF ENVIRONMENT AND FORESTRY (1997): Notification. Register No. DA/1, Dhaka.

HANCHETT, S. (1988): Coloured Rice. Symbolic Structure in Hindu Family Festivals, Dehli: Hindustan Publishing Corporation.

HARDIMAN, D. (1996): Small-Dam Systems of the Sahyadris. - In: ARNOLD, D. & R. C. GUHA (eds.): Nature, Culture, Imperialism. Essays on the Environmental History of South Asia, Dehli: Oxford University Press: 185-209.

HELBRECHT, I. & V. MEIER (1998): Einleitung. Methoden der Sozialforschung in der Geographie. - In: Geographica Helvetica 3: 87, 88.

HELFERICH, C. (1992): Geschichte der Philosophie, Stuttgart: J.B. Metzlersche Verlagsbuchhandlung.

HILLMAN, W. S. & D. D. CULLEY (1978): The Uses of Duckweed. - In: American Scientist 66: 442-451.

HIRSCHMAN, A. O. (1958): The Strategy of Economic Development, New Haven: Yale University Press.

HOERING, U. (1988): Zum Beispiel Bangladesh, Bornheim: Lamuv.

HOSSAIN, M. (1987): Green Revolution in Bangladesh: Its Nature and Impact on Income Distribution. BIDS Working Paper 4.

HOQ CHOWDHURY MD. M. & A. K. AZAD (1991): Pond Fish Production in Bangladesh. Problems and Prospects. - In: The Journal of Rural Development XXI/1: 97-121.

HOQUE, B. A. & M. M. HOQUE (1990): Environment and Health. - In: RAHMAN, A. et al. (eds.) Environment and Development in Bangladesh, Dhaka: University Press Limited: 180-187.

HOQUE, B. A. et al. (1995a): Partnership for Improving Water, Sanitation, Solid Waste and Hygiene Education System in Rural Bangladesh, Dhaka: ICDDR,B.

HOQUE, B. A. et al. (1995b): Technical Assistance to UNICEF on: Home Management of Water and Ingestion of Polluted Water in Urban and Rural Areas in Bangladesh, Dhaka: ICDDR,B mimeo.

HOQUE, B. A. et al. (1997): Workshop on Action Research on Social Mobilization for Sanitation. Proceedings, Dhaka: ICDDR,B.

HUNTER, W. W. (1973): Bardwan, Bankura, and Birbhum. - = A Statistical Account of Bengal 4, Dehli: DK Publishing House (1st edition 1877 London: Tübner & Co.).

HUQ, M. M. (1994): Technology transfer to Bangladesh: aid-dependence and failures in technology acquisition. - In: Science, Technology and Development 12/2-3: 225-241.

INTERNATIONAL CENTRE FOR DIARRHOEAL DISEASE RESEARCH, BANGLADESH (ICDDR,B): Annual Report, Dhaka: ICDDR,B.

INTERNATIONAL LABOUR OFFICE (ILO) (1972): Employment, incomes and equality. A strategy for increasing productive employment in Kenya, Geneva: ILO.

ILO (1976): Employment, growth and basic needs: A one-world problem, Geneva: ILO.

IQBAL, S. (1995): Practical Report. Shobuj Shona Bangladesh, Zürich: ETH mimeo.

ISLAM, A. & G. M. KAMAL (1993): Der Flutaktionsplan für Bangladesh und seine ökologischen Risiken. - In: Geographische Rundschau 45/11: 666-673.

ISLAM, S. (1997): World Bank to give $ 150m to check arsenic peril. - In: The Independent 21.10. 1997: 1.

ISLAM, M. S. & M. O. BATEMAN (1994): The spread and control of cholera in Bangladesh. - In: Waterlines 12/4: 20-23.

ISLAM, M. S. et al. (1996): Faecal Contamination of a Fish-culture Farm Where Duckweeds Grown in Hospital Wastewater Are Used as Fish-feed. - In: INTERNATIONAL CENTRE FOR DIARRHOEAL DISEASE RESEARCH, BANGLADESH (ICDDR,B): Fifth Annual Scientific Conference. Ascon V. Programme and Abstracts, Dhaka: 49.

ITN Newsletter Bangladesh (1997): The Arsenic Calamity in Bangladesh 2: 1-5.

JAHANGIR, B. K. (1982): Rural Society, Power Structure and Class Practice, Dhaka: Centre for Social Studies.

JAMAN, M. A., RAHMAN A. & A. HAI (1996): Barindra Prokolpo, Rajshahi: BMDA.

JANSEN, E. G., JAHANGIR B.K. & B. MAAL (1983): Dilemmas Involved in Defining and Delimiting Household Units in Rural Surveys in Bangladesh. - In: The Journal of Social Studies 21: 92-105.

JANSEN, E. G. (1990): Rural Bangladesh: Competition for Scarce Resources. - 3rd edition, Dhaka: University Press Limited.

JAPANESE ENVIRONMENT CORPORATION (JET) & ASSOCIATION FOR OVERSEAS TECHNICAL SCHOLARSHIP (AOTS) (1996): Environmental Protection, Dhaka 18./19. December: mimeo.

JESSEN, BRIGITTE (1990): Armutsorientierte Entwicklungshilfe in Bangladesch. Hilfe oder Hindernis für die Entwicklung? Berlin: Verlag für Wissenschaft und Bildung.

JHODA, N. S. (1989): Depletion of Common Property Resources in India: Micro-Level Evidence. - In: MC NICOLL, G. & M. CAIN (eds.): Rural Development and Population. A Supplement 10/15: 261-283.

JONAS, H. (1984): Das Prinzip Verantwortung. Versuch einer Ethik für die technologische Zivilisation, Frankfurt a. M.: Suhrkamp.

KAMANN, D. J. F. (1998): Modelling Networks: A long way to go. - In: Tijdschrift voor Economische en Sociale Geografie 89/3: 279-297.

KANTOWSKY, D. (1980): Sarvodaya. The Other Development, Dehli: Vikas Publishing House.

KHAN, A. A. (1997): Positive steps should be taken to combat arsenic contamination. - In: The Independent 09.08. 1997: 13.

KHAN, L.R. (1990): Round Ground Water Abstraction. - In: HUQ, S., RAHMAN A. A & G. R. CONWAY: Environmental Aspects of Agricultural Development in Bangladesh, Dhaka: University Press Limited: 135-153.

KHAN, M. D. & A. HOSSAIN (1994): Environmental Aspects of Surface Water Development Projects in Bangladesh. - In: RAHMAN, A. A. et al. (eds.): Environment and Development in Bangladesh. Vol. I, Dhaka: University Press Limited: 102-130.

KHAN, M. I. (1991): The Process of Technological Change in the Agriculture of a Bangladesh Village: Its Relevance to Mode of Production. - In: The Journal of Social Studies 53: 38-67.

KHAN, S. M. (1985): Culture Fisheries of Bangladesh: The Issue of Unused Ponds. - In: PANAYOTOU, T. (ed.): Small-Scale Fisheries in Asia. Socio-economic Analysis and Policy, Ottawa: International Development Research Centre: 261-268.

KHAN, S. M. (1990): Multipurpose Use of Ponds. - In: RAHMAN, A. A. HUQ, S. & G. R. CONWAY: Environmental Aspects of Surface Water Systems in Bangladesh, Dhaka: University Press Limited: 166-172.

KHIN, N. O. et al. (1993): Effectiveness of Potash Alum in Decontaminating Household Water. - In: Journal of Diarrhoeal Disease Research 11/3: 172-174.

KHONDER, S. A. (1996): Bangladesh's Economy, Environment and the Farakka Barrage. In: ASHRAF, A., ISLAM, F. & R. KUDDUS (eds.): Development Issues of Bangladesh, Dhaka: University Press Limited: 379-387.

KJELLERUP, B., JOURNEY W. K. & K. M. MINNATULLAH (1989): The Tara Handpump. The Birth of a Star, Washington: UNDP/World Bank Water and Sanitation Program.

KOTALOVA, J. (1996): Belonging to Others. Cultural Construction of Womanhood in a Village in Bangladesh, Dhaka: University Press Limited.

KROMREY, H. (1995): Empirische Sozialforschung, Opladen: Leske & Budrich.

LAL, D. (1997): The Poverty of 'Development Economics', London: The Institute of Economic Affairs.

LEVEBVRE, H. (1997): The Production of Space, Oxford, Cambridge: Blackwell.

LESER, H. (1997)[4]: Landschaftsökologie. - 4th edition, Stuttgart: Verlag Eugen Ulmer.

LEVINE, R. J. et al. (1976): Failure of Sanitary Wells to Protect Against Cholera and Other Diarrhoeas in Bangladesh. - In: The Lancet 10: 86-89.

LEWIS, A. W. (1954): Economic development with unlimited supplies of labour. - In: The Manchester School May: 139-191.

LEWIS, D. (1991a): Technologies and Transactions: A Study of the Interaction between New Technology and Agrarian Structure in Bangladesh, Dhaka: Centre for Social Studies.

LEWIS, D. (1991b): The „Offstage-Miracle": Carrying Out and Writing up Field Research in Bangladesh. - In: The Journal of Social Studies 52: 44-68.

LONG, N. (1992): From paradigm lost to paradigm regained? The case for an actor-oriented sociology of development. - In: LONG, N. & A. LONG (eds.): Battlefields of Knowledge. The Interlocking of Theory and Practice in Social Research and Development, London, New York: Routledge: 16-43.

MALIK, Y. K. & S. M. BHARDWAJ (1983): Politics, Technology and Bureaucracy in South Asia, Leiden: E. J. Brill.

MAJUMDER, R. M. K. (1998): A case of mass poisoning. - In: Weekend Independent 20.02. 1998: 17.

MCCOMMON, C., WARNER D. & D. YOHALEM (1990): Community Management of Rural Water Supply and Sanitation Services, Washington D. C.: UNDP/World Bank: Water and Sanitation Discussion Paper Series, DP No. 4, WASH Technical Report No. 67.

MCLANE, J. R. (1993): Land and local kingship in eighteenth century Bengal. South Asian Studies 53, Cambridge: Cambridge University Press.

MEADOWS, D. et al. (1972): Die Grenzen des Wachstums (The Limits to Growth). Bericht des Club of Rome zur Lage der Menschheit, Zürich: Ex Libris.

MEHMET, O. (1995): Westernizing the Third World. The Eurocentricity of Economic Development Theories, London, New York: Routledge.

MEIER, G. M. & D. SEERS (eds.) (1984): Pioneers in Development, New York: Oxford University Press.

MEIER, G. M. (1989): Leading Issues in Economic Development, New York, Oxford: Oxford University Press.

MEIER, V. (1998): Jene machtgeladene soziale Beziehung der „Konversation"... Poststrukturalistische und postkoloniale Geographie. - In: Geographica Helvetica 3: 107-111.

MINISTRY OF HEALTH (1996): Thana Health Complex Survey, Dhaka: mimeo.

MINISTRY OF IRRIGATION, WATER DEVELOPMENT AND FLOOD CONTROL, UNDP & WORLD BANK (1991): National Water Plan Project Phase II. Vol. I. Master Plan Organization, Dhaka.

MINISTRY OF LOCAL GOVERNMENT, RURAL DEVELOPMENT & COOPERATIVES (MLG,RD&C), UNICEF, UNDP & WORLD BANK (1994): Bangladesh SituationAnalysis Water Supply and Sanitation, Dhaka.

MOSSE, D. (1997): Local institutions and power: The history and practice of community management of tank irrigation systems in south India. - In: NELSON, N. & S. WRIGHT: Power and Participatory Development. Theory and Practice, London: Intermediate Techology Publications: 144-221.

NARMAN, ANDERS (1997): Development thinking - bridging the gap between theory and practice. - In: Geografiska Annaler 79B/4: 217-225.

NASH, L. (1993): Water quality and health. - In: GLEICK, P. H. (ed.): Water in Crisis: A Guide to the World's Fresh Water Resources, Oxford: Oxford University Press: 25-39.

NOHLEN, D. & F. NUSCHELER (eds.) (1992): Handbuch der Dritten Welt. Vol. 1, Bonn: Verlag J.H.W. Dietz Nachf.

NOVAK, J. J. (1993): Bangladesh. Reflections on the water, Dhaka: University Press Limited.

NURUZZAMAN, A.K.M. (1990): Perspectives on fisheries development in Bangladesh, Dhaka: BARC.

OPPENHEIMER, J. R. et al. (1978): Limnological studies of three ponds in Dacca, Bangladesh. - In: Bangladesh Journal of Fisheries 1/1: 1-28.

PITMAN, K.G.T. (1993): National Water Planning in Bangladesh 1985-2005. The Role of Groundwater in Irrigation Development. - In: KAHNERT, F. & G. LEVINE: Groundwater irrigation and rural poor. Options for development in the Gangetic Basin, Washington D. C.: The World Bank: 31-60.

PREBISCH, R. (1984): Five Stages in My Thinking on Development. - In: MEIER, G. & D. SEERS (eds.): Pioneers in Development, New York: Oxford University Press.

QADER MIRZA, M. M. (1998): Hydro-environmental aspects of Ganges Barrage Project.- In: The Independent 10.03. 1997: 8.

QUAIYUM, M. A. (1997): Arsenic pollution in Bangladesh. - In: The Independent 28.06. 1997: 13.

RAHMAN, A. MD. (1993): People's Self-Development. Perspectives on Participatory Action Research. A Journey through Experience, Dhaka: University Press Limited.

RAHMAN, M. MD. (1988): Land Relations in Colonial Rangpur: An Analysis of Long Term Changes, 1793-1940. - In: The Rajshahi University Studies Part A/XVI: 105-126.

RASHID, H. (1991): Geography of Bangladesh, Dhaka: University Press Limited.

RASHID, MD. H. et al. (1992): Use of local ponds (pukur) for rainwater harvesting and buffer storage for deep tubewell irrigation systems. Final Report (1989-92), Joydebpur, Gazipur: Irrigation and Water Management Division, Bangladesh Agricultural Research Institute (BARI).

REPETTO, R. (1986): World enough and time. Successful strategies for Resources Management, New Haven, London: Yale University Press.

REZA, A. (1990): Use of Aquatic Weeds: Water Hyacinth. - In: RAHMAN, A. A., HUQ S. & G. R. CONWAY: Environmental Aspects of Surface Water Systems of Bangladesh, Dhaka: University Press Limited: 173-176.

RIBAUX, C. A., ISLAM R. & A. MOTALEB (1999): WATSAN Partnership Project (WPP) in Bangladesh. Report of a Planning Mission, Dhaka, Berne: SDC mimeo.

ROMER, P. (1989): Endogenous technological change. Working Paper No. 3210, Cambridge MA: National Bureau of Economic Research.

ROSTOW, W. W. (1960): The Stages of Economic Growth. A Non-Communist Manifesto, Cambridge: Cambridge University Press.

RUTZ-IMHOOF, A. & D. TOCHTERMANN-PEDIO (1989): Private und öffentliche Entwicklungshilfe der Schweiz. Helvetas und ihre Basis, New York, Paris: Ruth & Tochtermann.

SADEQUE, Z. S. & S. TURNQUIST (1995): Handpump Financing Issues in Bangladesh. An Exploratory Study, Dhaka: UNDP/World Bank Water and Sanitation Program.

SADEQUE, Z. S. (1996): Nature's Bounty or Scarce Commodity - Competition and Consensus Over Ground Water Use in Rural Bangladesh. Paper presented at the Annual Conference of the Int. Ass. for the Study of Common Property, University of Berkley, California.

SAKAMOTO, M. (1996): Eutrophication. - In: BISWAS, A. K.: Water Resources. Environmental Planning, Management, and Development, New York: McGraw-Hill: 297-379.

SALAM, M. A. (1963): Village Water Supply Scheme Through Basic Democracies, Dhaka: DPHE mimeo.

SANJEK, R. (1996): ethnography. - In: BARHARD, A. & J. SPENCER: Encyclopedia of Social and Cultural Anthropology, London, New York: Routledge: 193-198.

SCHMUCK-WIDMANN, H. (1996): Living with the Floods. Survival Strategies of Char-Dwellers in Bangladesh, Berlin: asa-text 6.

SCHNEIDER, H. & M. H. LIBERCIER (eds.) (1995): Participatory Development. From Advocacy to Action, Paris: OECD.

SCHUMACHER, E. F. (1977): Die Rückkehr zum menschlichen Mass. Alternativen für Wirtschaft und Technik. "Small is Beautiful. A Study of Economic as if People Mattered", Rheinbeck: Rowohlt.

SCHULTZ, T. W. (1964): Transforming Traditional Agriculture, New Haven, London: Yale University Press.

SEN, A. (1997): Poverty and Famines. An Essay on Entitlement and Deprivation. - 7th edition, Oxford: Clarendon Press.

SEERS, D. (1969): The Meaning of Development. - In: International Development Review 11/ 4: 2-6.

SEERS, D. (1979): The Birth, Life and Death of Development Economics. - In: Development and Change 10/4 :707-719.

SEUR, H. (1992): The engagement of researcher and local actors in the construction of case studies and research themes. Exploring method of restudy. - In: LONG, N. & A. LONG (eds.): Battlefields of Knowledge. The Interlocking of Theory and Practice in Social Research and Development, London, New York: Routledge: 115-143.

SHAMIM, I. & K. SALAHUDDIN (1994): Energy and Water Crisis in Rural Households. Linkages with Women's Work and Time, Dhaka: Women for Women.

SHAW, R. (1992): 'Nature', 'culture' and disaster. Floods and gender in Bangladesh. - In: CROLL, E. & D. PARKIN (eds.): Bush base: Forest Farm. Culture, Environment and Development, London, New York: Routledge: 200-217.

SICH, D. et al. (eds.) (1993): Medizin und Kultur, Frankfurt a.M.: Peter Lang.

SIDDIQUI, A. (ed.) (1976): Bangladesh District Gazetters. Rajshahi, Dacca: Government of the People's Republic of Bangladesh, Ministry of Cabinet Affairs, Establishment Division.

SIMON, DAVID (1997): Development reconsidered: new directions in development thinking. - In: Geografiska Annaler 79B/4: 183-201.

SOMMER, B. et al. (1997): SODIS - an emerging water treatment process. - In: J Water SRT - Aqua, 46/3: 127-137.

SPACE RESEARCH AND REMOTE SENSING ORGANIZATION (SPARSSO) (1984): Report on FAO/UNDP Project in Bangladesh. Fisheries Resources Survey System. Supplementary Report on Large Water Bodies, Dhaka.

STEINBERGER, K. (1998): Bangladesch: Arsen im Wasser. Das Gift, das aus dem Brunnen steigt. - In: Süddeutsche Zeitung 23.10. 1998: 44.

STEINER, D. & B. WISNER (eds.) 1984: Humanökologie und Geographie/Human Ecology and Geography. Zürcher Geographische Schriften 28, Zürich: Geographisches Institut ETH.

STEWART, F. & P. STREETEN (1981): New Strategies for Development: Poverty, Income Distribution, and Growth. - In: STREETEN, P.: Development Perspectives: 148-174.

STREETEN, P. (1981): Development Perspectives, London, Basingstoke: Macmillan.

STOREY, A. (1994): The environmental transmission of cholera. - In: Waterlines 12/4: 4-7.

SWISS DEVELOPMENT COOPERATION (1995): Country Programme for Bangladesh 1995-2000. Bern: SDC mimeo.

SWISS NATIONAL SCIENCE FOUNDATION (1998): Rural Livelihood Systems and Sustainable Management of Natural Resources in Semi-Arid Areas of India. Priority Programme Environment Module 7. Project Nr. 5001 044780/1, Zürich: ETH/NADEL.

THE INDEPENDENT (1996): Ganges Water Treaty signed between India and Bangladesh 12.12. 1996: 1.

THE INDEPENDENT (1997): Farakka Barrage causing drought, says Sajeda 19.08. 1997: 2.

THE WORLD BANK (1987): World Bank Experience with Rural Development. Report No. 6883, Washington D. C.: The World Bank.

THE WORLD BANK (1990): Bangladesh. Review of the Experience with Policy Reforms in the 1980s. Report No. 8874, Washington D. C.: The World Bank.

THE WORLD BANK (1993): Water Resources Management, Washington D. C.: The World Bank.

THE WORLD COMMISSION ON ENVIRONMENT AND DEVELOPMENT (1987): Our Common Future, Oxford, New York: Oxford University Press.

TODARO, M. P.(1998): Economic Development. - 6th edition, London, New York: Longman.

TOUFIQUE KAZI, A. (1997): Some Observations of Power and Property Rights in the Inland Fisheries of Bangladesh. - In: World Development 25/3: 457-67.

ULLAH, M. (1983): Socio-economic Factors Affecting the Utilization of Village-ponds for Fish-culture, Noakhali: BIDS-CDR Research Centre.

UNDP 1993: Human Development in Bangladesh: Decentralization For Local Action, Dhaka: UNDP

UNDP & WORLD BANK (1996): Water Supply and Sanitation Programme: Country Plans FY 96. July 1995-June 1996, Washington D. C.

UNICEF (1997): Progotir Pathey. Achieving the Goals for Children in Bangladesh, Dhaka: BBS & Ministry of Planning.

VANSINA, J. (1985): Oral Tradition as History, Wisconsin: The University of Wisconsin Press.

WALTER, M. F. (1987): Role of ponds for irrigation in farming systems in Bangladesh. Consultancy Report, Dhaka: Bangladesh Agricultural Research Council (BARC), Winrock International Institute.

WEGELIN, M. et al. (1994): Solar water disinfection: scope of the process and analysis of radiation experiments. - In: J Water SRT - Aqua 43/3: 154-169.

WEGELIN, M. & B. SOMMER (1998): Solar Water Disinfection (SODIS) - destined for worldwide use? - In: Waterlines 16/3: 30-32.

WHITE, G. F., BRADLEY D. J. & A. U. WHITE (1972): Drawers of Water. Domestic Water Use in East Africa, Chicago, London: The University of Chicago Press.

WHO, DPHE & UNICEF (1990): Report on Study of Pond Sand Filters, Dhaka: mimeo.

WHO, WSCC & UNICEF (1996): Water Supply and Sanitation Sector Monitoring Report. Sector status as of 31 December 1994, Dhaka: mimeo.

WILLCOCKS, W. (1930): Lectures on the Ancient System of Irrigation in Bengal and its Application to Modern Problems, Calcutta: University of Calcutta.

YOUSSOUF, A. M. (1990): Openwater Fisheries and Environmental Change. - In: RAHMAN, A. A., HUQ S. & G. R. CONWAY: Environment and Development in Bangladesh, Dhaka: University Press Limited: 145-165.

ZEITLYN, S. & S. BRAHMAN (1994): Report on the Qualitative Assessment. Sanitation & Family Education (SAFE) Pilot Project, Dhaka: CARE International.